The East Asian Knowledge-based Economies

Sajit Chandra Debnath

University Education Press

Preface

This book is the outcome of research activities conducted during my doctoral studies. In it, the theories of the knowledge-based economy (KBE) have been advanced one step further, within the East Asian context. Many recent scholars have considered the KBE to be the main economic driver of today's economic growth. In the last couple of decades, many countries have shown high economic performance by knowledge creation and its diffusion to the various sectors of the economy. The economic ramifications of the creation of a KBE are that it would increase the competitiveness of any country and its stock of knowledge for future innovation activities. Many East Asian economies have shown tremendous success in economic development by transferring the traditional economic system into a KBE. This book explores the knowledge-based economies (KBEs) in East Asia by studying the factors contributing to the growth of KBE in the region.

One of the greater challenges of this study was to select an appropriate methodology to measure the contribution of knowledge and its output to the national economy. The usual methodology for measuring gross domestic product (GDP) and most other macroeconomic indicators cannot appropriately measure the impact of policy formulations on the KBE. Moreover, how to measure the performance of KBE, itself is yet to be identified and defined in the literature. The World Bank's knowledge assessment methodology is by far the most comprehensive methodology to identify the key variables of the KBE worldwide. Thus, this study investigates the key contributing factors of the KBE in East Asia by taking the World Bank's KBE index into consideration. A KBE framework is proposed based on the four pillars of the KBE indicated by the World Bank. The four pillars are as follows: economic incentives and institutional regimes, education and human resources, information and communications technology and a system for innovation. The intention behind using the KBE framework is to simplify systemic data collection and thereby facilitate the investigation of key factors of each pillar, factors affecting the development of the KBE. This will allow us to understand the economic ramifications of the KBE in the East Asian context.

Through the qualitative and quantitative analysis of the KBEs in East Asia, it has become evident that there are some key factors in each pillar of the KBE in East Asia. The countries that are better at developing these key factors are the most successful KBEs in the region. Japan, Korea, Taiwan, Hong Kong and Singapore have been the most successful countries in the region in developing the key determining factors to become KBEs. However, rapid demographic transition has been found to be one major challenge for these countries, as they hope to continue to supply the KBE with the human resources it requires. As a consequence, these countries have adapted the policy of attracting talented human resources from abroad, by providing them with opportunities equal to what the native population receives, as well as by raising the domestic birth rate.

I have benefited from many individuals and organizations that enthusiastically contributed to the completion of this book. I am afraid that without their help, assistance and cooperation, this book otherwise would have not been a success. I am grateful to Almighty that this book is finally finished in time. I also wish to convey my heartfelt gratitude to Professor A. Mani for his critical insights and bringing to light vital elements which have been the fuel in writing this book. Many thanks are due to Professor Yokoyama Kenji, Professor Jeremy Eades, and Professor Suzuki Yasushi for their critical comments and advice during the compilation of this book. I am also grateful to the Institute of Southeast Asian Studies, the National University of Singapore and the Nanyang Technological University, Singapore and the University of Malaya, the Prime Minister's Department, and Cyber Jaya, Malaysia for providing me with access to their valuable academic materials and industry statistics and other information related to this book.

I am greatly indebted to Ritsumeikan University for the funding to publish this book.

My heartfelt gratitude goes to my beloved family for always supporting and believing in my educational journey.

List of Figures

Figure No		Page
Figure 2.1	The Chronological Trajectory of the KBE	20
Figure 2.2	The Effect of Technological Change or Factor Substitution on the Production Function	21
Figure 3.1	Three Dimensions of the Social System with their Three Interactions	38
Figure 3.2	The First-order Interactions Generate a KBE as a Next Order System	39
Figure 3.3	Policy Framework for a KBE	41
Figure 3.4	Explaining Economic Growth - Differences in Approach	42
Figure 3.5	Proposed KBE Framework	43
Figure 5.1	Investment in Knowledge as Percentage of GDP, 1991-1998	64
Figure 5.2	Gross Expenditure on Research and Development as Percentage of GDP, 1994 and 2001	66
Figure 5.3	Early- and Expansion-stage Venture Capital Financing in OECD Countries/Regions, 1995-2001 (Share of GDP)	66
Figure 5.4	Total Researchers per Thousand Labor Force, 1990 and 2000	67
Figure 5.5	Business Enterprise Researchers as Percentage of Total Researchers, 1990 and 2000	67
Figure 6.1	Tariff & Nontariff Barriers, East Asia	76
Figure 6.2	Business Freedom, East Asia	77
Figure 6.3	Investment Environment, East Asia	78
Figure 6.4	Monetary System, East Asia	79
Figure 6.5	Financial System, East Asia	80
Figure 6.6	Domestic Credit to Private Sector, East Asia	81
Figure 6.7	Property Rights Protection, East Asia	81
Figure 6.8	Voice & Accountability, East Asia	83
Figure 6.9	Political Stability, East Asia	83
Figure 6.10	Government Effectiveness, East Asia	84
Figure 6.11	Regulatory Quality, East Asia	85
Figure 6.12	Rule of Law, East Asia	85
Figure 6.13	Control of Corruption, East Asia	86
Figure 6.14	Conceptual Framework of Economic Incentives and Institutional Regimes in the East Asian KBEs	87
Figure 6.15	Inward FDI Flows in East Asia, 1998-2007	88
Figure 6.16	Public Expenditure in Education in East Asia, 1997-2005	89

List of Figures   v

Figure 6.17	Total R&D Expenditure in East Asia, 1997-2006	89
Figure 6.18	ICT Expenditure in East Asia, 2000-2007	90
Figure 6.19	Overall Productivity in East Asia, 1998-2007	91
Figure 7.1	Science in Schools, East Asia	97
Figure 7.2	Youth Interest in Science, Asia and Pacific	97
Figure 7.3	Educational System in Asia-Pacific Countries, 2000-2009	99
Figure 7.4	University Education in the Countries of East Asia, 2000-2009	99
Figure 7.5	Knowledge Transfer in the Countries of East Asia, 2000-2009	100
Figure 7.6	Skilled Labor in the Countries of East Asia, 2000-2009	103
Figure 7.7	Qualified Engineers in the Countries of East Asia, 2000-2009	103
Figure 7.8	Labor Productivity in the Countries of East Asia, 1999-2008	103
Figure 8.1	Fixed Telephone Lines, East Asia	113
Figure 8.2	Mobile Telephone Subscribers, East Asia	113
Figure 8.3	Computers per Capita, East Asia	114
Figure 8.4	Internet Users, East Asia	115
Figure 8.5	Cyber Security, East Asia	116
Figure 8.6	Communications Technology, East Asia	117
Figure 8.7	Information Technology Skills, East Asia	117
Figure 8.8	Technological Cooperation, East Asia	118
Figure 8.9	Public and Private Sector Ventures, East Asia	118
Figure 8.10	Development and Application of Technology, East Asia	119
Figure 8.11	Technological Regulation, East Asia	120
Figure 8.12	Funding for Technological Development, East Asia	120
Figure 8.13	Exports of ICT Goods as a Share of Total Goods Exported (Percentage), 2000-2006	123
Figure 8.14	Total Volume of High-tech Exports Per Year, East Asia	124
Figure 8.15	Percentage of High-tech Exports Per Year, East Asia	125
Figure 9.1	Imports in the Industry Sector in East Asia, 1995-2007	132
Figure 9.2	Machinery & Transport Equipment Imports (% of GDP) and Per Capita GDP	132
Figure 9.3	Industrial Exports in East Asia, 1995-2007	133
Figure 9.4	Machinery & Transport Equipment Imports (% of GDP) and Per Capita GDP-2003	133
Figure 9.5	Royalty Payments (% of GDP) and Per Capita GDP (PPP)	137
Figure 9.6	Sectoral Composition of FDI Stock in 2002	138
Figure 9.7	Basic Research, East Asia	145
Figure 9.8	Capacity for Innovations in East Asia, 2007-2008	146
Figure 9.9	Quality of Scientific Research Institutions in East Asia, 2007-2008	146

Figure 9.10   University-industry Research Collaboration in East Asia, 2007-2008   *147*
Figure 9.11   Government Procurement for Technological Innovation, East Asia   *148*
Figure 9.12   Patenting Revealed Comparative Advantage in East Asia   *151*
Figure 9.13   Patent Citation in East Asia   *153*
Figure 9.14   Patents Citation Share in East Asia   *153*
Figure 9.15   Patent Citation Frequencies   *154*
Figure 9.16   Intellectual Property Rights, East Asia   *155*
Figure 9.17   Scientific Research, East Asia   *155*

List of Tables

Table No		Page
Table 1.1	Per Capita Income in 1965 and 2000 (in current USD)	*13*
Table 1.2	International Competitiveness Index for Selected East Asian and African Countries	*14*
Table 5.1	Contribution of the ICT-producing and ICT-using Sectors to Aggregate GDP Growth, 1990-1999	*65*
Table 5.2	School Enrollment, Primary (Percentage) in East Asia	*69*
Table 5.3	GDP Growth (Annual Percentage) in East Asia	*69*
Table 5.4	Foreign Direct Investment, Net Inflows (% of GDP) in East Asia	*69*
Table 5.5	Research and Development Expenditures	*70*
Table 5.6	USPTO Patents Granted	*71*
Table 7.1	Total Public Expenditure on Education in the Countries of East Asia, 1998-2007 (% of GDP)	*95*
Table 7.2	Total Public Expenditure on Education per Capita (USD) in the Countries of East Asia, 1998-2007	*95*
Table 7.3	Secondary School Enrollment (Percentage of relevant age group receiving full-time education) in the Countries of East Asia, 1995-2006	*96*
Table 7.4	Percentage of population that has attained at least tertiary education for persons 25-34 in the Countries of East Asia, 1997-2006	*96*
Table 7.5	Science Degrees, East Asia	*98*
Table 7.6	Labor with Secondary and Tertiary Education in the Countries of East Asia, 2004-2007	*102*
Table 7.7	Fertility Rate in the Countries of East Asia, 1999-2007	*105*
Table 7.8	Life Expectancy at Birth in the Countries of East Asia, 1999-2007	*105*
Table 7.9	Demographic Composition in East Asia	*106*

Table 7.10	Age Composition Changes in East Asia, 1960, 1990, and 2025	106
Table 7.11	Foreign Labor Force in the Countries of East Asia, 2000-2007	107
Table 8.1	Investment in Telecommunications, East Asia	112
Table 8.2	Broadband Subscribers, East Asia	116
Table 8.3	Global Production of Electronics, 2002-2005 (USD in billions)	121
Table 8.4	Exports of ICT Goods, 1996, 2000 and 2005 (USD in millions)	123
Table 8.5	Imports of ICT Goods, 1996, 2000 and 2005 (USD in millions)	124
Table 9.1	Machinery Import Share of Total Imports	131
Table 9.2	High-tech Exports in East Asia, 1998-2007	134
Table 9.3	Royalty Payments	136
Table 9.4	Total Expenditure on R&D (USD in millions)	141
Table 9.5	Total Expenditure on R&D Per Capita (USD in millions)	142
Table 9.6	Business Expenditure on R&D (USD in millions)	143
Table 9.7	R&D Performance in Different Sectors in East Asia	143
Table 9.8	Total R&D Personnel Nationwide Per Capita	144
Table 9.9	Total R&D Personnel in Business Per Capita	144
Table 9.10	Scientific Articles Published According to Author's Origin	145
Table 9.11	Number of Patent Applications Filed for Residents and Non-residents, East Asia	149
Table 9.12	Total Number of Patents Granted to Residents, East Asia	149
Table 9.13	USPTO Patents Granted, East Asia	150
Table 9.14	Patent Productivity, East Asia	152
Table 10.1	KBE Index for the East Asian KBEs	160
Table 10.2	Human Development Index Trends in East Asia	161

List of Abbreviations

APEC	Asia Pacific Economic Cooperation
BMRC	Bio-Medical Research Council
EU	European Union
FDI	Foreign Direct Investment
FTE	Full-time Work Equivalent
GDP	Gross Domestic Products
GERD	Gross Expenditure on Research and Development
GER	Gross Enrolment Rate

HDI	Human Development Index
HKSE	Hong Kong Stock Exchange
IK	Investment in Knowledge
ISEAS	Institute of Southeast Asian Studies
IT	Information Technology
ICT	Information and Communications, Technology
IMD	International Institute of Management Development
IDA	Infocomm Development Authority of Singapore
KAM	Knowledge Assessment Methodology
KBE	Knowledge-based Economy
KB	Knowledge Base
KI	Knowledge Inputs
KSF	Knowledge Stocks and Flows
KN	Knowledge Networks
MEXT	Ministry of Education, Sports, Science and Technology
MITA	Ministry of Information, Communications and the Arts
MSC	Multimedia Super Corridor
MNC	Multinational Corporation
NITA	National Information Technology Agenda
NSTP	National Science and Technology Plan
NSF	National Science Foundation
OBM	Original Brand Manufacturing
ODM	Original Design Manufacturing
OECD	Organization of Economic Cooperation and Development
OEM	Original Equipment Manufacturing
R&D	Research and Development
SERC	Science and Engineering Research Council
TFP	Total Factor Productivity
TSLN	Thinking Schools, Learning Nation
US	United States
VINNOVA	Swedish Agency for Innovation Systems
WCY	World Competitiveness Yearbook
WEF	World Economic Forum

The East Asian Knowledge-based Economies

CONTENTS

Preface i

List of Figures iv

List of Tables vi

List of Abbreviations vii

Chapter One: Discourse on the Knowledge-based Economy and East Asian Economic Growth 1

Introduction   1
Discourse on the KBE   3
KBE, the Contemporary Global Economy and the East Asian Miracle   11
KBE in the East Asian Perspective   13
Summary   16

Chapter Two: Definitions and Concepts of Knowledge-based Economy 17

Introduction   17
Definitions of KBE   17
Conceptualizing the KBE   19
Understanding the KBE   22
The Emergence of the KBE   25
Functionality in a Knowledge-based Economic System   26
Summary   27

Chapter Three: Growth Theories and Knowledge-based Economy 28

Introduction *28*
Discussion on Available Growth Theories - Are they enough to explain contemporary economic growth? *29*
The KBE Approach *34*
Developing the Theoretical Framework for a KBE *38*
Proposed KBE Framework *42*
Summary *49*

Chapter Four: The Challenge of Measuring the KBE 50

Introduction *50*
The Challenge of Measuring the KBE *50*
Different Methodologies Available to Measure the KBE *52*
Summary *58*

Chapter Five: Contemporary KBEs and East Asia 59

Introduction *59*
Contemporary Public Policy Directions and the KBE *59*
The KBE in OECD Countries *61*
The East Asian Economic Miracle and the Emergence of the KBE in East Asia *68*
Summary *73*

Chapter Six: Economic Incentives and Institutional Regimes in the Development of KBEs in East Asia ··· 74

Introduction *74*
Economic Incentives in East Asian KBEs *75*
Institutional Regimes in East Asia *82*
Economic Incentives, Institutional Regimes and Development of the KBE in East Asia *86*
The Impact of Economic Incentives and Institutional Regimes on Attracting FDI and Promoting the KBE in East Asia *88*
Summary *91*

Chapter Seven: Developing Education and Human Resources in East Asian KBEs ··· 92

Introduction *92*
Historical Background *92*
Public Spending on Education *94*
Developments in Secondary and Tertiary Education Sector *95*
Quality Education System for a Competitive Economy *98*
East Asia's Human Capital Development *100*
Demographic Transition *104*
Summary *107*

Chapter Eight: Information and Communications Technology in East Asian KBEs ··· *108*

Introduction *108*
Building the ICT Infrastructure in East Asia *109*
Relationship between FDI and ICT in East Asia *110*

ICT's Investment Facilitating Role in East Asia   *112*
Expanding ICT Services in East Asia   *112*
Role of ICT in Enhancing a Competitive Business Environment   *117*
ICT as Industry   *121*
Trade of ICT Goods and Services in East Asia   *122*
Macroeconomic Impact of ICT in East Asia   *125*
Summary   *126*

Chapter Nine: Innovations in East Asian KBEs   *128*

Introduction   *128*
Historical Background of Innovation in East Asia   *128*
Status of Research and Development in East Asia   *140*
Capacity for Innovation in East Asia   *145*
Moving Towards the Global Frontier of Innovation   *148*
Summary   *156*

Chapter Ten: Economic Ramifications of the KBE in East Asia   *157*

Introduction   *157*
Key Factors for KBE Development in East Asia   *157*
Present Status of the East Asian KBEs   *159*
Tracking the Overall Development of the East Asian KBEs   *161*
Proposed Framework for the KBE in East Asia   *162*
Future Trends for the KBE in East Asia   *162*
Policy Recommendations for the East Asian KBEs   *165*
Summary   *166*

References   *167*

Chapter One

Discourse on the Knowledge-based Economy and East Asian Economic Growth

Introduction

Classical economic theories have explained the phenomenon of economic growth in the traditional terms. They are inadequate, however, in explaining the influences and interactions of multiple factors, such as foreign direct investment (FDI), cross-country mobility of the factors of production (Economic Social and Commission for Asia and the Pacific, 1999), levels of democracy and inequality (Sen, 1999), technology and information flow (Orna, 1990), and integration and regionalism (Fort and Webber, 2006). Some economic concepts introduced by evolutionary economists have been more successful in describing economic growth than in describing the knowledge-based economy (KBE) (Leydesdorff, 2005:15). Traditional assumptions have constrained many economists and policy makers, preventing them from realizing that knowledge is the main driver of today's economy. However, recently, many scholars have been calling attention to this. Also in the face of fierce global competition, many developed countries have recognized the importance of the KBE. The European Union (EU), for example, has emphasized the importance of a KBE in reforming the economic base of EU countries (European Commission, 2000). During the European Summit in March 2000, the commission concluded, among many things, "the shift to a digital, knowledge-based economy, prompted by new goods and services, will be capable of improving citizens' quality of life and the environment." Compared with the 1990s, the world's gini-coefficient in 2005 was 0.67, an increase of 10 percent. This increase has largely been credited to the use and creation of knowledge through innovation. As a consequence, economists have now shifted their focus to the creation and diffusion of knowledge to explain the varying levels of economic growth and development present in today's world.

In the last two decades, many countries have shown high economic performance via knowledge creation and knowledge diffusion to various sectors of the economy. This has come to be described as the KBE (Debnath, 2008: 146). Many countries in East Asia have shown tremendous success in economic development by converting themselves from a traditional economic system into a KBE.

One of the challenges of this study is to select an appropriate methodology to measure the contribution of knowledge and its contribution to the national economy. The usual methodology for measuring gross domestic product (GDP), as well as most other macroeconomic indicators, cannot appropriately measure the impact of policy formulations on the KBE. Moreover, measuring the performance of the KBE itself is yet to be clearly identified and defined in the literature. The World Bank's knowledge assessment methodology is by far the most comprehensive methodology in identifying the key variables of the KBE worldwide. Thus, this study investigates the KBE in East Asia by taking the World Bank's KBE index into consideration. A KBE framework is proposed based on the four pillars of the KBE indicated by the World Bank. The four pillars are: economic incentives and institutional regimes, education and human resources, information and communications technology and innovation systems. The intention behind the KBE framework is both to simplify systematic data collection and facilitate the investigation of key factors for each pillar which affect the development of the KBE, as well as to understand the economic ramifications of the KBE in East Asian context.

Through qualitative and quantitative analysis of the knowledge-based economies (KBEs) in East Asia, it is evident that there are some key determining factors for each pillar. The countries that are better at developing these key determining factors are more successful in creating a KBE in the region. Japan, Korea, Taiwan, Hong Kong and Singapore are the most successful countries in the region that achieved superior performance in developing the key determining factors to become a KBE. However, rapid demographic transition has been found to be one major challenge for these countries, as they must continue to supply the talented human resources required by the KBE. These countries have adapted to the situation by a policy of attracting talented human resources from abroad, and by providing these workers with opportunities similar to those of their native population. This policy also assists in raising the domestic birth rate. On the other hand, China, Indonesia, Malaysia, the Philippines, and Thailand, though showing some progress in developing the key factors of KBE, still lag far behind the advanced KBEs mentioned above. Among the countries lagging behind, Malaysia has been performing comparatively well in terms of developing the key factors of a KBE. However, in general the developments in all these later countries are not as significant as they are in Japan, Korea, Taiwan, Hong Kong and Singapore.

Discourse on the KBE

What makes some countries grow faster and others slower? Since the days of Adam Smith, economists have been preoccupied with the answer to this question and have been searching for the causes of economic growth. To enhance productivity, Adam Smith (1776) invented the idea of division of labor, breaking down the work process into finer elements of a scale economy. He also argued that an economy of scale is the main driver of the macro-economy. The idea of breaking down the work process into finer elements, now known as work specialization, incurs cost, as it requires both knowledge accumulation and knowledge creation. Eliasson (1990:14-15) explains the process of knowledge creation and accumulation as follows:

> "Work specialization, however, came at a cost. It required *innovative knowledge* to be created. The more elaborate work specialization the more resources needed to *coordinate* production. Hence, there are explicit communications costs associated with organizing a specialized economy. Goods have to be moved *(transported)* and *information* has to be *processed* to guide and control specialized activities. Such coordination can be achieved *through the market* by what Adam Smith called the invisible hand, through management or *administrative methods* in production units. ⋯ ⋯ ⋯ Determination of division of labor and thereby information technology to coordinate economic action is a prime

function in any economy. The choice of organization technology is rarely made explicit. ⋯ ⋯ ⋯ Knowledge, once created through the organization technology (innovation) is diffused through the economy through imitation, or through various educational arrangements. Learning is an important category of economic activities that has to be considered to capture the whole economy at work."

Eliasson (1990:14-15)

It is true that Adam Smith's economic thoughts were well-taken by the capitalist world of the West, and that from there, they spread throughout the world. Throughout the twentieth century, almost all countries adopted the capitalist ideology either fully or partially. Looking at the success that capitalism had in bringing economic growth throughout the globe, Friedman (2006) argued that the world is flat. He supports this argument by mentioning various flatteners in wide use today, including work flow software, uploading, outsourcing, off shoring, supply-chaining, and in-sourcing. However, is the world really flat? If we look at economic development in different parts of the world, we can clearly see that development is very uneven across the world. Among the many observers of this uneven development is Michael Porter, who in 1998 noted that despite advances in communications and transportation technology, a number of industries, and particularly high-tech R&D, remain highly concentrated in particular geographical locations. As a consequence, some economies are growing much faster than others and as such, the KBEs are the leaders in innovation, all other economies are merely followers.

Friedman's argument can be better rephrased by the idea of 'great disruption', coined by Fukuyama (1999) in his book 'The Great Disruption'. However, before introducing this revolutionary idea of 'great disruption', he analyzes the changes in the post-Cold War world since 1992. Fukuyama (1999) mentions that the great disruption began over the past thirty years, and since then, the United States and other developed countries have undergone a profound transformation from industrial to information societies. He further mentions that during this disruption, knowledge has replaced mass production as the basis of wealth, power, and social interaction.

While neoclassical economists including Keynes (2003), and Solow (1997) were very much concerned with the determination of the optimum combination of labor and capital as a factor of production and growth, Joseph E. Schumpeter (1989) introduced the idea of 'creative destruction and entrepreneurship' in 1934 to explain the mystery of economic growth. This concept of creative destruction was well received by the world after the oil shock in 1973, and it remained popular until the end of the 1990s.

It was after the oil shock in 1973 that the U.S. policy-makers were at a loss as to how to respond, because economic stagnation was to be followed by a rapidly aging population. The development of Silicon Valley (Saxenian, 1994) paved the way in managing economic growth through innovation and the creation of a knowledge-based society. Presently, the Information Technology (IT) hub in Bangalore in India, Cyber Jaya in Malaysia, and other Science Parks in China, Korea, Taiwan, Singapore, and in other fast-developing countries have successfully applied this concept, and the concerned countries are thus developing faster than other countries in the region that are still unaware of the importance of a KBE. Creating a knowledge-based society has two economic ramifications: first, it increases the competitiveness of the country; and second, it expands its stock of knowledge for future innovative activities.

Knowledge, in and of itself, is a form of social capital that needs not exist within the boundaries of an individual company, and that needs not expire at the end of an individual's employment (Fukuyama, 1999:208). Informal networks, by creating and diffusing knowledge, are playing a critical role in technological development. This is largely because a great deal of knowledge is tacit and thus, is hard to be reduced to a commodity that can be bought and sold in an intellectual property market (Kash and Ryecroft, 1999). Fukuyama (1999:208) in this regard argued that, "the enormous complexity of the underlying technologies and of the systems integration process means that even the largest firms will not be able to generate adequate technical knowledge in-house". Though technology is transferred between firms through mergers, acquisitions, cross-licensing, and formal partnerships, or in case of country to country through FDI or any other agreements of exchange, the literature on technology development stresses the nature of R&D as one of the key elements in converting tacit knowledge into a usable commodity. Saxenian (1994:32-33) has argued that informal networks play a very important role in this process of converting knowledge into a usable commodity. According to her, by all accounts, the informal conversations in the informal networks are inescapable and are an important source of up-to-date information about competitors, customers, markets and technologies. Fukuyama (1999) has summarized social networks as follows:

> "The social capital produced by such informal social networks permits Silicon Valley to achieve scale economies in R&D not possible in large, vertically integrated firms. Much has been written about the cooperative character of Japanese firms and the way in which technology is shared among the members of keiretsu network. In a certain sense, the whole Silicon Valley can be seen as a single network organization that can tap expertise and specialized skills unavailable to even the largest vertically integrated Japanese firms and their keiretsu partners."
>
> Fukuyama (1999:210)

Economic ideology in the late twentieth century has changed drastically. Now, it focuses on knowledge creation and diffusion, popularizing the notion of the KBE in the developed world (so that those countries remain competitive in the global market) and in the developing world (so that those countries might accelerate their own economic growth). Dunning (1997: 53) explains this changing pattern by stating that in contrast to the land-based capitalism of the pre-industrial era and machine- and finance-based capitalism of the 19th and much of the 20th century, the capitalism of the 1990s is becoming increasingly knowledge-based. He further mentions that the territorial horizons of capitalism have continuously widened from the sub-national to the national and macro-regional levels and now, increasingly, to the global level, as well.

The changing phenomena in economic growth models recognized by the 'new' economic growth theorists indicate that the critical factors underlying growth are 'intangible' assets that create knowledge and generate innovation (Betcherman, 1997: 69). The economy, today, is really about the economics of coordination, innovation, selection and learning (Eliasson, 1989). As a result of globalization, the room to maneuver is diminishing in national macroeconomic and budgetary policies, and structural microeconomic policies (which affect the framework conditions determining a firm's competitiveness) are assuming increasing importance. In a KBE, a number of issues require particular policy attention, such as intangible assets, knowledge infrastructures and flows, intellectual property rights and so on (OECD Proceedings, 1997: 3-4). In most OECD countries, an increasing number of firms appear to be reorganizing their structures in response to greater international competition, greater international flows of investment and technology, and a shift towards a more KBE (Drake, 1997: 17).

The development of information and communications technology (ICT) has been a great element of the KBE. An information-based society has emerged globally, but large-scale trends involving ICT are emerging in regional economies, which have their own identity and regional specificity. These trends call for regional-specific responses from policy-makers who hope to reap the economic benefits of a blossoming information society (Dunnewijk and Wintjes, 2006:157).

In the ICT industry, which is characterized by science-based technologies, cooperation is driven by the needs of accelerating innovation and by joining complementary technological assets and competences. In this process, formal and informal agreements are implemented and most of the time, they are characterized by vertical integration for producing 'subsystems', such as Internet access, service providers and so on (Lazaric and Thomas, 2006:129). In this regard, Pyka and Hanusch (2006) claim:

"Beyond these processes stands the transformation of economies to so-called knowledge-based economies. The decisive difference with respect to traditional manufacturing-based economies has to be seen in the dominant role for economic welfare which is played today by knowledge creation and diffusion processes. However, only to push forward the scientific and technological frontiers (*exploration*) is not sufficient to cope with these pervasive developments. What additionally counts is to be prepared for permanent transformation process of the whole economic system which is strongly connected with the effective *exploitation* and use of various kinds of new knowledge in a preferably broad set of economic activities."

Pyka and Hanusch (2006:3)

The revolution in ICT led to a re-conceptualization of production and the re-conceptualization involves much more than a simple recalibration of the neo-classical production function; it involves a new "techno-economic paradigm" – *i.e.* the web of institutions, policies and practices by which economic activity is organized (Freeman and Perez, 1998). Soete (1997:135) explains the importance of ICT in a KBE saying:

"The ability of ICTs to codify information and knowledge over both distance and time brings about more global access. Knowledge, including economic knowledge, has become available world-wide. While local competencies to access or use such knowledge will vary widely, the access potential is there. In other words, ICTs bring to forefront the potential for catching-up, based on economic transparency of advantage, while at the same time stressing the crucial "tacit" and other competence elements in the capacity to access international codified knowledge."

Soete (1997:135)

We are living in an era characterized by the rise of the information society in a diverse, regional-specific reality. The foundation of this society is informationalism, which means that the defining activities in all realms of human practice are based on IT, organized (globally) in information networks, and centered on information (symbol) processing (Castells and Himanen, 2002:1). In regard to this, Castells and Hall (1994) state:

Chapter One: Discourse on the Knowledge-based Economy and East Asian Economic Growth

"Cities and regions are being profoundly modified in their structure, and conditioned in their growth dynamics by the interplay of three major historical processes: technological revolution, the formation of a global economy, and the emergence of an informational form of economic production and management. Technopoles, planned centers for promotion of high-technology industry, are the reality of these fundamental transformations, redefining the conditions and processes of local and regional development."

Castells and Hall (1994)

The world economy is undergoing dramatic change, with companies and markets everywhere becoming exposed to international competition, and the pros and cons of internationalization and competition are being increasingly acknowledged by developing countries (Micossi, 1997:113). The development of a society based on knowledge requires an open and competitive environment favoring innovation (Micossi, 1997:123). The European enlightenment pushed a dual platform that was both radical and revolutionary: reforming institutions to promote efficiency and innovation, and bringing the full force of human knowledge to bear on technology, without which, long-term economic growth in the West might not have happened (Mokyr, 2006:29-30). Regarding this, Dolfsma *et al.* (2006) argue:

"It is fair to say that any assessment of the contemporary role of knowledge must recognize that most economic activity rests on knowledge, not only in present society but in all forms of human society. Palaeolithic society was by any standards 'knowledge-based', and palaeontologistics have demonstrated the existence of well-formed bodies of knowledge with respect to animal behavior, materials, mining, symbolic communication and even medicine. In the most recent past, the industrial economy of the nineteenth century was intensively knowledge-based. At first sight many claims about the current 'knowledge economy' could plausibly have been made a hundred years ago. It is of course true that knowledge accumulates over time, that it changes the quality and quantity of output. Hence that today the knowledge intensity of production is likely to be much higher than ever before."

Dolfsma *et al.* (2006:1)

There is an obvious drift towards higher knowledge intensity in all economic sectors and flows of knowledge both tacit and explicit have an important positive effect on innovation performance. Flows of knowledge enable people to detect, adapt, adopt and use new knowledge and technologies, and in most countries, there exist "hubs" in which firms interact through dense knowledge networks and show above-average performance in terms of international competitiveness, growth and employment (Guinet, 1997:173-174). FDI is associated with firms and industries that use skilled labor intensively and that are closely associated with knowledge-incentive production. Much of the value of the multinational firms lies in various forms of knowledge-based assets rather than in physical capital (Markusen, 1997:83). Yashiro (1997), in this case, points out:

"The impact of movements of international capital and in particular of foreign direct investment will be even larger than that of free trade. ⋯ ⋯ ⋯ A country's acceptance of multinational firms implies that it imports not only foreign capital, but a combination of high-technologies and management skills, and a sales network abroad. Exports through the intra-firm trading network, which otherwise have taken a long time, are facilitated through the development of such "foreign domestic markets". The borderless economy gives multinational companies more freedom to choose the country in which they wish to locate their activities."

Yashiro (1997:125)

If we analyze the phenomenon above, we realize that the available literature recognizes the emergence of a KBE. Most scholars recognize this emergence of KBE as a fundamental change. Sheehan (1997), in this regard, argues:

"It is widely agreed that the global economy is in the early stages of an era of fundamental change, as the emerging information industries permeate all aspects of economic and social life. There is much emphasis on the necessity for improved methods of learning, as firms, individuals and institutions try to adjust to the new realities. But it is not so often realized that this is as much true of government as of any other group within society. Governments must learn- through a dynamic, iterative and often painful process- how to pursue the national interest effectively and efficiently in the new environment.

Sheehan (1997: 239)

Without building a proper base of knowledge, no economy can provide guarantees for steady growth. Meir Khon, *et al.*, (1992) argue that current productivity depends on the stock of knowledge. The reciprocal dependence of the stock of knowledge on the level of current production generates endogenous/traditional technological processes in a KBE. This is to increase the per capita output, capital stock and growth rates. Such growth is not possible in the neoclassical growth models, which assume that the economy will be stationary. Drucker (1985) argues that the Japanese success in adopting Western technologies without becoming a colony of the West is the result of a conscious decision made a hundred years ago to concentrate human resources on knowledge-based social innovations rather than technical innovations. Romer (1986) has also pointed out that knowledge-based growth models are consistent in explaining the divergence of growth rates, capital intensity and human mobility in the globe and thus, could be a complement to the standard neoclassical models. Poppo and Zenger (1998), in this regard, state that a knowledge-based theory of firm can be used to explain what makes some businesses grow steadily and others not.

KBE, the Contemporary Global Economy and the East Asian Miracle

In the contemporary global economy, where competition is fierce and uncertainty is associated with everything (Nonaka and Takeuchi, 1995), the importance of knowledge creation and diffusion is an absolute requirement in every sector of society. Knowledge creation is especially a high priority for any sector of society where government policies play a great role in integrating different sectors. Many OECD countries are completing this task successfully, while many others are lagging behind. Among the recent successful KBEs, Singapore is frequently cited as an example in the studies of policy-directed KBE (Bercuson, *et al.*, 1995 and Low, 2001) while other countries, such as Korea, Hong Kong, Taiwan and Malaysia are also considered to be emerging KBEs (Mani, 2005 and Mustapha and Abdullah, 2004) in the East Asian region. Surely, there are many other countries in other parts of the world, such as the United States, Canada, and countries in the EU, that are considered as KBEs in global economy.

The East Asian Miracle has left us with a great debate as to how to explain its model for growth. Until now, many scholars have criticized the neoclassical approach, saying that it does not adequately explicate the East Asian Miracle. Wade's 'state interventionist view' held the role of government to be key to East Asian economic growth, while Aoki's 'market enhancing view' took a different approach, explaining that East Asian economic development by way of a mechanism where government plays an important role in disciplining the market whenever necessary to avoid market collapse. However, none of these attempts fully explains the overall economic growth model in East Asia.

Many scholars have emphasized 'innovation' as one of the major factors in East Asian economic growth. During the high growth period, East Asian countries have made tremendous efforts in building appropriate technological and educational infrastructures to support the innovation process. Their governments have played a very important role by pursuing appropriate policies during this process. As a result, there is now a new attempt to understand East Asian economic growth from the 'KBE' standpoint, where knowledge is created and diffused for 'continuous innovation' by developing proper educational, technological and innovation infrastructures (Bercuson *et al.*, 1995; Low, 2001; Mani, 2005 and Mustapha and Abdullah, 2004). In this 'KBE' approach, the role of government is considered to be very critical to the development of educational, technological and innovation infrastructures. The four economic tigers of East Asia have been led by Japan, which many scholars claimed to represent a new pattern of economic growth (Kim, 1998). Some scholars came up with the "flying geese model" to explain the growth model of East Asian countries. The World Bank called the economic growth of East Asia an "Economic Miracle" (World Bank, 1993). Many recent scholars

(Weder, 1999; Stiglitz and Yusuf, 2001; Mustapha and Abdullah, 2004 and Mani, 2005) have pointed out that the East Asian countries mentioned above have been pursuing the government policies needed to transform their traditional economic system and create a KBE.

KBE in the East Asian Perspective

Most East Asian countries were poor in the mid-1960s, as shown in Table 1.1. There was no significant gap between the selected East Asian and major African countries in terms of per capita income. However, by the end of twentieth century, the selected East Asian countries achieved remarkable economic growth compared to African countries. Similarly, international competitiveness in selected countries in the two regions in Table 1.2, defined as (X-M)/ (X+M) where X and M are exports and imports, shows that although most of the East Asian countries had a negative international competitiveness index in the 1960s, similar to the African countries, they managed to overcome their structural constraints and become internationally competitive, whereas their African counterparts are still experiencing negative competitive indices.

Table 1.1 Per Capita Income in 1965 and 2000 (in current USD)

Country	1965	2000
Sub-saharan Africa		
Benin	120	390
Cameroon	140	580
Cote d'Ivoire	200	680
Ghana	230	330
Nigeria	120	260
South Africa	540	3,060
East Asia		
Japan	910	35,420
Korea	130	9,010
Hong Kong	690	26,410
Singapore	540	23,350
Malaysia	330	3,250

Source: WDI CD-ROM 2003.

Table 1.2 International Competitiveness Index for Selected East Asian and African Countries

Country	Year 1965	Year 2004
Sub-saharan Africa		
Cameroon	-0.38	-0.06
Ethiopia	-0.36	-0.62
Ghana	-.53	-0.70
Kenya	-0.25	-0.24
Nigeria	-0.49	0.24
South Africa	-0.04	0.06
East Asia		
Taiwan	0.09	0.11
Indonesia	-0.38	0.17
Japan	0.07	0.10
Korea	-0.33	0.06
Malaysia	-0.01	0.07
Singapore	-0.11	0.08

Source: Calculated based on data obtained from UNCTAD (2004).

It is therefore quite understandable why many scholars are now trying to understand what factors contributed most to the East Asian Miracle. Most countries in East Asia have experienced high levels of FDI, and this was appropriately used as an alternative source of foreign currency and was a major factor in capital formation in the development process. An essential difference with the market-oriented approach is that governments in East Asia used to intervene in certain phases of development, if it was necessary. Stiglitz (1996) pointed out that government policies in East Asia adapted to changing economic circumstances, rather than remaining fixed. As the economies grew more complex and the creation and diffusion of knowledge more vital, East Asian countries started transforming their economies into KBEs, allowing for all the sectors of the economy to find an appropriate interface for continuous innovation. This changed the role of the government from intervening to facilitating the operation of an interface which was conducive to economic growth.

Understanding the KBE in East Asia not only allows us to understand the secret to East Asian economic development; it also provides lessons to those countries that are still in the beginning of transforming their economies into KBEs. The economic system of any country is complex. This is more true when we are trying to study economic system not as a subsystem but as a fuller system encompassing a KBE. In East Asia, recently the development of the KBE has been a focus of many governments' policy formulations. The magnitude of this policy formulation towards a KBE dwarfs other aspects of the developmental landscape, and is widely recognized as a primary driving force behind the development of the KBE in East Asia. This transition of policy formulation from the traditional economy in East Asia towards a new one involves not merely the adoption of a new generation of technology; it requires a transition to a new economic framework - a KBE - whose nature and characteristics are profoundly different from that of the traditional economy.

Although policy formulation for the KBE in East Asia is rather new, knowledge and its management are not a new field of research. In the contemporary literature, knowledge and its management are generally discussed in the study of organizational behavior and its implications rather than in the broader arena of national affairs. It was not until the mid-1990s, with the publication of *The Knowledge Creating Company* (Nonaka and Takeuchi, 1995) and *Working Knowledge* (Davenport and Prusak, 1998), that knowledge management began to emerge as a recognized corporate discipline which later drew the attention of many other scholars from different disciplines, facilitating the study of the KBE from a multidisciplinary approach.

In East Asia, the KBE has begun to develop far and wide; this makes it essential to explore, in a collective manner, such as by pooling the intellectual resources within and beyond countries, the KBE that is directly related to current political events. Many scholars consider the economic system as a subsystem of a larger system in society. This assumption has hindered many scholars from studying the whole society and thus, many economic theories fall short in describing the economic development of East Asian countries. The East Asian economies are at different stages of development, with huge, diverse cultures and historical backgrounds. Thus, studying the economic system as a subsystem for East Asian economies is insufficient to understand the complex mechanism of East Asian economic growth. A more comprehensive approach, like that of the KBE, is needed.

In East Asia, it is a concern whether the education sector, private sector and government can cooperate to develop new products and technology through innovation, thereby achieving higher growth and long-term synchronous development. However, the cooperation among these different bodies requires a proper interface, an interface in which all sectors find cooperation beneficial. The successful East Asian KBEs, such as Japan, Korea, Hong Kong, Taiwan and Singapore, have been capable to create the interface required for innovation, where different sectors find cooperation easy and helpful, whereas some other East Asian economies have not been successful in transforming their economies into KBEs, as they have failed to create the interface needed for innovation, such as in Myanmar, Cambodia, and Laos (World Bank Policy Research Report, 1993). In this regard, China, Indonesia, Malaysia, the Philippines and Thailand have experienced limited success. Consequently, to understand the KBEs in East Asia, this study focuses on Japan, Korea, Taiwan, Hong Kong, and Singapore.

Summary

Based on the discussions in this chapter, we realize that although the arguments about the KBE are relatively new in the field, they have been debated seriously in the recent scholarly work of many economists, and these arguments have been given serious attention by policy-makers, as well. The OECD countries remain at the top of knowledge-based economic development, as East Asian countries joined the race later. Countries like Japan, Korea, Taiwan, Hong Kong, and Singapore have been in the forefront of KBE development in the East Asian region. The East Asian Miracle has enabled the advanced East Asian countries to transform their product economies into KBEs and thereby achieve high economic growth.

Chapter Two

Definitions and Concepts of Knowledge-based Economy

Introduction

The term 'KBE' is relatively new in the literature (OECD, 1996; Leydesdorff, 2006 and David and Foray, 2002). It was first introduced by the Organization of Economic Cooperation and Development (OECD). The OECD (1996:7) describes the KBE as an economy that is directly based on the production, distribution and use of knowledge and information. Later, Asia Pacific Economic Cooperation (APEC) extended this idea and came up with a definition of the KBE as "an economy in which the production, distribution, and use of knowledge is the main driver of growth, wealth creation and employment across all industries" (APEC, 2000:2). However, the KBE itself is yet to have a concrete definition and as a result, scholars in various disciplines have defined it in different ways. While some scholars think that high-technology is an integral part of the KBE, others argue differently, saying that even the old economies may be called KBEs. The point they raise here is whether the knowledge is used in the economic activities or not. This chapter sheds lights on this noteworthy debate of definitions and concepts of the KBE.

Definitions of KBE

Many scholars have attempted to define the KBE by looking at different aspects of investments in knowledge. In his attempt to define the KBE, Khan (2001:4) looks at the different possible components of 'Investment in Knowledge (IK)'. He tries to make a list of common components of IK, considering common factors like innovation, research and development, software, marketing, human capital, and organizational capital. Khan (2001:4) suggested a more concrete list of IK by saying that expenditures towards activities with the aim of enhancing existing knowledge and/or acquiring new knowledge or diffusing knowledge are called IK, such as research and development (R&D) expenditures, education expenditures, software expenditures, training expenditures, innovation expenditures, and industrial design expenditures.

The term "KBE" stems from the fuller recognition of the importance of knowledge and technology in modern OECD economies (Chartrand; 2006:8). Chartrand (2006:8) further argues that the importance of knowledge and technology diffusion requires better understanding of 'knowledge networks' and 'national innovation systems'. A knowledge economy is focused on the economy of production and management of knowledge (Drucker, 1969). The second conceptualization by Drucker that is frequently used refers to the use of knowledge to produce economic benefits; this second conceptualization provides a more concrete understanding of the first. The phrase was popularized, if not invented, by Peter Drucker as the heading to Chapter 12 in his book 'The Age of Discontinuity' (1969:263).

Despite all the difficulties, many scholars, institutions and organizations have tried to define the term KBE. The OECD (2005: paragraph 71) describes the KBE as an expression coined to describe trends in advanced economies towards greater dependence on knowledge, information and high skill levels, and the increasing need for ready access to all of these by the business and public sectors. The Work Foundation explains the KBE in a broader perspective. According to the Work Foundation (2007):

> "The ability to use, analyze and share knowledge is supposedly becoming one of the key drivers of economic growth and wealth creation across all the advanced industrialized economies. Knowledge and knowledge diffusion have been a key driver of economic development for centuries. What is new is that we have very powerful information and communication technologies that allow knowledge to be processed, analyzed, shared and used on an unprecedented scale and speed."
>
> The Work Foundation (2007: paragraph 4)

In their introduction to the topic, David and Foray (2002) warned against using the metaphor of the KBE. They cautioned that the terminology was coined recently, and noted that "it marks a break in the continuity with earlier periods, more a 'sea-change' than a sharp discontinuity" (David and Foray, 2002: 9). 'Knowledge' and 'information' should be more carefully distinguished by analyzing the development of a KBE in terms of codification processes (Cowan, David and Foray, 2000: 211-253). Indeed, some observers, such as David Wolfe (2002), argue that the so-called "new economy" should more properly be called "a learning economy" because of the transitory nature of knowledge.

Some scholars argue that failing to define terms concretely sometimes jeopardizes the analytical base of the KBE. Keith Smith (2002:7) says, "the weakness or even complete absence, of definition, is actually pervasive in the literature⋯ this is one of the many imprecisions that make the notion of 'knowledge economy' so rhetorical rather than analytically useful". The idea of the knowledge-driven economy is not just a description of high-tech industries. It describes a set of new sources of competitive advantage which can apply to all sectors, all companies and all regions, from agriculture and retailing to software and biotechnology.

However, developing better definitions of the KBE will be challenging due to its complex settings over a very broad terrain. As efforts so far indicate, we are yet to have a universal and concrete definition of the KBE; further research needs to be carried out to move beyond the current statistical constraints and accurately define KBE. This study does not aim to develop an appropriate definition of the KBE. It instead tries to understand the key factors that strengthen the KBE with respect to East Asia.

Conceptualizing the KBE

Generally, we use knowledge to codify the meaning of any information. Depending on one's level of knowledge or perspective about knowledge pertaining to certain information, the codified meaning may change. Moreover, knowledge itself can be codified. Leydesdorff (2005:17) argued that codified knowledge can be commercialized and thus, the KBE is a system that operates in recursive loops, loops in which one could expect it to be increasingly selective in terms of the information it retains. The knowledge-base of the KBE can be developed over time by an ongoing process of theoretically informed deconstructions and reconstructions (Cowan *et al.*, 2000: 211-253 and Foray, 2004).

In a KBE, knowledge operates by informing the expectations of the present based on past experience and at the same time, it predicts the future based on present events. So, the KBE is driven more by codified anticipation rather than by historical conditions (Lundvall and Borras, 1997). Leydesdorff (2005:18) also mentions that a technological trajectory follows the axis of time, while a KBE operates within the system in terms of operation, that is, against the axis of time (See Figure 2.1). He argues that before the emergence of a KBE, the economic exchange of knowledge was first developed as distinct from the exchange of commodities within the context of a market economy. He points out the case of the patent system, a typical product of industrial competition in the late nineteenth century, as an example, saying that patent legislation became crucial for regulating intellectual property when the knowledge market emerged and the patents began to package enough scientific knowledge to allow new knowledge contained therein to

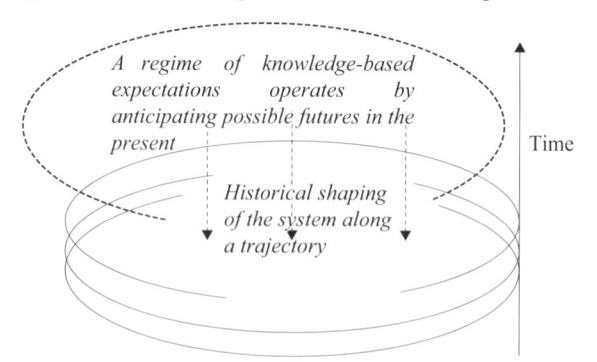

Figure 2.1 The Chronological Trajectory of the KBE
Source: Leydesdorff, 2005:18.

function at the interface of science and the economy. This process was incorporated into knowledge-based innovations and thus provided a format for codifying the contents of knowledge for purposes other than the internal requirements of quality control in scientific communication. Granstrand (1999) and Jaffe and Trajtenberg (2002) have also argued in the similar manner.

The creation and diffusion of organized knowledge has been one of the key sub-dynamics of the socio-economic system in many advanced countries for many years (Braverman, 1974). Schumpeter (1964) also argued that the dynamics of innovation upset market mechanisms. While market forces try to create equilibrium conditions at each moment, the innovative production function generates an orthogonal sub-dynamic along the time axis (Leydesdorff, 2005:19). Sahal (1981) considered the difference between the factor substitution, such as change of input factors along the production line and technological advancement, as a shift of the production function towards the origin (See Figure 2.2).

Both factor substitution and technological advancement interact with each other in the KBE through innovation reinforcement. This reinforcement occurs in some nations more than others because of differences in capability to invent,

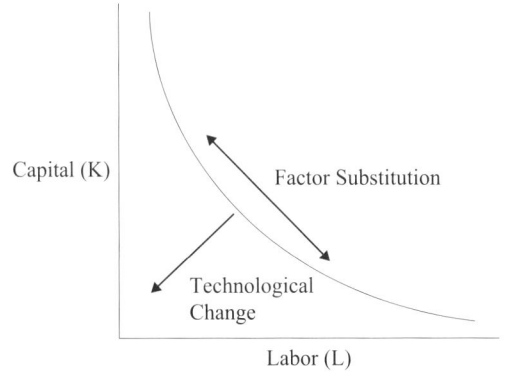

Figure 2.2 The Effect of Technological Change or Factor Substitution on the Production Function (Y=A.K.L)
Source: Adapted from Leydesdorff, 2005: 19.

produce, trade or retain value when cooperating or competing with other nations; differences in ability arise from a nation's economic conditions and its knowledge base (Lundvall, 1992; Nelson, 1993 and Leydesdorff, 2005). The interaction among the nation-states, knowledge creation and diffusion and economic trends therefore generates evolutionary dynamics as a system transition within a KBE (Schumpeter, 1964). In a KBE, this interaction is continuously disturbed at various interfaces and is never at rest, due to the nature of the KBE; even if any two of the sub-dynamics come to equilibrium, the third one will destabilize the equilibrium or another factor, such as globalization, for instance, can cause erosion of relative stability in nation-states by changing the conditions of innovation systems (Leydesdorff, 2005:21). The historical progression of the KBEs varies among countries, and integration at the national level still plays vital role in realizing a KBE.

Understanding the KBE

The capacity to generate and apply knowledge efficiently has been a tool of innovation, competition and economic success since long ago (Knowledge Economy Forum, 2002: 4). However, classical economic theories failed to consider knowledge as an important component of an economy's productivity, although this is now a very important force for the economic and social development of any country. Many contemporary scholars have argued for knowledge to be recognized as an important component of the KBE, given its contribution to a country's overall economic and social development. In an increasingly globalizing world, physical barriers, such as distance or terrain, are becoming increasingly irrelevant; at the same time, knowledge is becoming more and more important to competitiveness both locally and globally. As knowledge flows both vertically and horizontally, it creates better matches between R&D and downstream innovation, and thereby increases the rate of innovation.

The Knowledge Economy Forum (2002) organized by the World Bank has mentioned the following modern facets as a way to understand the KBE from a broader perspective:

> "The increase in global trade and foreign direct investment in recent years, itself facilitated by the ease of information flows, accelerates the impact of these changes. In an increasingly global economy, where knowledge about how to excel competitively and information about who excels are both more readily available, the effective creation, use and dissemination of knowledge is increasingly the key to success, and thus to sustainable economic and social development that benefits all. Innovation, which fuels new job creation and economic growth, is quickly becoming the key factor in global competitiveness.
>
> The impact of global information flows, and of the knowledge economy, on governmental and societal institutions is no less profound or important. In information-rich environments where knowledge flows freely and communications are abundant and multi-directional, pressures increase on governments to be more transparent, accountable and participatory. At the same time, the ability of governments to access and control information, and the uneven access to information and knowledge among sectors of society can, in certain circumstances, increase inequality and further entrench existing political and social elites. Unequal access to education and training can perpetuate and deepen inequality.
>
> The growth of a global KBE creates great opportunities, and poses great challenges, for all countries, but particularly for those that are still struggling to combat widespread poverty and create sustainable development that reaches all, or those dealing with difficult transitions from centralized forms of economic organization. To create these opportunities and navigate these risks, a country must do three difficult things. It must develop a coherent, multi-faceted national strategy for building and sustaining a KBE. It must develop this strategy in a participatory, broad-based fashion that includes and empowers all major sectors of society, including the private sector, educators, scientists and innovators, civil society, the media and others. And it must implement this strategy in a sustained and patient fashion, carefully balancing competing priorities, difficult tradeoffs, and interdependent changes with different time horizons, all in the context of

opening progressively to a fast-paced, rapidly changing, unpredictable and highly competitive global economy."

Knowledge Economy Forum (2002:4-5)

The Knowledge Economy Forum (2002:5-6) also recognized four essential dynamics for building a KBE such as:

1. *Creating an appropriate economic incentive and institutional regime* that encourages the widespread and efficient use of local and global knowledge in all sectors of the economy, that fosters entrepreneurship, and that permits and supports the economic and social transformations engendered by the knowledge revolution;
2. *Creating a society of skilled, flexible and creative people*, with opportunities for quality education and life-long learning available to all, and a flexible and appropriate mix of public and private funding;
3. *Building a dynamic information infrastructure*, and a competitive and innovative information sector of the economy that fosters a variety of efficient and competitive information and communications services and tools available to all sectors of society. This includes not only "high-end" information and communication technologies (ICTs) such as the Internet and mobile telephony but also other elements of an information-rich society such as radio, television and other media, computers and other devices for storing, processing and using information, and a range of communication services.
4. *Creating an efficient innovation system* comprising firms, science and research centers, universities, think tanks and other organizations that can tap into and contribute to the growing stock of global knowledge, adapt it to local needs, and use it to create new products, services, and ways of doing business. Designing and implementing a coherent and sustained response to these challenges is not easy, particularly for developing countries and countries in transition, which face additional burdens from limited resources, weak institutional capacity, and a legacy of centrally-controlled economic development.

The various modern facets of a KBE given by the Knowledge Economy Forum provide us with a general understanding of what contributes to the development of a KBE, and the four essential dynamics mentioned therein portray its basic skeleton. In the absence of a universal definition, the factors mentioned above by the Knowledge Economy Forum (2002) help us to understand the basic mechanism of the KBE in the contemporary world.

The Emergence of the KBE

During the formation of national systems in the nineteenth century, knowledge production was first considered as exogenous (List, 1841) although people like Marx had closely observed the technological advancement that took place during the era of industrialization. Leydesdorff (2005) translated Marx (1857) as follows:

"Nature does not build machines, locomotives, railways, telegraphs, self-acting mules, etc. These are the products of human industry; natural resources which are transformed into organs of the human control over nature or one's practices in nature. (···) The development of fixed assets shows the extent to which knowledge available at the level of society is transformed into immediate productive force, and therefore, the extent to which the conditions of social life have themselves been brought under control of the general intellect and have been transformed accordingly. Crucial is the degree to which the socially productive forces are produced not only as knowledge, but as immediate organs of social practice, that is, of the real process of living".

Marx (1857:594, translated by Leydesdorff, 2005)

Given the legitimacy and stability of various nation states after 1870, national systems of innovation could gradually be developed among the axes of economic exchange and organized knowledge creation and diffusion (Rosenberg, 1982). The market economy functions mainly to bring about equilibrium by clearing the imbalances in the system, whereas the political economy tries to regulate the market. The equilibrium of these two gets interrupted by innovations in technology as knowledge is created and diffused throughout the economic system. In a KBE, the knowledge creation and diffusion system works, therefore, as a third sub-dynamic along with the two other sub-dynamics of markets and political systems (Schumpeter, 1964; Whitley, 1984 and Leydesdorff, 2005). These three function in a complex dynamic, wherein independent variables at one moment in time may become dependent at the next moment and consequently, the economic and political mechanisms do not control anything, but rather provide a feedback mechanism enabling the development of scientific and technological knowledge. This process results in the emergence of the KBE in nation states.

Functionality in a Knowledge-based Economic System

The emergence of the KBE reinforces the capacity of the economic system to develop solutions through continuous innovation. In a KBE, future-oriented planning is considered more important than current trends in the market, because institutions and markets usually develop historically, whereas the knowledge-based structure of expectations functions in an anticipatory mode (Leydesdorff, 2005:25). The dynamics of innovations in a KBE are, thus, non-linear (Allen, 1994). Such non-linearity is the natural consequence of complex interaction of different sub-dynamics in a KBE.

Although historically, interactions among the sub-dynamics were first enhanced by national proximity, dynamic scale effects endangered by innovation became more important than static ones, as the economic and technological dimensions became more and more globalized. This was first realized by multinational corporations and later became the concern of national governments in advanced, industrialized countries after the global oil crisis in the 1970s (Galbraith, 1967; Brusoni *et al.*, 2000 and OECD, 1980). Creating a functional KBE became the priority of these countries, as they recognized knowledge-based innovations to be the main driver of their economic growth (Freeman, 1982 and Irvine and Martin, 1984). Globalization induces an oscillation in which the nation states use their resources for the continuation of an 'endless transition' through knowledge creation and diffusion to compete in a global KBE. Under these circumstances, in many cases, the institutional make-ups of the nation states must undergo a restructuring (Etzkowitz and Leydesdorff, 1998).

The creation and diffusion of knowledge in a KBE does not have a single frame of reference yet (Leydesdorff, 2005:29) and thus the governance or make up of a KBE can only be based on a set of assumptions about the relevant systems. Given this, in this book, I have investigated the determining factors of the KBE in East Asia so as to understand its governance and regional composition.

Summary

After reviewing the definitions and concepts of the KBE, we can say that although the scholars are yet to provide us with a universal definition of the KBE, the application of the KBE is extremely important for economic development in the competitive world of the twenty-first century. The discussion on conceptualizing and understanding the KBE, along with its emergence and functionality, provides us with a general picture of what the KBE is all about. In the absence of a concrete definition of the KBE, a KBE framework is developed in the next chapter so as to share our understanding of the developmental patterns in KBE and the various factors involved in this process.

Chapter Three

Growth Theories and Knowledge-based Economy

Introduction

One of the greater challenges of studying the KBE is to develop an appropriate theoretical framework to comprehend KBE growth. Growth models currently available are able to measure gross domestic product (GDP) and most other macroeconomic indicators specified by the United Nations System of National Accounts; these models are structured around input-output tables that map inter-sectoral transactions (OECD, 1996). However, theories and models needed for understanding KBE growth are yet to be identified and defined in the literature. There are various obstacles to the creation of intellectual capital accounts parallel to the accounts of conventional fixed capital (OECD, 1996: 29). Presently, we only have some indirect and partial indicators of the growth of the KBE, because many unquantifiable factors are involved in a KBE. For example, knowledge remains difficult to be quantified, as are other factors of the KBE, such as knowledge stocks and flows, knowledge distribution and the relation between knowledge creation and economic performance (OECD, 1996:29).

In measuring the performance of the KBE, basic problems also emerge in designing a conceptual theoretical framework that includes the different national accounts, and that uses a traditional measurement system for traditional goods and services (OECD, 1996:30). Conceptualization becomes more complex because of the fast changing nature of the inputs and outputs of the KBE. Again, most often the qualitative factors involved in the KBE are difficult to be measured and at the same time, they are also difficult to be used in a conceptual framework. This chapter deals with the theoretical conceptualization of the KBE and develops a simplified model that will guide our discussion in the following chapters.

Discussion on Available Growth Theories - Are they enough to explain contemporary economic growth?

Currently existing economic theories help to understand and explain fast changes in economic growth. Economic growth phenomena seen in the neo-classical era are not identical to those of today. As a result, new theories have been developed in order to explain new notions of economic growth. After the neo-classical theory, there have been many other theories and concepts, such as the Keynesian view, Schumpeter's 'creative destruction' approach, and the developmental state view, coined by economists to make sense of the changes and new phenomena seen during economic growth of the twentieth century onward. One key element that was neglected by the traditional economists is technological change and its contribution to economic growth. Jewkes *et al.* (1956) pointed out three reasons for this negligence: 1. Economists were generally ignorant of science and technology and felt unprepared to venture into this unknown territory; 2. There were very few statistics to guide them; and, 3. Ever since the Great Depression of the 1930s, they had been mainly preoccupied with the problems of cyclical fluctuations in the economy and the unemployment associated with these fluctuations. This section debates the shortcomings of the existing economic growth theories.

There have been many critics of the economic growth theories invented up until now; these critics hold that current theories are inadequate to explain economic growth in a holistic manner. Many scholars have argued that the existing theories do not take into account social learning processes, and, as a result, whenever any revolutionary change takes place in economic growth, the existing theories will be unable to explain the new phenomenon. Freeman (1988) argues:

"In its anxiety to be the 'theoretical physics of social sciences' and to achieve logical elegance and mathematical formalization, neo-classical economics elaborated and refined quantitative equilibrium analysis and mathematical models, which, although useful as modeling exercise on highly restrictive assumptions, neglected some of the crucial elements involved in the long-term behavior of the system. They, therefore, appeared to non-economists and to other social scientists to be concerned with endless elaboration and refinement of assumptions which lacked both realism in relation to certain fundamental features of the system's behavior and rigorous falsifiability of the predictions derived from the models."

Freeman (1988:3)

Neo-classical Growth Theory

Neo-classical growth theory is one of the most popular economic growth theories that are available in economic literature today. Throughout the twentieth century, many scholars have debated the strengths and weaknesses of this theory. One of the major problems with this theory is that it makes too many assumptions about an ideal economic situation which does not actually exist. Sheehan (1997) analyzed the assumptions of the neo-classical economic theory in the following manner:

"As it is well known, the standard neo-classical model on which so much of our policy and institutional structure is based is one which takes as given the existence of an adequate supply of firms with necessary skills and capabilities; which assumes full information and complete markets, including in relation to future technological developments and the skill inputs to production; which assumes that technological change is external to the economic system, taking place as a result of the independent development of science rather than the intentional action of profit-seeking agents; which abstracts from increasing returns and feedback mechanisms, which otherwise might lead to increasing polarization of economic outcomes for regions and countries, and so on. It is now clear that in these and other ways the basic neo-classical model falls far short of describing central features of modern economies."

Sheehan (1997: 239)

A lack of theoretical discussion in economics on concepts such as *knowledge* and *information*, particularly in science and technology literature and in the broader field of innovation, has been recently acknowledged. Bateira (2006) explains this situation as the outcome of a defensive attitude adopted by the large number of economists who refrain from interdisciplinary dialogue, or even admit that the discipline should 'economize' this kind of speculation, arguing as follows:

> "While mainstream economists continue to apply neoclassical analysis to the production, transmission and management of knowledge, a 'new economics of science' appeared in the 1990s. This strand combines neoclassical analysis with contributions of new institutionalism, and identifies information with codified knowledge, which can be treated as commodity. Despite these innovations, knowledge is still conceptualized as a personal stock that determines the so-called collective knowledge of organizations and the 'general level' of society's knowledge."
>
> Bateira (2006:222-223)

Developmental State View

The developmental-state view considers market failures to be more pervasive for developing economies and thus, looks to government intervention as a substitute mechanism for resolution of these more common market failures (Aoki *et al.*, 1997:1). Johnson (1982) points out that the "soft authoritarian character" of the state was the source of East Asia's autonomy, merging with Wade's conception of the developmental state. Toner and Butler (2004: 81-102) summarized Wade's arguments on *'Governing the Market'* based on the particular political and economic conditions that were propitious for the development of the Northeast Asian developmental states:

1. The particular national histories of Northeast Asian states which resulted in these states entering the postwar period with 'authoritarian regimes or tightly circumscribed democracies'. Japan also provided a model for neighboring states which had undergone an unprecedented rapid transformation in the prewar era from a feudal state into an industrial power. These histories facilitated the establishment of clear national development strategies directed at both resource creation and resource allocation. Political and bureaucratic control or influence was made through a wide range of industry policy instruments—such as controls over credit, import and export licenses, public sector research and

development (R&D), and government procurement;
2. The Cold War gave the United States an overriding interest in the Northeast Asian states that abutted the Soviet Union and China. The United States fostered 'their state-led capitalisms in order to prove that capitalism was superior to the communist systems next door'. This support took the form, *inter alia*, of the United States acting as the principal market for the developmental states' exports; and
3. The change in the postwar strategy of multinational corporations, whose investment in developing countries had hitherto been restricted largely to primary production. The scope of such investments was significantly widened to include manufacturing industry, including the "re-location" of these activities from developed economies.

Although the cooperative dynamism of the developmental state was supported by Evan's concept of embeddedness (Evans, 1995) and Weiss's concept of 'Governed Interdependence' (Weiss, 1998), a major weakness of these conceptual frameworks is that state-society relations are limited to government-business relations – an elite coalition (Edigheji, 2005:12). Pointing out how society at large is not adequately addressed in the developmental-state approach, Seddon *et al.* (1995:326) note, "Effective insulation from immediate pressures of special interests enables policy-makers to respond swiftly and effectively to new circumstances; but the capacity to identify and implement appropriate policies to promote effective medium- and longer-term development requires the maintenance of strategic relations with wider civil society". Toner and Butler (2004) also state the limitations of Wade's developmental-state model:

> "Finally, and very briefly, the principal purpose of *Governing the Market* was to prove the existence and efficacy of intelligent state action directed at creating and allocating resources within Northeast Asian economies. A principal means of achieving this objective was to criticize neoclassical orthodoxy by contrasting actual developmental state action with neoclassical prescriptions for development. *Governing the Market* was not attempting to detail and prove the

efficacy of some underlying economic model for such state action.

While Wade at various points in his book explicitly and implicitly suggests such an alternative model, he does not develop it fully. In this sense the purpose of *Governing the Market* was negative - to disprove the explanatory power of neoclassical orthodoxy, rather than to positively describe and confirm an alternative economic theory of growth and development."

Toner and Butler (2004: 81-102)

Market Enhancing View

Aoki *et al.* (1997) suggested a third view based on the neo-classical market-friendly view and developmental-state view, the 'market-enhancing' view, where instead of viewing the state (that is to say, government) and the market as the only alternatives, and mutually exclusive substitutes, the role of government policy to facilitate or complement private-sector coordination is examined (Aoki *et al.*, 1997:1). This new approach is capable of explaining the role of government in bringing out the proper form of cooperation from the private-sector. The East Asian Miracle is, thus very well, explained by applying the market enhancing view.

However, East Asian countries have been greatly influenced by the presence of technological change and rapid innovation, which are missing in the market-enhancing view. Thus, although the market-enhancing view explains the political economy fairly well, it fails to explain the complex dynamism of economic growth, in which technological development and innovation play extremely important role. As a result, this new view cannot explain the economic growth of the post-East Asian Miracle, as technological advancement and greater innovation have become huge sources of economic growth.

Breaking into Traditional Theories - Schumpeter's 'Creative Destruction'

While most of the currently available theories have failed to include technological progress and innovation, Joseph Schumpeter almost alone among the major twentieth-century economists, did attempt to place technological change at the heart of his system and address problems of social and institutional change. His idea of 'creative destruction' breaks into the traditional economists' idea of technology being exogenous. Freeman (1988) acknowledges the contribution of Joseph Schumpeter as follows:

"Among the positive merits of Schumpeter's work were his consistent emphasis on innovation as the main source of dynamism in capitalist development, his sense of historical perspective, his recognition of the importance of the conceptual distinctions between invention, innovation and diffusion of innovations, and his recognition of the vital importance of the links between organizational, managerial, social and technical innovations. This led him, like other great economists (such as Smith, Mill and Marx), to a unified theory of the disparate social sciences and a general theory of global development."

Freeman (1988:5)

However, Schumpeter could not develop a formalized model that explained the international trade or international diffusion of technology which might have helped him to address the development pattern in the so-called 'Third World' peripheral areas (Freeman, 1988:5). Although Schumpeter's studies pointed out the relationship between the technological revolutions and long cycles of economic development, they do not show any general mechanism in this relation whereby government, universities and research and development centers work in a complex yet dynamic system - the main essence of the KBE.

The KBE Approach

All the views of economic development so far discussed fall short in describing economic development from a complete or holistic perspective. One of the reasons for this may be due to the fast changing nature of economic development brought on by technological advancement and innovation. The neoclassical model attempts to explain the economic development process from a very simple point of view. It was developed in a period when we could not realize how big the impact of technological advancement and innovation would be once an economy started developing. As a result, technology is considered as exogenous, which cannot be justified by looking at the post-industrialization development of the industrialized economies or at some of the newly emerging economies, such as India and China. With regard to this, Wentzel (2006) comments as follows:

"Invention, innovation and entrepreneurship (collectively referred to as imagineering), while not totally disregarded, have attracted relatively little attention in mainstream economic research. A possible reason for this is that economists tend to pay more attention to phenomena that they can place within mathematical or economical model. Entrepreneurship and invention do not fit well into such models, and it is therefore difficult to generate consistent results from their incorporation into economic models.

Another reason for superficial treatment of imagineering, especially invention, is not seen as so important and that it is therefore sufficient to treat as exogenous to the analytical systems of economists. Schmookler's (1955) counter-argument would be that imagineering is not only a form of economic activity (which is sufficient to merit extensive attention from economists) but it also affects economic development. Mokyr (1990) argued that technologically progressive economies have always shown considerable flair in invention and innovation, and by implication, those are the economies where imagineering is given most attention. As the economy becomes ever more knowledge-based, these arguments gain in strength, and may lead economists to change their views and look deeper into dynamics of imagineering."

Wentzel (2006:13)

The developmental-state view, although is able to explain the role of government in the developmental stage of economy, fails to explain the mechanism of economic development once a country has crossed a certain developmental threshold. One of the reasons that this view does not take technology and innovation into account may be because of how challenging it is to understand the impact of technology and innovation during the initial developmental stage. However, technological advancement and innovation are an integral part of today's economic growth system. So, there is a need for a new approach or view to explain contemporary economic growth mechanisms. With respect to this, Toner and Butler (2004) are correct to observe as follows:

> "That Wade was, of course, aware of this apparent in the conclusion to his *opus* where he appeals 'for economists to accept the challenge of constructing a theoretical rationale for the non-neoclassical East Asian facts'. Such a theory first and foremost will contribute to explaining why the 'governed market' policies worked and secondly will challenge on a theoretical level the neoclassical prescriptions that Professor Wade's book so successfully challenged on an empirical level. The body of theory and evidence associated with the 'cumulative causation' school can furnish such a rationale."
>
> Toner and Butler (2004: 81-102)

From the discussions so far, it is clear that we need some new approach to tackle the complex dynamism of economic growth from a holistic perspective. Some economic concepts introduced by evolutionary economists have been more successful in describing economic growth than the 'KBE' concept has, and this assumption of a qualitative transition in economic conditions has become commonplace among policymakers and mainstream economists (Leydesdorff, 2006:42). Many recent revolutionary economists (Leydesdorff, 2005) have come out with the new 'knowledge economy' approach to explain the complex matrix of new economic development. The new economy is, in the literature, considered to be a 'KBE' where along with other components of the economy, technological advancement and innovation are also discussed. With respect to this, Salavisa (2006) argues as follows:

> "While invested with qualitatively different objectives the state cannot simply discard its old forms of social and economic intervention. For the state, the big challenge to be met is how to favor the rise of the knowledge-based society while also dealing with the old society, which remains. New and old problems appear intimately interlinked at a time when nation-states are under great strain due to the convergence of various phenomena: globalization of information,

finance and commodities' market; volatility of multinational companies' strategies; budgetary restrictions: adverse demographic trends, namely in the EU; and the inertia of the state itself as an institution, among others."

Salavisa (2006:182)

Dolfsma (2006:200) points out the importance of understanding knowledge accumulation and diffusion, now that we realize our economies are KBEs. This requires economists to study much more carefully what knowledge is, and how it accumulates or dwindles away. A further consequence is that developments in the economy may also need to be evaluated differently from before. Recent scholars have pointed out the importance of so-called communities of practice in a knowledge economy, and the prominence of those communities that has been recognized in several fields of enquiry, such as the knowledge-based theory of firm, open source software development or industrial clusters (Muller, 2006:77). Economic firms are institutions, sustained by corporate law and fiscal arrangements and they are basic units of the market economy and drivers of change. Stam and Garnsey (2006:102) state that in the KBE, new firms have proliferated as a result of the lowering of barriers to entry by information technologies and the associated emergence of new economic activities; however, it is still difficult to understand the contributions these newcomers may make to the economy or the basis of the growth on which their innovative contributions depend.

R&D, both on a domestic and international level, is an integral part of a KBE. Ferne (1997: 207) asserts that the variety and scope of international R&D programs and activities has rapidly become a major feature of the global scientific and technological scene and that these activities range from structured and closely monitored efforts launched by governments to informal groupings of researchers who join forces in areas of common interest, and increasingly include R&D alliances between firms.

Developing the Theoretical Framework for a KBE

The KBE approach is capable of incorporating technical and institutional change into mainstream economic analysis and policy-making, rather than treating it as part of the rag-bag of 'residual' or 'exogenous' factors (Freeman, 1988:1). In this section, we attempt an alternate formulation of some of the main issues, based on critiques of the existing mainstream economic theories, so as to develop the theoretical framework for a KBE.

In designing the conceptual framework for the KBE, Leydesdorff (2005: 20) references a three-dimensional social system (See Figure 3.1). In his argument, he states that the three dimensions reflect different micro-operations of the social system because people (1) are differently positioned, (2) can maintain relations of exchange, and (3) learn from these relations with reference to their local positions. He further argues that this three dimensional system is continuously disturbed by interactions of various interfaces and is never at rest (Leydesdorff, 2005:21). Based on this social framework, he then develops his own three dimensional framework for the KBE (See Figure 3.2). In his reconstructed framework, innovation, which is an outcome of the KBE, is emphasized as having spillover effects on other economic activities in a KBE. Dosi (1982) also differentiates the stabilization of innovations

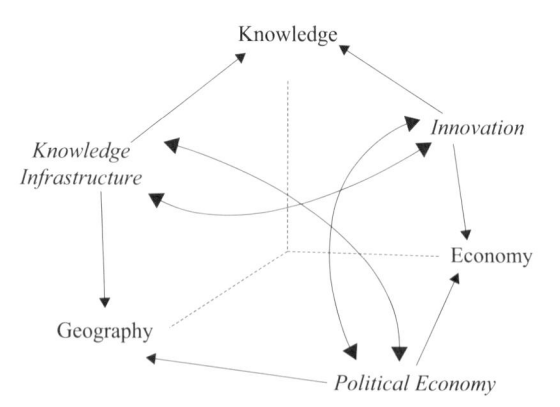

Figure 3.1 Three Dimensions of the Social System with their Three Interactions
Source: Leydesdorff, 2005:20.

along the technological trajectories and the knowledge base (KB) as a next-order regime that remains emergent as a paradigm. Leydesdorff (2005: 23) mentions that as innovations are further developed along trajectories, a KBE becomes reflexively available as an evolutionary mechanism for restructuring the historical trajectories on which it builds. With respect to his framework, he further argues:

> "The carriers of a KBE entertain as dually layered network: one layer of institutional relations in which they constrain each other's behavior and one layer of functional relations in which they shape each other's expectations with reference to the future. The second order interaction term remains as a historical result of the first order interactions in the knowledge infrastructure. An evolving knowledge base (KB) can be developed under the condition that various interactions find their own resonances, that is, in a self-organizing mode."
>
> Leydesdorff (2005:24)

Figure 3.2 shows how the first-order interactions generate a KBE as a next order system, and how in a KBE, all the components of knowledge, innovation, economy, political economy, geography and knowledge infrastructure interact with each other through knowledge creation and diffusion. The diagram in Figure 3.2 provides the whole picture of an already created KBE wherein components intermingle with each other and create new knowledge. However, for any country to become a KBE, it has to create the infrastructure first and then, the fuller system

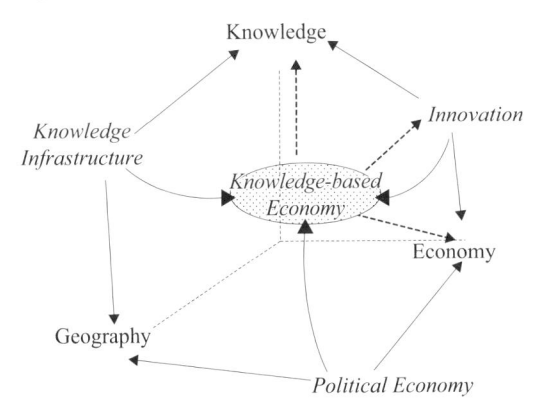

Figure 3.2   The First-order Interactions Generate a KBE as a Next Order System
Source: Leydesdorff, 2005:24.

of a KBE, which is rather complex. Although the interactions among different components of KBE are well explicated in Figure 3.2, it does not illustrate any concrete growth pattern of a KBE.

As a consequence, a further simplified framework of a KBE, which can portray its determinants and show how they are inter-related in a continuous flow, could provide us with a simpler framework to understand the development of a KBE. Realizing the necessity of a more simplified framework of a KBE, I proposed a relatively simpler framework for a KBE in 2007 (Figure 3.3) (Debnath, 2007:14). In this framework, the KBE itself is the dependent variable, influenced by the independent variable (policy formulation). However, between the KBE and the policy formulation, intervening variables play a bridging role, and as such, the change in the intervening variables should to be studied to reveal how policy formulations affect the development of a KBE. The arguments for the Figure 3.3 framework are as follows:

"A KBE is an economy where knowledge acquisition, sharing, creation, and application are the main drivers of growth, wealth creation and employment. For this knowledge acquisition, sharing, creation, and application there must be investment in developing the KBE infrastructure, which largely consists of Educational Infrastructure, Technological Infrastructure and Scientific Infrastructure. The knowledge inputs (KI) that involve R&D, technological development, patent rights, employment of engineers and technicians, and innovations, the knowledge stocks and flows (KSF) that include embodied knowledge and diffusion of knowledge in society, and the knowledge networks (KN) that incorporate government-industry partnerships, government-academia partnerships, industry-academia partnerships, and government-industry-academia partnerships all are included in the KBE infrastructure."

Debnath (2007:13)

The KBE infrastructure (educational, technological and scientific) is considered to be the intervening variable, a variable that is developed based on policy formulation (See Figure 3.3). As a consequence, the KBE is the overall outcome of the investment in the KBE infrastructure, and it is the dependent variable in the framework. In this framework, the KBE infrastructures are considered to be

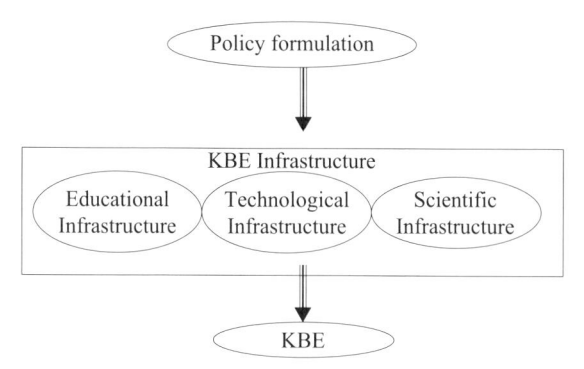

Figure 3.3 Policy Framework for a KBE
Source: Debnath, 2007:14.

intervening variables in a KBE policy framework, resembling the developmental state approach, and thus, having certain limitations defining the KBE from a holistic point of view. We have therefore considered a new framework for this study, and, based on the discussions above, will present it in the following section.

Much has been written about the necessity of a major shift in investment in KBE infrastructure, because the role of knowledge-based workers and expected behaviors is very different from the traditional models of growth (Porter, Takeuchi and Sakakibara, 2000). In a KBE, knowledge needs to be continuously re-created and re-constructed through dynamic inputs in the KBE infrastructure. The role of the government here is not to control but to stimulate, and to provide policy directions and address other facilities that are required for the sound development of the KBE infrastructure.

The underlying purpose of proposing a KBE framework in this study is to better structure data collection and analysis for the countries to be studied. The three KBE frameworks (See Figure 3.1, 3.2 and 3.3) described earlier function as the basis for the proposed framework (See Figure 3.5) to identify the determining factors of a KBE. We have already discussed about the neoclassical market-friendly approach, the state-interventionist developmental state approach, a combination

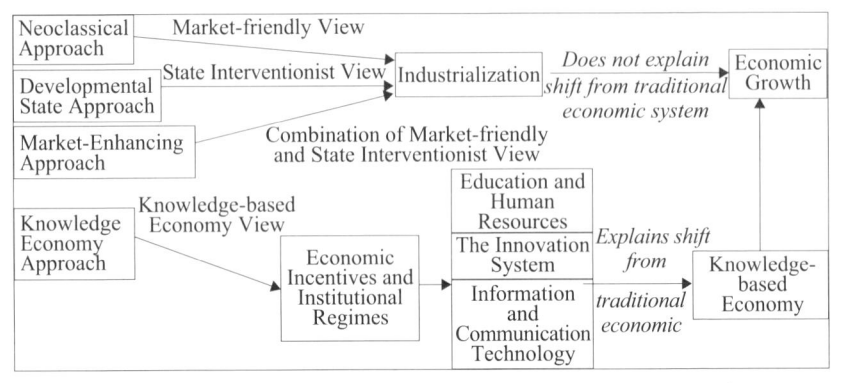

Figure 3.4 Explaining Economic Growth - Differences in Approach
Source: Developed by the author.

of both the market enhancing view and also the newly developed knowledge economy approach. From this earlier discussion, we can clearly see that the first three approaches do not take into consideration technological advancement and innovation as determining factors in the economic system (See Figure 3.4).

The knowledge economy approach is the only approach that considers technological advancement and innovation as determining factors in the economic system, and which is able to describe post-industrialization economic development. Joseph Schumpeter breaks away from the former three views by considering technology and innovation as inevitable forces for the economy. Thus, the knowledge economy approach can be one solution for defining today's knowledge-based economic growth, wherein all three views above are partially accurate. This approach looks at the economic growth from a holistic point of view by taking the whole society into account.

Proposed KBE Framework

The proposed KBE framework is developed based on the earlier stated frameworks and the World Bank's four pillars of the Knowledge Economy Framework. The World Bank's KBE framework includes the following pillars (World Bank

Knowledge Assessment Methodology, 2008):
- An economic and institutional regime to provide incentives for the efficient use of existing and new knowledge and the flourishing of entrepreneurship;
- An educated and skilled population to create, share, and use knowledge well;
- An efficient innovation system of firms, research centers, universities, consultants and other organizations to tap into the growing stock of global knowledge, assimilate and adapt it to local needs, and create new technology;
- Information and communications technology to facilitate the effective creation, dissemination, and processing of information.

This framework establishes the collective nature of a KBE's foundations, such as education, information and communications technology and innovation systems, which are spurred on by government through different policy and institutional settings. Figure 3.5 shows the relationship among the four pillars, such as the role of government, education for creating the skilled human resources, information and communications technologies (ICT) infrastructure and the innovation system. In Figure 3.5, the rectangular boxes inside the circle represent the four pillars of a KBE. The thin solid black arrows show the first-order development of KBE infrastructure. They show that the role of government is to guide better education

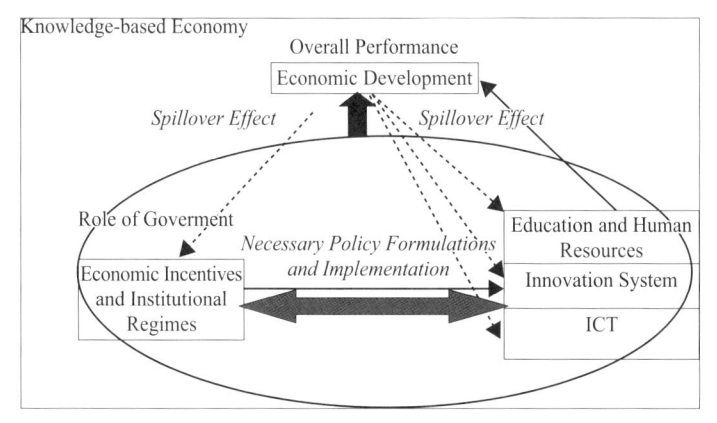

Figure 3.5   Proposed KBE Framework
Source: Developed by the author based on the World Bank's Knowledge Assessment Methodology.

and human resource development, better ICT development and better innovation system development, thereby enhancing overall economic growth in the initial stage. At this stage or in later stages, overall economic growth will have spillover effects on all four pillars, as shown by the dotted black arrows in the figure. Once the first-order development is working steadily, second-order developments take place, wherein all four pillars interact with each other, mutually or independently, as shown by the solid black color double-faced arrow in Figure 3.5, leading to the creation of a complete KBE. This creation ultimately contributes to economic growth, as indicated by the thick black color single-faced arrow in Figure 3.5.

Role of Government

As knowledge itself has significant indivisibilities and scale effects, it is likely to suffer from under-investment unless there is public intervention. It is no coincidence that societies that have high private expenditure on R&D also have significant public programs to support private R&D, increasingly at the small and medium enterprise level (World Bank Working Paper, 2004:9). Hence, it is important that the government plays a key role in setting up the correct incentives, in terms of policies and institutions, to enable the other determinants of a KBE. Just as investments in education are characterized by the need for similar synergies, the public role in establishing access to ICT infrastructure is crucial. Similar to the case of the global environmental commons, the collective nature of the knowledge economy demands meticulous attention to incentives in order to ensure an optimal mix of public and private involvement.

Governments' policy formulations aim to bring balance between internal resources and capabilities (strengths and weaknesses) and external environmental relations (opportunities and threats). Policy formulation for a KBE is a part of the national policy formulation for a country which is trying to exploit knowledge and make a difference within a competitive environment (Rollo, 2002). In formulating the policies for a KBE on how to acquire, share, create and apply knowledge so as to excel within a competitive environment, a country has to take all its environmental contexts into consideration and complement them with internal strengths so as to find out what policy would allow for maximum return on investment. The better the fit of a KBE's policy formulation to its context, the better its country can be expected to perform.

The policy formulations for a KBE can either be to consolidate and intensify the economic and social divisions of a KBE between and within nations, or they can be to provide the foundations for equitable participation in a new economy, an economy in which knowledge, intellect, and the establishment of effective and accessible information infrastructure are the keys to economic development. A KBE is capable of sustained growth providing more and better jobs and greater social cohesion; this is an ongoing challenge for many policymakers. Since mid-twentieth century, most countries have been trying to build strong KBEs, with a vision of a social and human dimension, as well as strategic objectives, determined by each country's government.

The duty of governments is to ensure that social, human and economic issues are taken into consideration in their research activities, and to inform their citizens about all social aspects relating to the scientific and technological progress made in areas all fields covered. Given the recent birth of the KBE concept, as well as its importance for re-launching and modernizing an economy, it is necessary to promote research and analysis in this field to support national and community policies. Thus, the KBE framework involves a holistic approach whereby knowledge can be learned and created in all sectors of society.

Education and Human Resources Development

One important sector for governments to promote is that of education, as education can create the human resources needed in any economy. During the industrialization and post-industrialization period, countries around the world have spent considerable sums of money on the development of education, so as to meet the demands of increased competition in the global economy. The trend continues today. For the KBEs, especially, this trend in education carries great weight, as they are trying to achieve economic growth through knowledge creation and diffusion. The main objective of the education system in a KBE is to bring out the best in every schoolchild, developing sound morals and skills needed to meet the demands of a rapidly changing world. Education in the KBEs plays a very important role in promoting social and economic changes by expanding the pool of professionals and executives, as government's education policy in a KBE is designed to create the human resources that a KBE requires for sustainable development. The education policy in all KBEs has thus emphasized the scientific and technological aspects of education. However, other fields of studies also deserve attention. Kong (2004), in this regard, observes as follows:

> "In most recent times, even while great emphasis has come to be placed on the life sciences in particular, and increasingly nanoscience and nano-engineering, a simultaneous acknowledgement of the importance of broad-based multidisciplinary learning is also evident. In all these varied thrusts, one motivation remains paramount – finding an educational emphasis that will provide the country with the requisite human resources to fuel the economy. .... Thus, educational strategies have in large part been used to meet economic needs through the production of a suitably qualified workforce."

(Kong, 2004:1)

In the KBEs, the governments' main goal in formulating education policies has been to expand science and technology education so as to meet the demand for scientific and technological human resources in the competitive global economy. Time to time, governments re-examine their educational policies and re-enforce the old policies alongside new initiatives; in some cases, they also create new policies. Kong (2004), points this out:

> "In responding to these key developments in the economy, educational policies have been once again re-examined. It became necessary to reshape education towards placing a higher premium on innovation, flexibility, entrepreneurship, creativity and a commitment to life-long learning. The role of science and

technology remains important but increasing attention has come to be given to broad-based multi-disciplinary efforts in curricula, including some expectations that scientists and engineers learn humanistic modes of inquiry".

(Kong, 2004:5)

To foster greater creativity and innovation among students, many countries have launched special programs in education focused on developing students' active learning and critical thinking skills, as well as schools' creative and critical thinking culture. In recent policy formulations for education, many governments are moving towards making IT, biotechnology and some other core science subjects obligatory for undergraduate study. Special policies, too, have been formulated to address life sciences and biotechnology. In the years since 2000, governments have created a number of ways to provide funding for R&D in universities.

ICT Development

In the last few decades of the 20th century, information and communications technology (ICT) has transformed the world. It is becoming increasingly effective in fostering growth both in developed and developing countries. By connecting people and places, ICT has played a vital role in national, regional and global development and holds enormous promise for the future.

Governments of many countries, especially those in the KBEs, have realized that to compete at the global frontier, an innovation-based KBE requires a well-developed technological infrastructure, a set of capability-focused technology policies, as well as an institutional environment that stimulates innovation and entrepreneurship. The current KBEs need further technology creation to compete in the technological frontier to propel their economies (Koh and Wang, 2003:3). For instance, over the last four decades, Singapore, which is one of the leading KBEs in East Asia formulated policies that have shifted from emphasizing *'using* technology to creating it' (Koh and Wang, 2003:16). Wong (2003) pointed out the following four main phases in Singapore's technological transition with respect to the global technological frontier: (a) an industrial take-off phase from the 1960s to the mid-1970s, when there was high dependence on technology transfer from foreign Multinational Corporations (MNCs); (b) from the mid-1970s to the late-1980s, when there was rapid growth in local technological process development within MNCs and the development of local supporting industries; (c) from the late-1980s to the late-1990s, when there was rapid expansion of applied R&D by MNCs and by publicly funded R&D institutions; and, (d) from the late-1990s onwards, when there was emerging emphasis on high tech start-ups and a shift towards technology creation capabilities. Since the last couple of decades, when ICT started booming, many governments took initiative in broadening and deepening their technological capabilities to meet the demands of the 21st century.

Innovation System Development

The role of government policies on innovation system development takes on added importance as countries move to innovation-based growth in the global KBE era. In terms of the development of scientific capability, there was a sustained shift from learning to use with high reliance on multinational corporations (MNCs), to learning to adapt and improve via "learning by doing" within MNCs as well as "learning by transacting" in local firms acquiring external technology. The next shift was learning to innovate, mainly, through applied R&D in product or process, and finally, learning to pioneer by creating indigenous technology and commercializing it in the marketplace through new ventures (Koh and Wang, 2003:17). In discussing Singapore's Third National Science and Technology Plan, Koh and Wang (2003) state:

> "Reflecting the shift in focus to basic research under the Third National Science and Technology Plan, the NSTP was re-organized in 2000 to focus on promoting research and developing R&D manpower, taking on a role similar to that of the National Science Foundation (NSF) in the United States. Two research councils were set up; namely, the Bio- Medical Research Council (BMRC) to award research grants and develop R&D manpower in the life sciences, while the Science and Engineering Research Council (SERC) was set up to oversee research in selected scientific and technological fields. In 2000, the Singapore

government announced a strategic push to promote life sciences research and industry development, following the completion of the Global Genome Mapping project."

(Koh and Wang, 2003:25)

Singapore was ranked number one in terms of its innovation policy, winning top scores for its effectiveness in protecting intellectual property, as well as for its support of R&D through various tax incentives and grants in the 2002-2003 period according to the WEF (World Economic Forum) Global Competitiveness Report. The same can be said about other KBEs in the East Asian region. Realizing the force of globalization, not only the industrialized or KBEs are working hard to create a sustainable scientific infrastructure for innovation and invention to compete in global level; developing countries, too, are catching up very fast in this regard.

Summary

The proposed KBE framework shows that in creating a KBE where knowledge acquisition, sharing, creation and application abound, a country has to work to harmonize *policy and KBE inputs according to its own characteristics and circumstances*. In the event that circumstances are unfavorable, the country has the option of adjusting its policy and/or KBE infrastructure so as to create a better fit within its context, or to change its context to be conducive to policy and/or KBE factors. A limitation of the proposed framework is that it is derived from a theory with limited empirical evidence of the correlation between national policy formulation and KBE inputs. Another limitation is that due to the complex nature of this study, many other inputs and factors also overlap and cannot be clearly defined. However, in the absence of a concrete definition of a KBE, the proposed KBE framework provides us with a general picture of the KBE. In this chapter, a brief description of the theoretical considerations is presented along with the research framework for a KBE. The proposed KBE framework is the guiding tool for discussions in following chapters so as to understand the various key factors of a KBE in East Asian economies.

Chapter Four

The Challenge of Measuring the KBE

Introduction

The greatest challenge in studying the KBE is the absence of an appropriate research methodology to measure it. Such a methodology could create enormous acceptance for the KBE to be used as a theory in the study of economic growth theory. However, researchers of the KBE have used a variety of methods to describe its emergence, though only a few of them have actually attempted to quantify and measure the KBE. This chapter shall shed light on the challenge of measuring the KBE.

The Challenge of Measuring the KBE

The development of the heterogeneity of quality inputs and outputs makes it extremely difficult to measure the inputs and outputs of the KBE. It is difficult to measure the inputs appropriately, as both tacit and explicit knowledge is qualitative in nature. On the other hand, we still lack appropriate statistical techniques for quantifying the output of knowledge creation as a component of the output of a KBE. The quality input and quality output in a KBE are the two intangibles (Eliasson, 1990:16) that truly matter in an advanced KBE, and, at the same time, these two intangibles make it enormously difficult to appropriately measure the KBE. Eliasson (1990) argues as follows:

> "The modern industrial nations may be entering a phase in which the most important and the most rapidly growing inputs and outputs – knowledge and quality, respectively- are not measured at all. Our economic sensors will only be able to pick up a noisy reflection of the ongoing "hidden" production process, namely positive return to these un-measurable quantities, reflected in

above-normal returns to measured capital in the capital market."

Eliasson (1990:16-17)

Ever since the evolutionary economists (Leydesdorff, 2006:262) introduced the concept of a 'KBE', they have faced the problem of how to measure this new type of economic configuration. Although the idea of the KBE is well-received by the evolutionary economists because of its practical implications in many countries around the world, the measurement of the KBE remains a challenge. Many scholars actually have doubted the feasibility of measuring the KBE because of its elusive nature (Skolnikoff, 1993; Leydesdorff, 2001b and Foray, 2004). Storper (1997:28) considers technology, organization and territory as the 'holy trinity' for regional development not to be studied as an aggregate of the composing elements, but in terms of relations between and among these elements. Pointing out the difficulties in operationalizing the relational paradigm to measure the KBE, he argues:

"Technology involves not just tension between scale and variety, but that between the codifiability or noncodifiability of knowledge; its substantive domain is learning and *becoming*, not just diffusion and deployment. Organizations are knit together, their boundaries defined and changed, and their relations to each other accomplished not simply as input-output relations or linkages, but as untraded interdependencies subject to a high degree of reflexivity. Territorial economies are not only created, in a globalizing world economy, by proximity in input-output relations, but more so by proximity in the untraded or relational dimensions of organizations and technologies. Their principal assets - because scarce and slow to create and imitate - are no longer material, but relational."

Storper (1997:28)

It is clear to many eminent scholars that measuring the KBE poses difficulties. Despite the ambiguous nature of inputs and outputs of the KBE, some scholars have tried to measure it. However, their work has yet to bring about any general methodology for measuring the KBE.

The usual methodology for measuring gross domestic product (GDP) and most other macroeconomic indicators is specified by the United Nations System of National Accounts; it is structured around input-output tables that map intersectoral transactions (OECD, 1996). However, an appropriate, general methodology to measure the impact of the KBE on economic growth is yet to be identified and defined in the literature. There are various obstacles to the creation of intellectual capital accounts parallel to the accounts of conventional fixed capital (OECD, 1996: 29). So far we only have some indirect and partial indicators of the growth of KBE because of various unquantifiable factors involved. For example, knowledge is very hard to be quantified, so are the other aspects of the KBE, such as knowledge stocks and flows, knowledge distribution and the relationship between knowledge creation and economic performance (OECD, 1996:29).

Different Methodologies Available to Measure the KBE

The economy of the twenty-first century has been largely expressed as a KBE wherein knowledge, by virtue of being created and diffused, plays a central role for economic development. However, the process of knowledge creation, accumulation and diffusion is very complex, and this probably poses the biggest obstacle for economists to suggest a generalized methodology to measure the KBE (or to come up with a standard model for the KBE). As a consequence, the process of knowledge creation and diffusion in a KBE remains mostly a mystery. However, despite the difficulties of defining any specific methodology to measure the KBE or to draw a framework for it, many recent scholars have attempted various methodologies to understand the KBE.

Morone and Taylor's Simulation Model

Morone and Taylor (2006) developed a simulation model to investigate the complex learning process that occurs through informal networks in the KBE. They explain the model as follows:

"We assume a population of N agents and a global environment consisting of a grid of cells. Each agent is initially assigned a random position in the grid, and interacts with her/his closest neighbors. Not all the cells of the grid are occupied by agents, and those occupied contain only one agent. We specify a wrapped grid (that is a torus) so that there are no edge effects- where we might have different behaviors due to the boundaries of the grid."

Morone et al. (2006:203)

Morone *et al.* (2006:205) defined Γ_x as the set of initial acquaintances of agent x (or first generation connections), $\phi_{x,t}$ as the set of acquaintances of the acquaintances time t (or next generation connection), the individual $m_t \in \phi_{x,t}$ who is added at each t, $\vartheta_{x,t}$ as the set of acquaintances dropped at time t and the individual $n_t \in \vartheta_{x,t}$ who is dropped at each t. Morone *et al.* (2006), taking the total set of acquaintances for individual x at time t- T defined their model as follows:

$$\Phi_{x,T} = (\Gamma_x \cup \phi_{x,T}) \setminus \vartheta_{x,T} \tag{1}$$

In this model, it is assumed that agents exchange knowledge by means of face-to-face interactions, and every time a knowledge transfer occurs, the new knowledge acquired is confronted and linked with existing knowledge. Using this model, Morone *et al.* (2006:223) draw the following conclusion:

"We found a critical level, by tuning the visibility parameter, above which convergence in knowledge levels occurs. A converging long-run equilibrium was also achieved by increasing the ICT penetration. Nonetheless, we showed how this latter option was less efficient, as convergence was slower. We conclude from this finding that a more effective measure aimed towards generating more evenly-distributed knowledge flows should focus upon enhancing local-network connectivity rather than extending the cyber-network coverage."

Morone et al. (2006:223)

It is clear that the results of the methodology above have failed to find positive results for ICT penetration in a KBE; this goes against the mainstream knowledge-based economists' argument that ICT is a fueling tool for knowledge creation and diffusion in a KBE (Castells and Hall, 1994; Soete, 1997; Freeman and Perez,

1998; Castells and Himanen, 2002 and Pyka and Hanusch, 2006).

Los's Nonlinear Regression Approach

Los (2006) used a nonlinear regression approach by using the Abramovitz (1979) simple regression equation (1) and Verspagen's (1991) point of departure equation (2) to test the catch up process of countries in a knowledge-based global economy, where $\dot{g}i$ represents the productivity gap, a refers to the innovation by the leader, β refers to the ability of countries to benefit from the pool of technology spillover and δ is considered to be an indicator of the 'intrinsic learning capability' of a country.

$$\dot{g}i = a+\beta g_i^0 + \varepsilon_i \qquad (1)$$
$$\dot{g} = a+\beta g e^{-g/\delta} \qquad (\delta>0) \qquad (2)$$

Los (2006:237) argued for this methodology by saying that the nonlinear regression framework is attractive in the following ways:
1. It is derived from a simple but elegant theory of productivity growth;
2. It yields sensible results; and
3. It survives exposition to specification tests against linear specifications.

However, the results from this methodology do not contribute to the understanding of the macro picture of today's complex KBE. Los (2006:247) also mentioned the limitation of this study, saying, "The methods were implemented for a small dataset on labor productivity dynamics for aggregate economies in the period 1960-2000. We did not find evidence for two or more regimes if the labor productivity gap to the world leader (the USA) was used as an indicator of social capabilities". The results of this methodology do not explain the 'East Asian Miracle' or how countries in East Asia such as Singapore and Malaysia are transforming their economies into KBEs. As a consequence, although Los's efforts to use the nonlinear regression analysis to understand the complex build-up of a KBE in a country did make some contribution to the literature on the KBE, it is not sufficient to explain the current developments in East Asian KBEs.

Leydesdorff's Triple Helix Model

Leydesdorff (2006) proposed the Triple Helix model as a way to understand the University(U)-Government(G)-Industry(I) relationship. In his study of the Triple Helix model, mutual information in three dimensions is defined as:

$$T_{UI} = H_U + H_I - H_{UI} \qquad (1)$$
$$T_{UIG} = H_U + H_I + H_G - H_{UI} - H_{IG} - H_{UG} + H_{UIG} \qquad (2)$$

The mutual information between two dimensions of the probability distribution such as in university-industry relations, is called *transmission T*. The transmission is defined as the difference between the sum of the two uncertainties minus their combination (1). In this case, H_U stands for the uncertainty in the distribution of the variable(s) measured in the university domain, H_I similarly for the uncertainty in the industrial domain, and H_{UI} for the uncertainty in the combined system. This last uncertainty is reduced with the co-variation or mutual information between the two relating systems, since it follows Equation 1. The mutual information *T* is zero if the two distributions are independent, but otherwise it is positive. A double helix is observable and can be measured from Equation 1 by applying the entropy law (Georgescu-Roegen, 1971); since mutual information in two dimensions is always positive, a co-evaluation between two systems generates a probabilistic entropy. The T_{UIG} can be positive or negative depending on the terms of Equation 2. The uncertainty of the variables measured in each interacting system (H_U, H_I, and H_G) is reduced at the systems level by the relations at the interfaces between them (H_{UI}, H_{IG}, and H_{UG}), and the three-dimensional uncertainty (H_{UIG}) adds positively to the uncertainty that prevails.

Leydesdorff (2006) explained the rationale behind proposing the new Triple Helix model as follows:
"The Triple Helix can be elaborated into a neo-evolutionary model which enables

us to recombine sociological notions of meaning processing, economic theorizing about exchange relations, and insights from science and technology studies regarding the organization and control of knowledge production. The further codification of meaning in scientific knowledge production can add value to the exchange. This model can serve as heuristics, but should not be reified. Its abstract and analytical character enables us to explain current transitions towards a Knowledge-based Economy as a new regime of operations."

Leydesdorff (2006:45)

The Triple Helix in *the Internet, Science Citation Index, National subdomains and languages on the Internet*, and *U.S. Patent Data* has been tested by Leydesdorff (2006). The results of the tests above have supported the rationale behind using this methodology, as it does help to understand the outputs of the KBE by using the empirical data. Although the Triple Helix model is able to explain some notions of a KBE, its capability to explain the making of the KBE has not been tested. Thus, this model serves as a tool to understand only some traits of a KBE.

World Bank's Knowledge Assessment Methodology

The World Bank proposed the *Knowledge Assessment Methodology* (KAM) to assess, across the world, countries' readiness for the knowledge economy (Chen and Dahlman, 2005). The main purpose of the KAM methodology is to identify sectors or specific areas where specific countries may need to focus on so as to realize a full-scale KBE. The KAM is further improved on in great detail in Chen and Gawande's (2007) "Underlying Dimensions of Knowledge Assessment: Factor Analysis of the Knowledge Assessment Methodology Data". The general factor analysis model (Equation 1) of the World Bank is derived from the notation and material in this section, borrowed from Reyment and Joreskog (1993, Sections 2, 4) where $\mathbf{X}$ is the data matrix of p variables, $\mathbf{F}$ is the matrix of $k < p$ factors, and N is the sample size. The $k \times p$ "factor loadings" matrix $\mathbf{A}'$ is used to linearly sum the factors to predict each column of $\mathbf{X}$. What cannot be predicted is collected in the error matrix $\mathbf{E}$.

$$\mathbf{X}_{(N \times p)} = \mathbf{F}_{(N \times k)} \mathbf{A'}_{(k \times p)} + \mathbf{E}_{(N \times p)} \tag{1}$$

At present, the KAM is widely used both internally and externally in the World Bank, and frequently facilitates engagements and policy discussions with government officials from client countries. Chen and Gawande (2007) point out the rationale for using the factor analysis of the knowledge assessment methodology data by saying, "Formal analysis employing KAM data is faced with the problem of which variables to choose and why. Rather than make these decisions in an ad hoc manner, we recommend factor-analytic methods to distill the information contained in the many KAM variables into a smaller set of 'factors'". In factor analysis of the knowledge assessment methodology both principal components and true factor analytic methods have been examined to provide a clear political-economic meaning of the factors so as to construct comparisons over time. Chen and Gawande (2007) stated the contribution of the KAM as follows:

"A contribution of the paper is identifying the political-economic dimensions in the KAM data and measuring them for (ordinal) comparisons over time. We embrace the idea of a simple structure of the dimensions and allow these dimensions to be correlated with each other. The output from the factor analysis is used to graphically analyze how countries have changed their rankings on the underlying dimensions over the 1995-2002 period."

Chen and Gawande (2007:34)

However, the World Bank considered the three key variables for each pillar of the KBE such as economic incentives and institutional regimes, education and human resources, information and communications technology and innovation in this methodology and came up with a KBE index for all the countries of the world. This methodology, although it provides us with a general understanding of key variables for each pillar of the KBE worldwide, does not reflect regional or country-specific characteristics. For instance, the variables that the World Bank considered for using in the knowledge assessment methodology may not be equally important for all the regions of the world. There may be other factors that contribute to a region more than the selected three factors of each KBE pillar used in this methodology.

Summary

After reviewing the contemporary research methodologies on the KBE, we can say that there is no perfect single methodology available for carrying out research on it. Among the available methodologies discussed in this chapter, the World Bank's Factor Analysis Model seems so far to be the most powerful tool to measure the KBE; however, this model alone is not sufficient to describe the mechanism of constructing a KBE, as it reveals the comparative readiness of countries for a KBE merely through quantitative data analysis. At this juncture, our KBE framework in Chapter Three would provide us with the guiding tool needed to understand KBEs in East Asia. These KBEs will be discussed in the following chapters.

Chapter Five

Contemporary KBEs and East Asia

Introduction

To understand the impact of government policy on a country transitioning to the KBE, we must consider the nature and outcomes of specific type of policies currently in place. Advanced OECD countries are pioneers in transforming their economies into KBEs by formulating appropriate policies; most East Asian economies, though, are latecomers in this regard. This chapter is structured into two parts. The first part comments on the development of the KBE in the advanced OECD countries, with reference to government policies and outcomes observed in them, and the second part discusses how countries in East Asia have attempted to follow after the advanced OECD economies in their pursuit to become KBEs.

Contemporary Public Policy Directions and the KBE

In a KBE, national policies play a very important role in creating the infrastructure required for growth. In the process, the KBE involves all levels of the economy, from the individual level to national one. The magnitude of policy formulation towards a KBE dwarfs all other aspects of the developmental landscape, and is widely recognized as a primary driving force behind the process of globalization. This transition in policy formulation does not just involve the adoption of a new generation of technology, but rather is a transition to a new economic framework - a KBE - whose nature and characteristics are profoundly different from that of the earlier economy.

Although policy formulation for a KBE is quite new, knowledge and its management are not a new research area. In the contemporary literature, knowledge and its management are generally discussed in the study of the organizational behavior. However, it was not until the mid-1990s with the publication of *The Knowledge Creating Company* (Nonaka and Takeuchi, 1995) and *Working Knowledge* (Davenport and Prusak, 1998) that knowledge management began to emerge as a recognized corporate discipline which later drew the attention of many other scholars from different disciplines, and that enabled the KBE to have a multidisciplinary approach used in its analysis.

Thus, policy formulation turns out to be very important for realizing a KBE, and, naturally, policy makers get involved in this process. Wide-ranging work has begun and must continue on subjects such as governance, economic policy issues, the functioning of the internal market, employment policies, regional development policies and issues relating to social integration and cultural minorities. It is essential to explore, in a collective manner, new topics which probe and investigate the KBE, and which are directly related to current political events, by pooling the intellectual resources within and beyond individual countries.

The aim of governance and public administration in a given country is to contribute to factors which spread knowledge as well as the phenomena underlying a knowledge-based society. These activities take into account all the economic, political, social, cultural and cognitive aspects of knowledge, its dynamics and its scientific and technological content and interactions. Administrative reforms should be aimed at several areas, such as improving the production, dissemination and use of knowledge, as well as its effects on economic and social development, so as to achieve an overall understanding of the following: first, how a knowledge-based society can promote the societal objectives of sustainable development, social and geographic cohesion and improvement in the quality of life in the country; and, second, through comparative scenarios made not only between countries but also at the regional level, how improvements can be made. This will form the basis for the formulation and implementation of strategies for transition towards a knowledge-based society at the national and regional levels.

The KBE in OECD Countries

Available literature (Colecchia and Schreyer, 2001; Khan, 2001 and OECD, 2001a, 2001b, 2001c, 2002a, 2002b, 2002c and 2002d) argues that the OECD countries are the leading KBEs of the world. This section, therefore, examines their policies so as to understand the role of government, and the consequences of these policies in some of the OECD countries.

In all the KBEs of OECD countries, governments play a significant role by formulating policies appropriate for the KBE. Countries such as Australia, Canada, Hungary, Ireland, South Korea, and Spain have introduced comprehensive policy frameworks to guide the development of science, technology and innovation so as to create sustainable KBEs (OECD, 2002). To improve efficacy, many countries are creating stronger linkages among different policies to enlarge the functional area of the KBE. In doing so, their governments have to regularly measure the effectiveness of policies and update them to suit the changing patterns of science, technology, R&D and innovation in a given KBE.

In the twenty-first century, the governments of OECD countries have made administrative and organizational structural changes to promote the KBE. Among prominent initiatives, are the establishments of national councils and inter-ministerial bodies, as well as the reorganization of government structures, so as to meet the demand for increased coordination, governance and steering of the components of the KBE (OECD, 2002:15). Increasingly, many OECD countries are designing policies to strengthen their industries for R&D and innovation, in parallel with the governments' own efforts in R&D.

Policies to increase public funding for R&D and innovation in the OECD countries were mentioned in the 'OECD Science, Technology and Industry Outlook 2002'. After roughly a decade of fiscal restraint and stagnation in government support for R&D, many OECD countries set specific targets to increase national investment in R&D and innovation. One major breakthrough in policy formulation has been increased funding for science and technology in certain sectors. Many governments have identified priorities in particular fields of science and technology other than the public funding of R&D for traditional public missions such as basic science, health, military and the environment. In many OECD countries, ICT, biotechnology, and nanotechnology have received special attention (OECD, 2002:16).

Significant reforms in universities and public research institutions are also being addressed by the national policy formulations of many countries. The governments involved are trying to create organizations that have greater autonomy and less subject of government control. This is creating a competitive edge at certain universities and public research institutions, as most of the funding they are given is based on performance (OECD, 2002:16).

Recent policy formulation in the KBEs is designed not only to facilitate government-led R&D and innovation, but also to promote private sector industrial R&D and innovation. In some countries, the tax regime has become more favorable for business R&D and innovation (OECD, 2002:17) while in others, national R&D programs have been designed to support specific industrial sectors.

One of the most important goals in formulating policy for a KBE is to enhance competitiveness among different industries, both in manufacturing and in the service sector. In a world of globalization, it would be impossible for any industry to survive without creating a distinct and competitive niche for itself in the market. In doing so, countries also need to protect infant industries by giving them adequate support in science and technology. Many countries, in this regard, may require technology transfer from other countries.

Looking at the contemporary KBEs, we can definitely consider the United States to be one of the most successful countries in the world in terms of creating a functional KBE. The United States transformed itself from being a good copier in the nineteenth century to a great inventor by the last half of the 20th century (Thurow, 1999:100). Americans spend a great deal of money and human resources on R&D. With the creation of Silicon Valley, the KBE in the States experienced rapid growth. Of the total R&D expenditure made in the States, big firms contribute almost 84% (Thurow, 1999:108) and play the most important role in new inventions. The wise government policy of the country to attract the most brilliant pool of workers from all over the world, is giving the country long-term sustainability in the development of its KBE.

Sweden is another example of a successful KBE. The government established the Swedish Agency for Innovation Systems (VINNOVA) in January 2001 to focus public efforts on areas of strategic importance, aiming to raise efficiency and better adapt to the needs of target groups (OECD, 2002:70). Among the many activities of VINNOVA, are sponsoring R&D, promoting research cooperation among universities, research institutes and businesses, stimulating knowledge creation and diffusion, and developing the role of integrated research activities in the national innovation systems.

The key ingredients of the KBE are R&D, ICT infrastructure, quality education and the creation of quality human resources. Presently, OECD countries are the leading KBE nations in the world. In most of them, investment in and exploitation of knowledge are the key drivers of R&D, innovation, economic growth and overall social well-being. The investment in knowledge creation and diffusion activities, such as science, technology, R&D, ICT and innovation, influences macroeconomic variables, such as employment, production and trade. This, in turn, leads to economic prosperity by supporting the emergence and expansion of new industries, encouraging organizational changes, and driving productivity improvements (OECD, 2002a).

During the last two decades, most countries' expenditures in R&D, higher education, and ICT grew more rapidly than gross fixed capital formation (OECD, 2002:13). OECD countries' efforts towards the KBE are helping them to improve productivity through creation and diffusion of knowledge, especially in the area of information technology. The growing ICT sector is helping member countries to thrive in the information network, receiving the maximum benefit given the resources available. This, in turn, propels technology- and knowledge-based industries, the heart of the KBE, to grow faster than ever before. As a consequence, in OECD countries, the production and application of scientific and technological knowledge have become a more collective effort, linking industries, academia and the government (OECD, 2002:13).

The outcome of policy formulation for the KBE can be seen in many sectors. Although different KBEs achieve different outcomes, there are some definite outcomes from policy formulation. In many countries, investment in knowledge has increased, although different countries have different areas of investment depending on their area of specialization (Khan, 2001). As shown in Figure 5.1, three main areas of investment are R&D, higher education and software development.

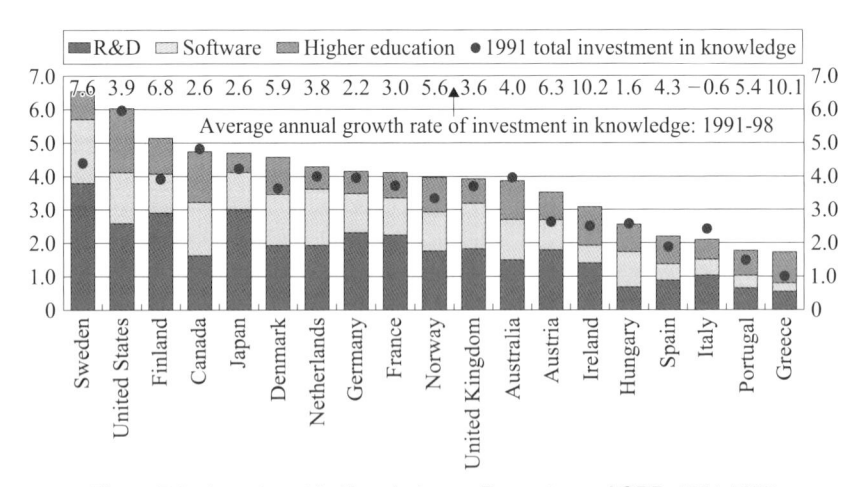

Figure 5.1 Investment in Knowledge as Percentage of GDP, 1991-1998
Source: OECD, 2002:25.

Table 5.1 Contribution of the ICT-producing and ICT-using Sectors to Aggregate GDP Growth, 1990-1999

		Canada	Denmark	Finland	France	Germany	Italy	Japan	Netherlands	United Kingdom	United States
1990-1995	ICT-producing sector	0.21	0.24	0.29	0.17	0.06	0.17	0.32	0.12	0.32	0.37
	ICT-using Sectors	0.43	0.1	-0.48	0.12	0.4	0.41	0.55	0.5	0.39	0.56
	Non-ICT sector	1.07	1.17	-0.34	0.63	0.94	0.71	0.65	1.43	0.99	1.38
1995-1999	ICT-producing sector	0.35	0.23	1.48	0.45	0.4	0.28	0.4	0.63	0.63	0.78
	ICT-using Sectors	0.88	0.84	1.02	0.3	0.56	0.43	0.38	0.129	0.87	1.89
	Non-ICT sector	1.95	1.27	2.57	1.11	0.86	0.71	0.31	1.74	1.32	2.02

Source: OECD, 2002:30.

As indicated in Table 5.1, one of the significant outcomes in KBE policy formulation is the increasing investment in ICT. ICT is considered to be a critical element in the transition towards the KBE, because of its ability to widely increase productivity in information processing and exchange and in the organization of working processes (OECD, 2002:27). In the twenty-two OECD countries, ICT production represented approximately 9.5% of business sector value added in 1999, compared to 8% in 1995 (OECD, 2002c). The impact of this ICT investment has significantly contributed to the GDP growth in many countries (Colecchia and Schreyer, 2001). In many countries, the increasing share of ICT in aggregate investment has directed the shift in composition of capital stocks aimed at assets with higher marginal productivity, *i.e.* an improvement in the overall quality of investment stock (Scarpetta *et al.*, 2000).

Realizing the importance of science and technology for a KBE, the governments in many countries have pursued appropriate policies to invest more in science and technology. This investment has reliably resulted in the rise of scientific and technological productivity. The gross expenditure on research and development

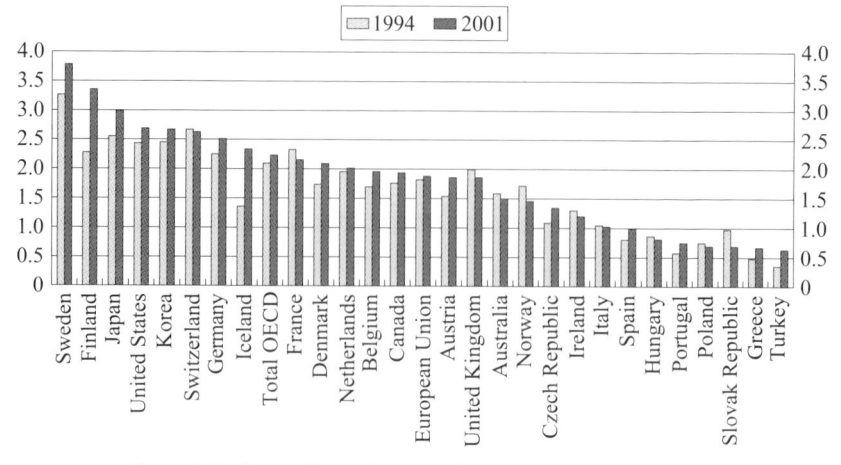

Figure 5.2 Gross Expenditure on Research and Development as Percentage of GDP, 1994 and 2001*
* Or the nearest available year.
Source: OECD, MSTI database, May 2002.

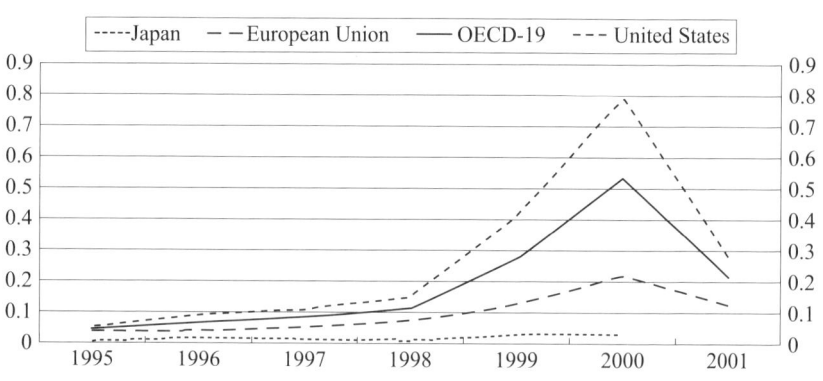

Figure 5.3 Early- and Expansion-stage Venture Capital Financing in OECD Countries/Regions, 1995-2001 (Share of GDP)
Source: OECD, 2002:35.

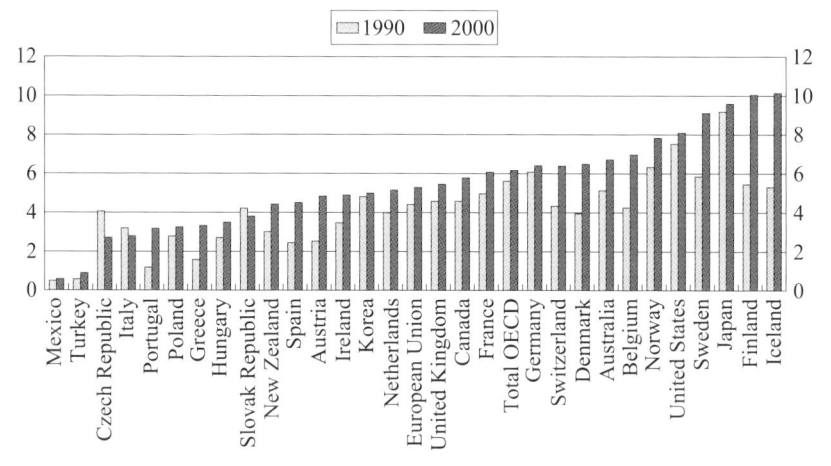

Chapter Five: Contemporary KBEs and East Asia   67

Figure 5.4 Total Researchers per Thousand Labor Force, 1990 and 2000*
*or nearest available years.
Source: OECD, 2002:44.

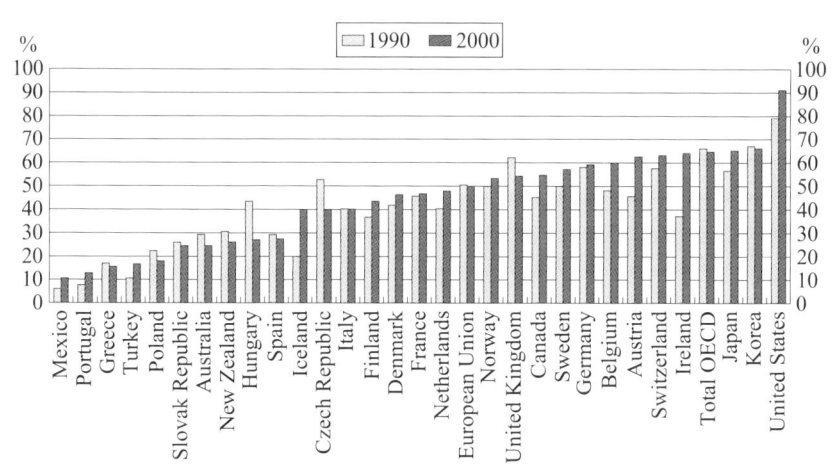

Figure 5.5 Business Enterprise Researchers as Percentage of Total Researchers, 1990 and 2000**
**or nearest available years.
Source: OECD, 2002:45.

(GERD) continues to rise in many countries even now, and this is especially significant in OECD countries (See Figure 5.2).

Parallel to the increase in GERD, private sector financing in R&D has also increased in many countries as a result of policy initiatives taken by concerned governments. However, in some countries, like France and the United Kingdom, private sector expenditures have declined in relation to government policies. At the same time, venture capital financing also started declining as of 2000 (See Figure 5.3). Despite this decline, governments and the private sector continue investing enormously in the high-tech sector.

One of the most important factors in the KBE is the rapid expansion in its pool of researchers. This phenomenon is particularly prominent in OECD countries. The total researchers per thousand in the labor force reached 6.2 in 2000, compared to 5.6 in 1990 (OECD, 2002:44) (See Figure 5.4). In this regard, the business sector is the main source of employment. According to *OECD Science, Technology and Industry Outlook 2002*, more than two-thirds of total researchers in OECD countries were in the business enterprise sector in 2000 (See Figure 5.5). However, industry and academia, along with government, support the work of R&D in the KBEs through cooperation and coordination.

The East Asian Economic Miracle and the Emergence of the KBE in East Asia

Many economies in East Asia have achieved unprecedented growth in output and living standards over the recent decades. It was only when the economies were hit hard by the Asian financial crisis that growth began to slow down. During the period of 1965 to 1990, most countries in East Asia experienced rapid growth.

Among the East Asian countries, Japan, Hong Kong, Taiwan, Singapore and South Korea have been most successful, and these countries, by creating the

Table 5.2   School Enrollment, Primary (Percentage) in East Asia

Country	1997	1998	1999	2000	2001	2002	2003	2004	2005	2006
China	N/A	N/A	N/A	N/A	117	116	115	N/A	N/A	111
Hong Kong	N/A	N/A	100	103	105	106	N/A	N/A	N/A	N/A
Japan	N/A	N/A	101	101	101	101	100	100	100	N/A
South Korea	N/A	N/A	95	98	100	102	104	105	105	105
Taiwan	101	100	100	100	100	100	100	101	100	100
Indonesia	N/A	N/A	N/A	109	112	113	114	115	115	N/A
Malaysia	N/A	N/A	98	97	97	95	97	100	N/A	N/A
Philippines	N/A	N/A	113	N/A	112	111	112	112	111	N/A
Singapore	N/A	N/A	83	81	79	78	78	78	78	N/A
Thailand	N/A	N/A	106	106	106	108	108	110	109	108

Source: World Development Indicators 2008 and Statistical Yearbook of the Republic of China 2006 (calculated in rounded figures).

Table 5.3   GDP Growth (Annual Percentage) in East Asia

Country	1997	1998	1999	2000	2001	2002	2003	2004	2005	2006
China	9	8	8	8	8	9	10	10	10	11
Hong Kong	5	(5)	3	10	0	2	3	8	7	7
Japan	2	(2)	(0)	3	0	0	1	3	2	2
South Korea	5	(7)	9	8	4	7	3	5	4	5
Taiwan	7	5	6	6	(2)	5	4	6	4	5
Indonesia	5	(13)	1	5	4	4	5	5	6	5
Malaysia	7	(7)	6	9	0	4	6	7	5	6
Philippines	5	(1)	3	6	2	4	5	6	5	5
Singapore	8	(1)	7	10	(2)	4	3	9	7	8
Thailand	(1)	(11)	4	5	2	5	7	6	4	5

Source: World Development Indicators 2008 and Statistical Yearbook of the Republic of China 2006 (calculated in rounded figures).

Table 5.4   Foreign Direct Investment, Net Inflows (% of GDP) in East Asia

Country	1997	1998	1999	2000	2001	2002	2003	2004	2005	2006
China	5	4	4	3	3	3	3	3	4	3
Hong Kong	N/A	9	15	37	14	6	9	21	19	23
Japan	0	0	0	0	0	0	0	0	0	(0)
South Korea	1	2	2	2	1	0	1	1	1	0
Taiwan	N/A	N/A	N/A	N/A	N/A	N/A	N/A	N/A	N/A	N/A
Indonesia	2	(0)	(1)	(3)	(2)	0	(0)	1	3	2
Malaysia	5	3	5	4	1	3	2	4	3	4
Philippines	1	4	2	3	0	2	1	1	2	2
Singapore	14	9	20	18	18	8	13	18	13	18
Thailand	3	7	5	3	4	3	4	4	5	4

Source: World Development Indicators 2008 and Statistical Yearbook of the Republic of China 2006 (calculated in rounded figures).

infrastructure needed, are leading the race to transform their industrial economy into a KBE. All the economies mentioned above have showed greater performance in education reform and in GDP growth; and most of them have also received a great deal of FDI (See Tables 5.2, 5.3 and 5.4). The same can be said for investment in R&D. Most countries in East Asia have invested in R&D during last few decades (See Table 5.5). Patents granted in East Asia also increased by 17.6 percent during the 2000-2004 period compared to the 1990-2000 period (See Table 5.6).

Japan has long been the most successful KBE in the region. Japan's prolonged recession after the bubble burst motivated the country to further advance the already available KBE. Realizing the need to strengthen administration and make it more compatible with science and technological innovation, Japan merged the Ministry of Education, Science, Sports and Culture, and the Science and Technology Agency into Ministry of Education, Culture, Sports, Science and Technology (MEXT)

Table 5.5 Research and Development Expenditures

	R&D Spending 2002		R&D as % GDP*	
	US$ Bill. (PPP)	% of World	1992	2002
East Asia	111.7	13.5	0.7	1.2
Hong Kong	1.1	0.1	0.3(b)	0.6
Korea	20.8	2.5	1.9	2.5
Singapore	2.2	0.3	1.2	2.2
Taiwan	12.2	1.5	1.8	2.3
Indonesia	0.3	0.0	0.1(c)	0.1(a)
Malaysia	1.5	0.2	0.4	0.7
Philippines	0.4	0.0	0.2	0.1
Thailand	1.1	0.1	0.2	0.2
China	72.0	8.7	0.8	1.2
World	829.9	100.0	1.7	1.7
Developed	645.8	77.8	2.3	2.3
Japan	106.4	12.8	2.9	3.1
USA	275.1	33.1	2.6	2.6
Developing	184.1	22.1	0.6	0.9
Latin America	21.7	2.6	0.5	0.6
Emerging Europe	30.3	3.7	1.0	1.2

Source: UNESCO (2004, 2006). Note: (a) 2001, (b) 1995 and (c) 1994.
*Regional data are sum of R&D divided by sum of PPP GDP.

(OECD, 2002:92). The new ministry plays a leading role in promoting and coordinating integrated strategic research conducted by national research institutions, as well as basic research conducted by universities. Additionally, Japan has also developed the Council for Science and Technology Policy so as to strengthen the administrative leadership of the Cabinet and the Prime Minister; this has improved Japan's ability to foresee the future demand for R&D and innovation and thus, helps the government to facilitate, as it arranges R&D and innovation activities through the integration of different disciplines (OECD, 2002:92). The government has also launched the 'Rika-e Initiative' to enhance science and technology education, and improve public science and technology literacy with the help of digital learning materials (OECD, 2002:78).

Hobday (1995, 2000) stresses the role of Original Equipment Manufacturing (OEM) subcontracting in fostering industrial exports and technology transfer in Korea and Taiwan. In these cases, the supplier undertakes production according

Table 5.6   USPTO Patents Granted *

	Number of Patents		Patents per 1000 People		
	1990-2000	2000-2004	1990-2000	2000-2004	% Change
East Asia (9)	2239	12108	0.14	0.72	17.6
Hong Kong	184	616	3.15	9.32	11.4
Korea	633	4009	1.44	8.67	19.7
Singapore	36	382	1.09	9.87	24.6
Taiwan	1307	6593	6.30	30.17	17.0
Indonesia	6	15	0.00	0.01	8.8
Malaysia	13	64	0.07	0.28	15.3
Philippines	6	18	0.01	0.02	10.4
Thailand	6	43	0.01	0.07	20.9
China	48	368	0.00	0.03	22.9
World	107361	182523	1.98	2.95	4.1
Developed (21)	104170	168017	12.88	19.58	4.3
Japan	22647	35687	18.23	28.54	4.6
USA	59024	97104	23.00	33.56	3.9
Latin America (11)	173	368	0.04	0.08	6.3
Emerging Europe (9)	205	348	0.07	0.12	5.6

* Annual averages.
Source: US Patent and Trade Office.

to the design specifications of the foreign buyer, who then markets the product under its own brand name and through its own international distribution channels. China is another addition to the recent OEM countries. Its rapid rise in this area is creating huge competition in the OEM sector in East Asia.

Foreign direct investment (FDI) is one of the strongest contributors to the East Asian economic growth (See Table 5.4). Economic growth in East Asia has contributed to growth in output and living standards over recent decades. However, lack of proper institutional settings in many sectors of the East Asian economies resulted in huge economic slowdown during the Asian financial crisis.

Hong Kong, Singapore and Malaysia, by creating infrastructure needed, also have been pursuing policies to transform their industrial economies into KBEs. These economies have shown greater performance in education reform and GDP growth, and most of them have also received large volume of FDI (See Tables 5.2, 5.3 and 5.4). Although the Singaporean government announced its full policy towards the KBE in 1998 (MITA, 1998) [1], it has been adopting short-term policies for different sectors of knowledge creation since independence. Soon after the independence in 1965, Singapore has been forced to take drastic measures to cope with cultural and colonial barriers. In terms of national policy formulation, education and family planning were addressed as top priorities (Booth, 1999). That sowed the seeds for the KBE in Singapore. Within a very short time, the schooling rate increased rapidly at all levels. Mani (2005) has noted that during the 1960-1965 period, Singapore appears to have a better human capital endowment with gross primary enrollment (Gross Enrolment Rate, GER) exceeding 100%, secondary GER reaching 39%, and tertiary GER reaching around 10%, which was better even compared to Korea during the same period. In 1996, Singapore achieved secondary GER of 67%, while tertiary GER reached about 28.7%. These observations indicate that Singapore is a front runner in educational achievements within East Asia. By the late 1980s, the total mean years of education in Singapore rose to seven, second only to the Philippines (with eight years) in East Asia (Easterly *et al.*, 1999:22). Besides education, by the year 1996, Singapore had the highest number of scientists and engineers out of all other East Asian countries. These efforts were reflected clearly in annual GDP growth. Singapore is the only country in East Asia with an average GDP growth rate at or even higher than 7% for the period from 1960-1996. The most recent data available (See Tables 5.2, 5.3 and 5.4) also indicate Singapore's superior performance in education, GDP growth and FDI inflows. Given these facts, it is clear that Singapore's policy since independence has been to construct a solid educational base for the nation, a base that has propelled the country toward realizing a KBE. Current government policies deal with different components of the KBE from a holistic perspective.

Summary

Reviewing the contemporary state of KBEs, we can say that the application of the KBE is *sine quo non* for increasing the growth rate and building up a competitive base to compete in the global market. Many indicators of KBE have been discussed in this chapter using the examples of OECD countries. While the OECD countries are pioneers in transforming their economies into KBEs, most East Asian countries started transforming their economies into KBEs in the late twentieth century. In this sense, the East Asian KBEs enjoyed certain benefits as latecomers. However, not all the East Asian economies have been successful in this regard. Countries like Japan, Korea, Taiwan, Hong Kong and Singapore have shown extraordinary success, while countries like Malaysia, Thailand, China and Philippines have joined the race late. Other East Asian economies are still largely lagging behind.

Chapter Six

Economic Incentives and Institutional Regimes in the Development of KBEs in East Asia

Introduction

The fundamental challenge in an emerging KBE is to harness knowledge for development by providing an enabling environment of competitive education system, highly qualified human resources, excellent information and communications technology (ICT) and innovation infrastructures. Science and technology are at the heart of knowledge-based economic growth and development. However, diffusion and transfer of technology for economic development are not straightforward. Identifying the factors, policies and institutional arrangements that promote technology diffusion is the first step in ensuring a country has access to and uses technologies developed by technology leaders. As such, it is needless to say that the whole process of knowledge creation and diffusion in a KBE heavily depends on appropriate government policies, policies that are usually the outcome of economic incentives and institutional regimes. Many East Asian governments have shown remarkable success in creating a KBE by pursuing appropriate policy. In this regard, governments play a very crucial role, because knowledge creation and diffusion cannot simply depend on market mechanism alone. An appropriate framework for economic incentives and institutional regimes is necessary to facilitate interaction among different sectors in a KBE. This chapter attempts to explain the role of economic incentives and institutional regimes to promote a KBE in East Asia.

Economic Incentives in East Asian KBEs

Economic incentives are very crucial to the growth of the KBE. Without appropriate economic incentives, it is difficult to foster growth. Openness towards trade (Chen and Dahlman, 2005), stable financial and monetary systems that allow minimal price distortions and create sound investment opportunities (Heritage Foundation, 2009), competitive business and investment environments and the presence of appropriate property rights legal system are some of the main factors in economic incentives that encourage entrepreneurship and competition. These factors ultimately lead to continuous innovation in knowledge-based economic growth.

Openness

Openness refers the openness of an economy to imports of goods and services from around the world, as well as the ability of citizens to interact freely as buyers and sellers in the international marketplace (Heritage Foundation, 2009:13). In most East Asian KBEs, the presence of greater trade freedom has been contributing to high growth for the last couple of decades. The weighted average tariff rate in Japan and Korea was 1.5 percent and 7.4 percent in 2006, respectively. Import and export restrictions, import quotas, services market access barriers, non-transparent and burdensome regulations and standards, restrictive sanitary and phytosanitary rules, state trade in some goods, subsidies, and inefficient customs administration add to the cost of trade in Japan; in Korea, though, it is prohibitive tariffs, import restrictions, quantitative restrictions, services market access barriers, some import taxes, use of "adjustment" tariffs and taxes to increase import costs, burdensome and non-transparent standards and regulations, weak enforcement of intellectual property rights, and subsidies that add to the cost of trade (Heritage Foundation Online, 2009). Japan and Korea have less trade freedom than Hong Kong and Taiwan (See Figure 6.1).

Taiwan's weighted average tariff rate was 2.4 percent in 2006. The government has been improving the trade regime, but import and export bans and restrictions,

Trade Freedom

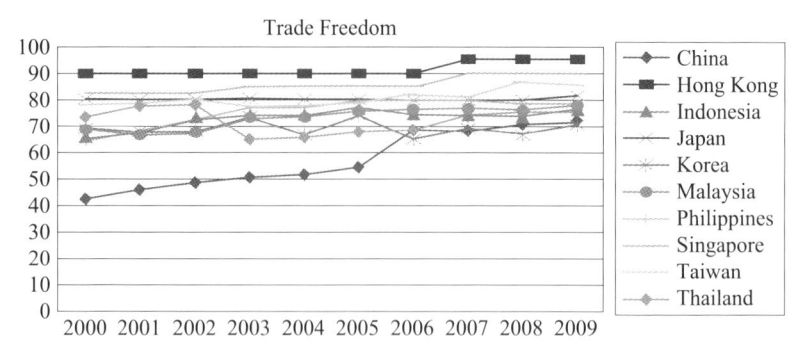

Figure 6.1　Tariff & Nontariff Barriers, East Asia
Source: The Heritage Foundation's Trade Freedom score, 2009.

services market access barriers, import taxes and fees, burdensome standards and certification requirements, restrictive pharmaceutical regulations, cumbersome sanitary and phytosanitary rules, state trade in rice, and weak enforcement of intellectual property rights all add to the cost of trade. The weighted average tariff rate in Hong Kong and Singapore was, however, 0 percent in 2006. In Hong Kong, restrictive pharmaceuticals regulation, market access restrictions for some services, limited import licensing, and issues involving the enforcement of intellectual property rights add to the cost of trade; in Singapore, though, it is import restrictions, services market barriers, import taxes, import licensing, non-transparent regulations, burdensome sanitary and phytosanitary rules, and export incentive programs that add to the cost of trade.

Supportive Business Environment

A supportive and helpful business environment refers to an individual's right to create, operate, and close an enterprise with ease; this should not encourage the rise of unnecessary regulatory rules that would be barriers to the free conduct of entrepreneurial activities (Heritage Foundation, 2009: 12). The major East Asian KBEs have maintained helpful business environments for businesses to flourish and contribute to economic growth.

In the case of Japan, Korea, Taiwan, Hong Kong, and Singapore, the business

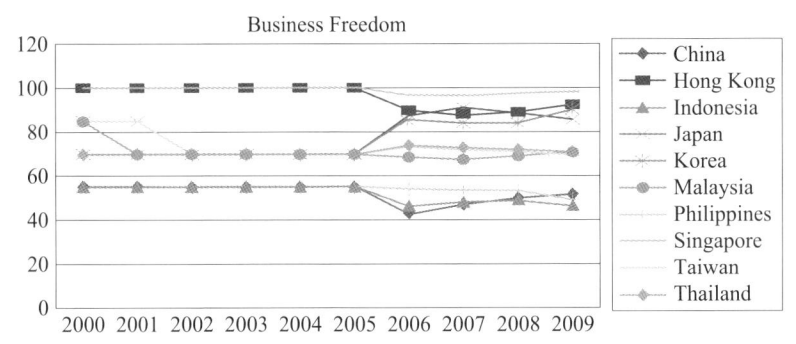

Figure 6.2 Business Freedom, East Asia
Source: The Heritage Foundation's Trade Freedom score, 2009.

environment is regulated through a system, which provides smooth procedures for businesses to open, operate or close. In all these countries, starting a business and obtaining necessary licenses take much less time than the world average. However, Singapore and Hong Kong have relatively better business freedom than Japan, Korea and Taiwan (See Figure 6.2).

Suitable Investment Environment

In an investment-friendly environment, capital flows to where it is needed most, and there, returns are greatest. The state plays an important role in facilitating such an investment-friendly environment, so that both the investor and those seeking capital can find a match. The alternative lowers entrepreneurial activity, hindering economic growth (Heritage Foundation, 2009: 14). Foreign investment is officially welcomed and inward directed investment is subject to few restrictions in Japan and Korea. There are no controls on the holding of foreign exchange accounts or on transactions, current transfers, repatriation of profits, or real estate transactions by residents or non-residents in Japan, while the Korean government offers such incentives as cash grants and zero–corporate tax zones, has a one-stop shop for foreign investments, and assigns an official to facilitate each project. However, regulatory administration in Korea is still non-transparent and can appear to be arbitrary [2].

Investment Freedom

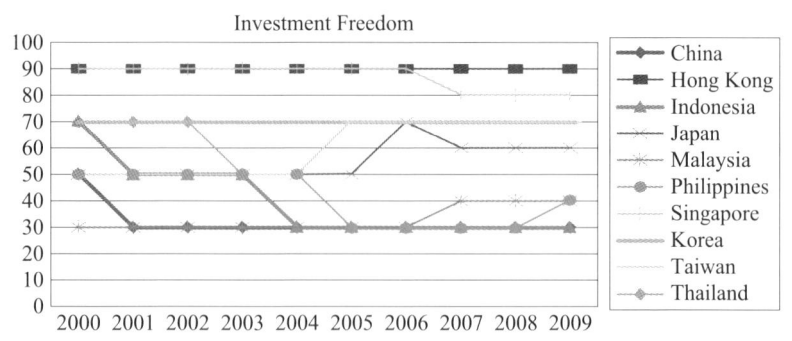

	China
	Hong Kong
	Indonesia
	Japan
	Malaysia
	Philippines
	Singapore
	Korea
	Taiwan
	Thailand

Figure 6.3   Investment Environment, East Asia
Source: The Heritage Foundation's Investment Freedom score, 2009.

In Taiwan, foreign and domestic investments are equal under the law, and private investment is welcomed in most sectors. There are relatively few restrictions on converting or transferring direct investment funds; however, there are quantity restrictions on the level of total outbound investment, and investments in China are subject to additional restrictions. In the case of Hong Kong and Singapore, foreign and domestic businesses are treated equally, and nearly all sectors are open to 100 percent foreign ownership; there are no controls or requirements on current transfers, payments, or repatriation of profits [3]. In creating an investment-friendly environment, Hong Kong and Singapore have performed better than Japan, Korea and Taiwan over the last ten years (See Figure 6.3).

Functional Monetary System

A sound monetary system is necessary for a stable currency and market-determined prices. A stable monetary system with monetary freedom is necessary to create long-term value in the economy. The value of a country's currency is controlled largely by the monetary policy of its government, a policy that ought to maintain stability, and ensure inflation does not distort pricing, resources are not misallocated, the cost of doing business does not rise unnecessarily, and a free society, in which people can rely on market prices for the foreseeable future, is not undermined (Heritage Foundation, 2009:14).

Monetary Freedom

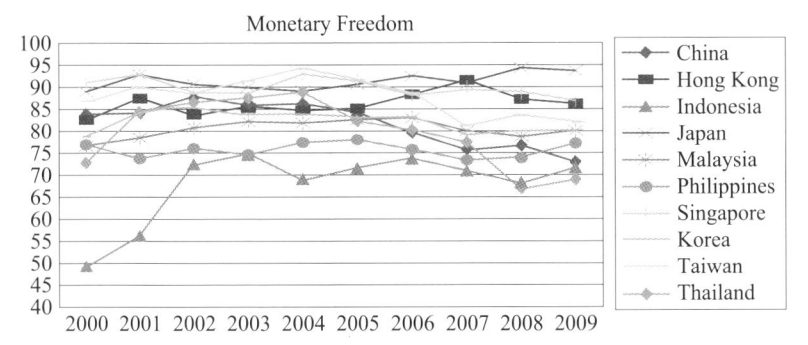

Figure 6.4 Monetary System, East Asia
Source: The Heritage Foundation's Monetary Freedom score, 2009.

Inflation in Japan has been extraordinarily low, averaging 0.01 percent between 2005 and 2007 while Korea, Taiwan, Hong Kong and Singapore experienced average inflation rates of 2.5 percent, 1.5 percent, 1.9 percent and 1.7 percent respectively during the same period. According to the Heritage Foundation's Monetary Freedom score, Japan is the leading country in East Asia in this regard, followed by Singapore, Hong Kong, Taiwan and Korea (See Figure 6.4).

Sound Financial System

Virtually all countries provide some type of prudent supervision of banks and other financial services to ensure that financial service firms meet basic fiduciary responsibilities (Heritage Foundation, 2009: 14). Most East Asian countries have developed quite strong financial systems, as they experienced high economic growth during the high growth era. Almost all these countries' financial systems are subject to government control to prevent the financial disasters that some economies experienced during the Asian financial crisis and the current global financial crisis. Deregulation and competition in Japan have led to consolidation in an effort to create banks large enough to be major players abroad, while Japanese corporations maintain tight relationships with the banks so as to have access to cheap credit and lessen their accountability in the event of failure. The Japanese government supports bank mergers to speed up the transformation of the financial sector, and it continues to update laws and regulations to facilitate them.

Korea's modern financial sector has become more open and competitive, providing positive momentum for reforms in other sectors. After the 1997 Asian financial crisis, the government succeeded in recapitalizing banks and non-bank financial institutions. Taiwan's modern financial sector has become more competitive as many restrictions on financial activities, particularly those of foreign financial institutions, have been reduced. Hong Kong is a global financial center with a regulatory and legal environment focused on enforcing prudent minimum standards and transparency.

Singapore's financial sector is also very modern and competitive. Although the capital market is quite strong in all the mentioned East Asian countries, the Tokyo Stock Exchange and Hong Kong Stock Exchange (HKSE) are the two of the ten most capitalized stock exchanges in the world. If we look at the Heritage Foundation's Financial Freedom score, which is an indicator of sound financial systems, we see that Hong Kong is the leading center in East Asia (See Figure 6.5).

Domestic credit to private sector is one of the important components of a sound financial system. In the selected East Asia countries, although there is a negative trend in domestic credit to the private sector, as compared to the percentage of GDP, they still provide huge domestic credit to the private sector (See Figure 6.6).

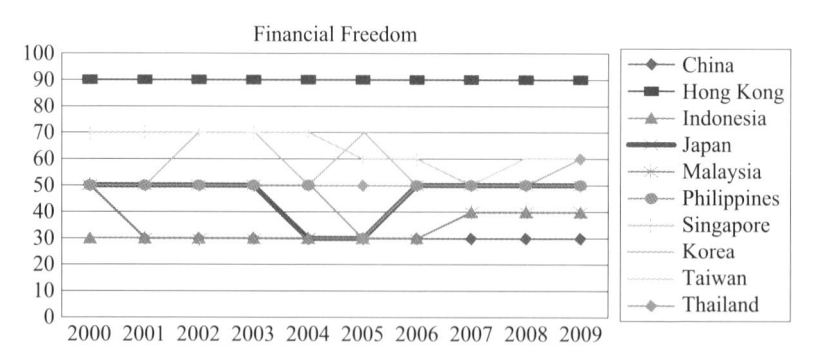

Figure 6.5 Financial System, East Asia
Source: The Heritage Foundation's Financial Freedom score, 2009.

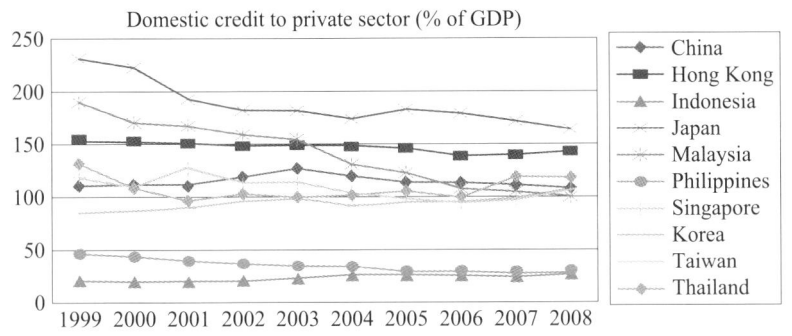

Figure 6.6 Domestic Credit to Private Sector, East Asia
Source: World Bank, 2009.

Property Rights Protection

The ability to accumulate private property is the main motivating force in a market economy, and the rule of law is vital to a fully functioning free-market economy (Heritage Foundation, 2009:14-15). A secure property rights system, requiring an effective and honest judicial system available to all, equally and without discrimination, gives citizens the confidence to undertake commercial activities, save their income, and make long-term plans, because they know that their income and savings are safe from expropriation or theft. In most of the selected countries in East Asia, real and intellectual property rights are generally secured. However, in Hong Kong and Singapore, property rights are more strongly protected than Japan, Korea and Taiwan (See Figure 6.7).

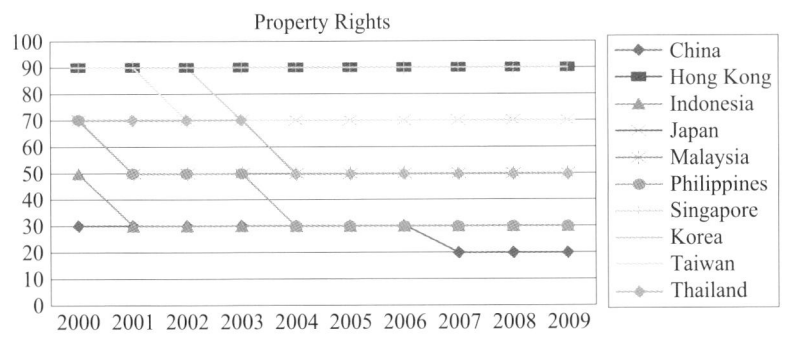

Figure 6.7 Property Rights Protection, East Asia
Source: The Heritage Foundation's Property Rights score, 2009.

Institutional Regimes in East Asia

A government that is effective, accountable and free of corruption, as well as has an appropriate legal system that ensures the rule of law and regulatory efficiency, is necessary to support and enforce the basic rules of business; these rules should allow for a fair and competitive business environment in which innovation is a continuous process (Chen and Dahlman, 2005:8-9). Many scholars have argued that good governance is absolutely necessary to have a functional and institutional regime, a regime that would include an effective, impartial and transparent legal system that protects property and individual rights; public institutions that are stable, credible and honest; and government policies that favor free and open markets. In East Asia, these conditions encourage FDI and presumably private domestic investment as well, by protecting privately held assets from arbitrary direct or indirect appropriation. Generally, 'good governance' indicators have six dimensions: i) Voice & Accountability, ii) Political Stability, iii) Government Effectiveness, iv) Regulatory Quality, v) Rule of Law, and vi) Control of Corruption (Kaufmann *et al.*, 1999). Using the data from 1996-2008 for the six indicators stated above, a comparative analysis has been conducted for the selected East Asian countries.

Voice and Accountability

Voice and Accountability is a composite indicator and comprises a number of individual indicators measuring various aspects of the political process, civil liberties and political rights. This index measures the extent to which citizens of a country are able to participate in the selection of government including measuring the independence of the media, which plays an important role in monitoring those in authority and holding them accountable for their actions. Figure 6.8 asserts that all the selected East Asian countries indeed performed well in terms of voice and accountability measures of good governance.

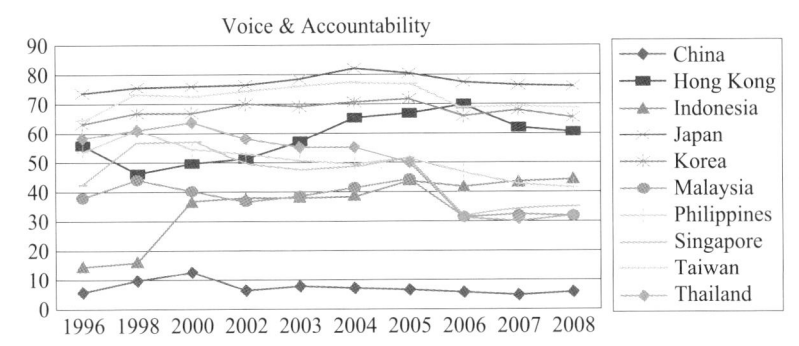

Chapter Six: Economic Incentives and Institutional Regimes in the Development of KBEs in East Asia   83

Figure 6.8   Voice & Accountability, East Asia
Source: Computed data collected from Worldwide Governance Indicators, 1996-2008 available at http://info.worldbank.org/governance/wgi/sc_country.asp.

Political Stability

The Political Stability Index combines several indicators, all of which measure perceptions of how likely it is that the government in power will be destabilized or overthrown by unconstitutional and/or violent means [4]. Figure 6.9 indicates that almost all the selected East Asian countries have been performing well in terms of political stability.

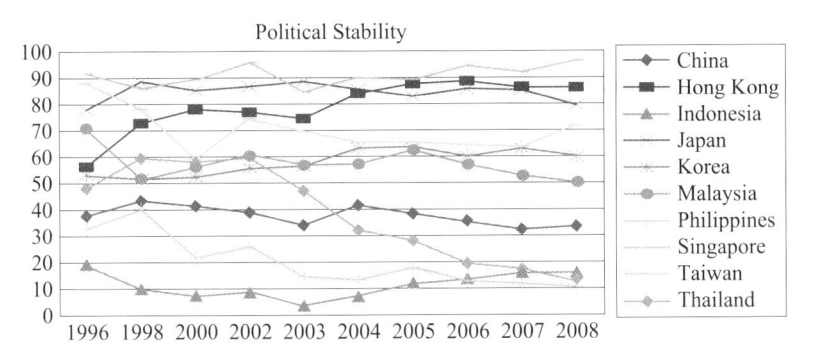

Figure 6.9   Political Stability, East Asia
Source: Computed data collected from Worldwide Governance Indicators, 1996-2008 available at http://info.worldbank.org/governance/wgi/sc_country.asp.

Government Effectiveness

Government Effectiveness combines into one grouping perceptions of the quality of public service, the quality of the bureaucracy, the competence of civil servants, the independence of the civil service from political pressures, and the credibility of the government's commitment to its policies [5]. Figure 6.10 indicates that all the East Asian countries have performed consistently well in terms of government effectiveness. China is performing above the 60% level while other East Asian countries' performance in 2007 was above the 80% level.

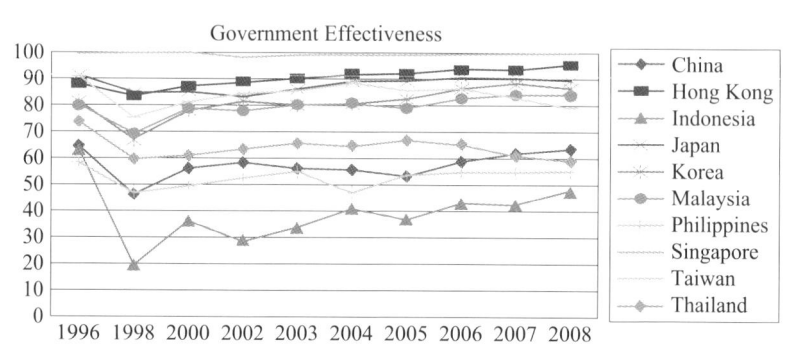

Figure 6.10   Government Effectiveness, East Asia
Source: Computed data collected from Worldwide Governance Indicators, 1996-2008 available at http://info.worldbank.org/governance/wgi/sc_country.asp.

Regulatory Quality

Regulatory Quality measures the incidence of anti-market policies, such as price controls or inadequate bank supervision, as well as perceptions of the burdens imposed by excessive regulation in areas, such as foreign trade and business development [6]. Figure 6.11 shows the regulatory quality in East Asian countries. From the graph, it is evident that all the selected East Asian countries are performing well above the 70% level.

Rule of Law

Rule of Law includes several indicators, all of which measure the extent to which agents have confidence in and abide by the rules of society. These indicators

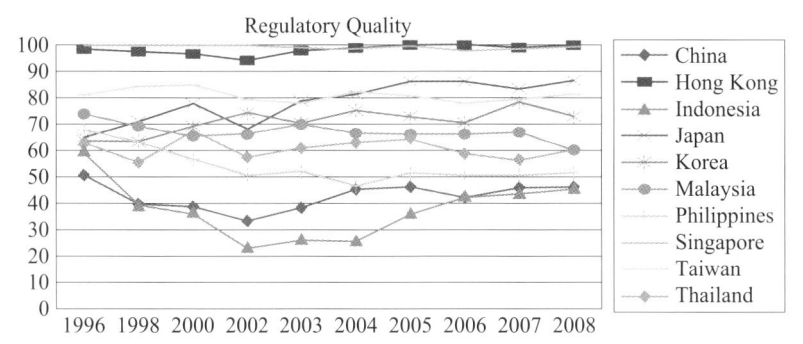

Chapter Six: Economic Incentives and Institutional Regimes in the Development of KBEs in East Asia   85

Figure 6.11   Regulatory Quality, East Asia
Source: Computed data collected from Worldwide Governance Indicators, 1996-2008 available at http://info.worldbank.org/governance/wgi/sc_country.asp.

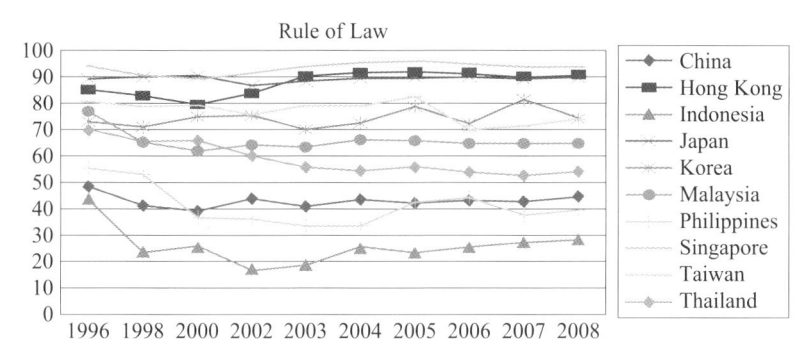

Figure 6.12   Rule of Law, East Asia
Source: Computed data collected from Worldwide Governance Indicators, 1996-2008 available at http://info.worldbank.org/governance/wgi/sc_country.asp.

include perceptions of the incidence of both violent and non-violent crimes, the effectiveness and predictability of the judiciary, and the enforceability of contracts [7]. In terms of the rule of law, all the selected East Asian countries are performing well above the 70% level (See Figure 6.12).

Control of Corruption

The Control of Corruption indicator corresponds to "graft" measures of corruption, notably, corruption measured by the frequency of "additional payments to get things done" and the effects of corruption on the business environment [8]. From Figure 6.13, we can see that all the East Asian countries are performing above

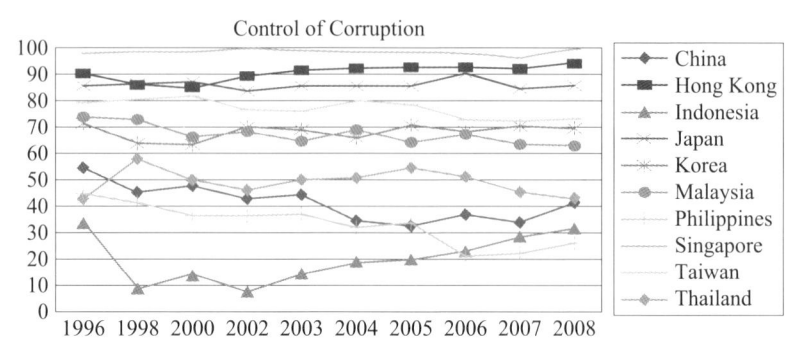

Figure 6.13 Control of Corruption, East Asia
Source: Computed data collected from Worldwide Governance Indicators, 1996-2008 available at http://info.worldbank.org/governance/wgi/sc_country.asp.

the 70% level in controlling corruption. Only China has performed poorly in this regard when compared to the other advanced KBEs in the region, coming in at the below average level of 50%. China's performance has been declining since 2003.

If we combine all the six indicators of good governance, we can see that Singapore, Hong Kong, Japan, Korea and Taiwan have been performing well above the 70% level, far better than other East Asian countries. A combination of good economic incentives and healthy institutional regimes has helped the selected East Asian countries to become KBEs.

Economic Incentives, Institutional Regimes and Development of the KBE in East Asia

A good institutional framework should ensure the flow of knowledge between bodies of scientific research and parties exploring technological application. A good institutional framework should also ensure the flow of information between researchers and users. Here, the government plays a crucial role, as knowledge creation cannot depend on market mechanism alone. As the market for knowledge is often characterized by imperfections (meaning, that social and private returns derived from knowledge in any area of knowledge creation can widely differ), any 'market failure' may lead to private underinvestment in knowledge (UNCTAD, 2007). Thus, policies to support knowledge creation through government funding, government procurement, tax subsidies, intellectual property rights protection, and so on, as well as knowledge diffusion through the establishment of libraries, communication networks, and access cost subsidies, etc. must be formulated by the government.

Having postulated that the role of government is indispensable in creating a KBE, in this chapter, we propose that economic incentives and institutional regimes are also determining factors, required for creating a sound KBE.

Figure 6.14 shows the relationship among the three components of economic incentives and institutional regimes, FDI inflows and domestic investments, and development of KBE infrastructure in the East Asian context. The two black arrows show the first-order development of KBE infrastructure, indicating that economic incentives and institutional regimes attract more FDI and enable more domestic investment to flow in and develop KBE infrastructure in the initial stage. Once first-order development is steadily underway, second-order developments take place in which all three components interact, either mutually or independently, to improve and coalesce into a complete KBE.

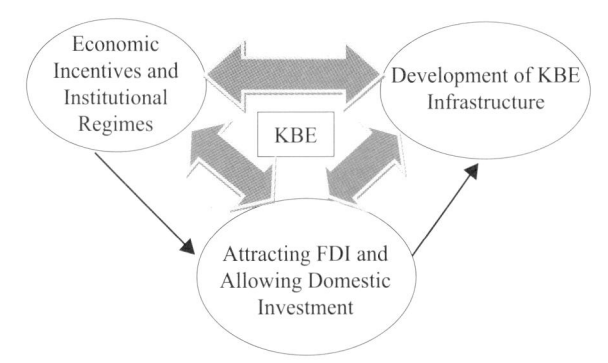

Figure 6.14 Conceptual Framework of Economic Incentives and Institutional Regimes in the East Asian KBEs
Source: Developed by the author.

The Impact of Economic Incentives and Institutional Regimes on Attracting FDI and Promoting the KBE in East Asia

The role of economic incentives and institutional regimes in promoting the KBE in East Asia has long been apparent: incentives and regimes are able to attract a large volume of FDI and increase domestic investment to build up KBE infrastructure and achieve higher economic growth. FDI can increase competition in the host economy, making domestic companies more efficient and improving living standards. A recent study found that for a one-percent increase in FDI in developing economies, there will be a GDP per capita growth of about 0.5% (McLean and Shrestha, 2002). As shown in Figure 6.15, almost all the East Asian countries have positive FDI inflows. This indicates that the stable socio-political environment in East Asian countries, a product of good governance, is one of the core reasons for the large volume of FDI inflows in East Asian countries as compared to South Asian or African ones.

In terms of FDI inflows, China has performed much better than other East Asian countries, though FDI has played a major role in advancing all the East Asian KBEs. However, the inward FDI within China flows disproportionately into provinces with less corrupt governments and governments that better protect

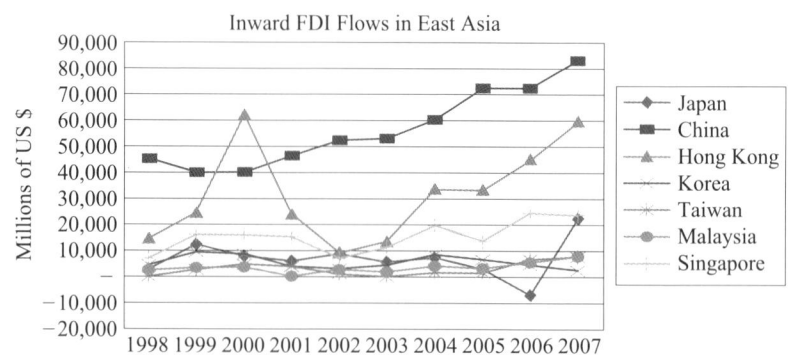

Figure 6.15 Inward FDI Flows in East Asia, 1998-2007
Source: IMD online 2009.

private property rights. This, therefore, suggests that if China had higher quality governance across all provinces, the country as a whole would have attracted even more FDI. Among the East Asian countries, China attracts the highest FDI, as China has maintained political and ideological stability along with its growing wealth. Since China ranks at the bottom in the good governance rankings among the East Asian countries selected, its success in attracting FDI should largely be attributed to a spectacular growth track record, a relatively wise use of the government's executive power, relative political stability, good infrastructure, an abundant and educated labor force, and a huge domestic market. If China wants to catch up with the other East Asian KBEs, it has to further improve its economic incentives and the quality of its institutional regimes.

Domestic investments in Eucation, Research and Development (R&D) and

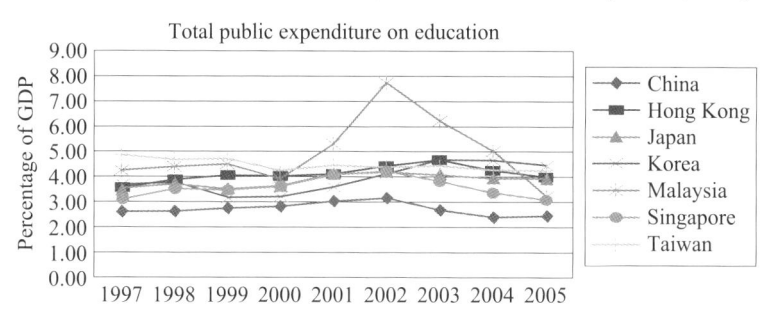

Figure 6.16 Public Expenditure in Education in East Asia, 1997-2005
Source: Government Finance Statistics Yearbook 2007.

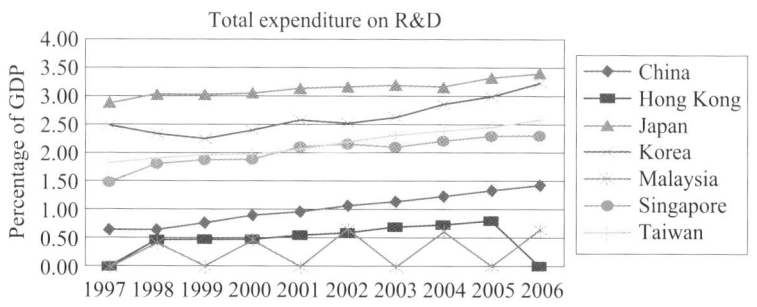

Figure 6.17 Total R&D Expenditure in East Asia, 1997-2006
Source: UNESCO online database (http://stats.uis.unesco.org).

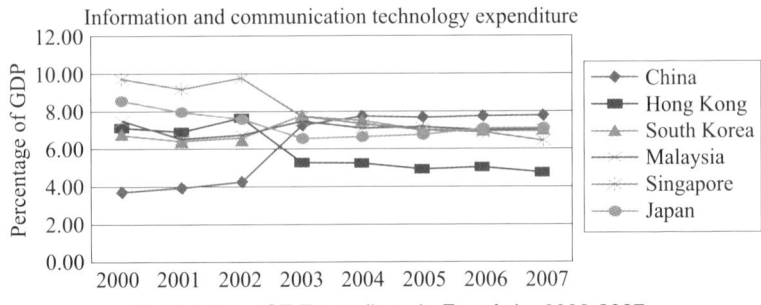

Figure 6.18 ICT Expenditure in East Asia, 2000-2007
Note: Taiwan's data is not available.
Source: World Development Index Database.

ICT have been quite steady for most of the East Asian countries above, indicating that their governments, while attracting more FDI, have also striven to develop knowledge-based economic infrastructure (See Figure 6.16, 6.17 & 6.18).

Among the East Asian countries, Japan, South Korea, Hong Kong, Singapore and Taiwan have shown superior performance in maintaining high-quality economic incentives and institutional regimes. If we consider the knowledge base of each country, which is measured by investments in KBE infrastructure and FDI inflows, we can see that the same countries have developed more by strengthening the knowledge base of their economies in all the other pillars of the KBE, including education and human resources, innovation infrastructure, and ICT infrastructure.

Now, if we investigate the six good governance indicators further, we will find that Japan, Korea, Taiwan, Singapore and Hong Kong are leaders, and that Malaysia has been performing better than China, taking sixth position in all indicators. The positive impact of having good governance has been observed in the growth of the overall productivity of East Asian countries. Overall productivity refers to economic stability, and we can see from Figure 6.19 that countries that lead in terms of economic incentives and institutional regimes in East Asia are also leading economic growth in the region.

GDP per Person Employed

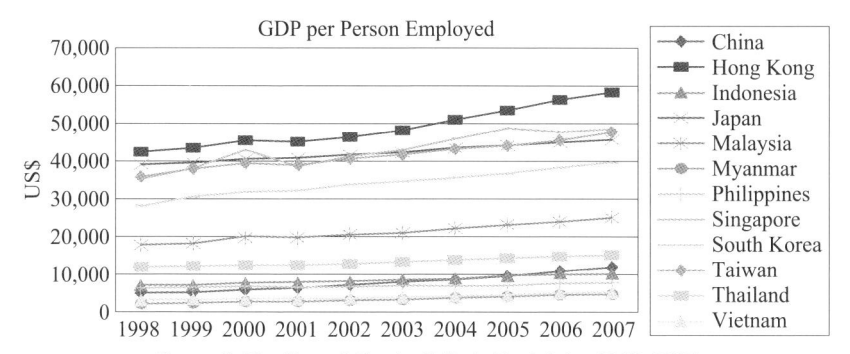

Figure 6.19   Overall Productivity in East Asia, 1998-2007
Source: The Conference Board and Groningen Growth and Development Centre, Total Economy Database, September 2008 [9].

Summary

From the analysis given above, it is clear that there is a positive correlation between economic incentives and institutional regimes, and the creation of the KBE in East Asia. In East Asia, good governance has played an important role in attracting FDI, thereby developing knowledge-based economic infrastructure needed for the KBE.

From this discussion and analysis of various empirical data, it is evident that advanced KBEs in East Asia, such as Japan, Korea, Taiwan, Hong Kong and Singapore, have been highly successful in the development of functional economic incentives and institutional regimes. Openness, a supportive and suitable business environment, a functional monetary system, a sound financial system, and property rights protection have been the key contributing factors to economic incentives in the East Asian countries. In terms of institutional regimes, voice and accountability, political stability, government effectiveness, regulatory quality, rule of law and control of corruption are all, key contributing factors. These key factors of the economic incentives and institutional regimes have contributed greatly to the development of a functioning KBE in East Asia.

Chapter Seven

Developing Education and Human Resources in East Asian KBEs

Introduction

Adam Smith (1776) invented the idea of 'division of labor' to enhance productivity by breaking down the work process into finer elements of scale economy, which is the main driver of the macro-economy. The idea of breaking down the work process into finer elements led to the concept of 'work specialization' which calls for knowledge accumulation and creation. One of the fundamental challenges in an emerging KBE is to develop a competitive educational infrastructure by which a KBE can find the highly skilled workforce it needs. Many East Asian countries have formulated appropriate policies in order to create a competitive education infrastructure, cultivating and training human resources for absorption into the KBE. A competitive educational infrastructure is a pre-requisite for any KBE aiming to create knowledge workers it needs. In a rapidly changing competitive world, a transformation of the educational sector is required for creating and maintaining a KBE. This Chapter, in this regard, addresses broad issues related to the development of a competitive educational infrastructure in the East Asian KBEs.

Historical Background

A number of historical factors have influenced the educational development of the major East Asian KBEs. Colonization has been a common feature of East Asian societies, although countries differ greatly in terms of colonial period and the extent of colonization. All the advanced economies of East Asia except Japan have been under either Japanese or Western colonization and some have been colonized by both. The Japanese defeat in World War II, as well as strong domestic movements against colonial occupation, brought independence to most of the countries in East Asia. Hong Kong was the last to get independence from the British in 1997. Although the end of the colonial era changed the political landscape of these countries, most of them were able to keep certain good traditions of the colonial period. The education sector, in this regard, particularly maintained the legacy of the colonial era and was rebuilt on colonial era foundations. The education sector in Korea and Taiwan was influenced by the Japanese education system during the colonial era, and that influence continued even after the colonial era ended. The case of Singapore and Hong Kong is also similar, although with respect to British rule. However, since then, all these countries have adjusted their education system to focus more on job creation, revising curricula and reorienting educational policies to new perceptions of national interest (Bray and Lee, 2001:4).

Rapid economic growth may be the most notable post-colonial feature of advanced countries in East Asia, such as Korea, Taiwan, Hong Kong and Singapore (Morris, 1996). Japan was the leader in the "five nations' flying geese model of East Asian development" (Kojima, 2000). This economic development also shaped the education sector in the East Asian countries drastically. There has been huge investment in the education sector in almost all the newly independent countries. This heavy commitment towards education has helped the East Asian economies to create an educated workforce eventually attracting the attention of external investors. Later, the 'adopt and adapt' policies and the spillover effects from FDI boosted the economic growth of East Asia. High commitment to education and training has been very influential factor in the rapid development of both human resources and the economy. Bray and Lee (2001) have stated, with respect to the heavy investment in education in East Asia, that the tigers' single biggest source of comparative advantage is their well-educated workers.

Strong international competition, due to globalization, has forced the governments in advanced East Asian countries to reconsider the state's role in the education sector. The privatization of the education sector in the East Asian KBEs has reduced the state's role, and allowed the education sector to become competitive. This has had a positive impact on overall student enrollment and student mobility, both across the region and across the globe.

Among the East Asian countries, Japan was the first country to develop a comprehensive educational infrastructure. Other East Asian countries, such as Korea, Taiwan, Hong Kong, and Singapore have aspired to build an educational infrastructure molded after education infrastructure of Japan. As the economy of these countries has grown, concerned governments have taken vigorous steps to build comprehensive educational infrastructure and create the human resources needed to attract more FDIs; this has been the case ever since the era of high Japanese economic growth. As the KBE has advanced in East Asia, the governments of most East Asian countries have announced broader education reform policies so as to create a competitive educational infrastructure.

The development of a competitive educational infrastructure is one of the most basic requirements for becoming a KBE. Two other segments of infrastructure, namely ICT and Innovation, are also highly dependent on the development of the education infrastructure. Thus, any country trying to become a KBE must focus on building up the educational infrastructure as the first step. The East Asian Economies are no exception to this.

Public Spending on Education

Public spending on education has been the single most important driving force in the education sector in most East Asian countries. The advanced KBEs of East Asia, such as Japan, Korea, Taiwan, Hong Kong and Singapore spend more than 3% of their GDP on the education sector (See Table 7.1). As seen in Table 7.2, Japan spends more than any other East Asian country (in terms of public expenditures) on education per capita, indicating that Japan still strongly focuses on creating and maintaining a globally competitive educational infrastructure. Other East Asian

Table 7.1 Total Public Expenditure on Education in East Asia, 1998-2007 (% of GDP)

Countries	1998	1999	2000	2001	2002	2003	2004	2005	2006	2007
China	2.63	2.76	2.78	3.01	3.15	2.67	2.42	2.45	2.26	2.85
Hong Kong	3.81	4.03	3.96	4.08	4.35	4.64	4.21	3.93	3.52	3.33
Indonesia	0.49	0.76	0.60	0.58	0.73	1.04	0.77	1.06	1.36	1.28
Japan	3.67	3.57	3.66	4.16	4.11	4.07	3.98	4.09	3.89	N/A
Korea	3.74	3.16	3.03	3.41	3.84	4.37	4.36	4.14	4.22	N/A
Malaysia	4.42	4.48	3.95	5.28	7.76	6.25	5.05	5.13	5.39	5.72
Philippines	3.43	3.16	2.90	2.79	3.25	2.98	2.64	2.48	2.39	2.47
Singapore	3.52	3.47	3.67	4.07	4.17	3.83	3.35	3.02	3.15	3.00
Taiwan	4.83	4.88	4.05	4.36	4.43	4.45	4.37	4.30	4.20	4.04
Thailand	4.36	4.25	4.19	4.00	3.96	3.92	3.94	4.02	4.12	4.41

Source: IMD World Competitiveness Online.

Table 7.2 Total Public Expenditure on Education per Capita (USD) in East Asia, 1998-2007

Countries	1998	1999	2000	2001	2002	2003	2004	2005	2006	2007
China	21.51	23.78	26.32	31.22	35.66	39.40	45.61	N/A	45.61	70.86
Hong Kong	965.41	989.46	999.27	1,006.66	1,051.07	1,086.70	1,024.95	1,017.91	974.92	996.32
Indonesia	2.29	5.16	4.83	4.54	6.75	11.39	9.17	12.22	22.30	24.73
Japan	1,120.75	1,230.59	1,346.69	1,337.66	1,265.06	1,659.04	1,417.45	N/A	1,324.95	N/A
Korea	279.97	301.76	343.87	363.69	464.81	587.89	655.42	N/A	830.53	N/A
Malaysia	142.81	154.63	157.73	203.87	318.83	275.18	246.26	168.95	316.44	392.81
Philippines	30.57	32.15	28.87	25.51	31.39	29.51	27.63	28.78	31.69	39.29
Singapore	738.39	723.92	844.96	841.59	882.37	852.11	867.41	844.41	995.12	1,090.16
Taiwan	587.25	635.64	612.71	580.47	584.98	597.67	626.39	667.77	672.58	676.99
Thailand	79.70	84.31	82.26	73.27	79.06	87.18	97.62	109.57	130.33	164.97

Source: IMD World Competitiveness Online.

KBEs, such as Korea, Taiwan, Hong Kong and Singapore are also well ahead of the latecomers, such as Malaysia, China and Thailand, in terms of per capita spending on education (See Table 7.2).

Developments in Secondary and Tertiary Education Sector

Public spending on education has had a clear impact on secondary school enrollment in most of the East Asian countries listed below (See Table 7.3). Here, too, the advanced KBEs performed better than the latecomers. A sound secondary education system has been the key in creating a massive, semi-skilled workforce during East Asia's high growth period.

The governments of advanced East Asian KBEs have been very active in formulating policies to facilitate higher enrollment in tertiary level education. This is because of the growing need for highly skilled human resources in a competitive KBE. The governments involved have been forced to create a very competitive tertiary educational infrastructure. The outcome of these government efforts is very evident in Table 7.4. Most of the advanced KBEs in the region attained more than 50% tertiary enrollment among those 25 to 34 years of age by 2006. Together with

Table 7.3 Secondary School Enrollment (Percentage of relevant age group receiving full-time education) in East Asia, 1995-2006

Countries	1997	1998	1999	2000	2001	2002	2003	2004	2005	2006
China	N/A	N/A	N/A	88.60	88.70	90.00	92.70	94.10	95.00	97.00
Hong Kong	76.00	76.40	74.70	75.00	73.79	74.27	75.00	75.99	77.14	77.91
Indonesia	N/A	54.41	56.17	48.20	55.86	56.93	54.29	56.14	57.44	60.37
Japan	100.00	N/A	99.36	99.46	99.56	99.67	99.82	99.90	99.99	98.69
Korea	99.00	97.20	94.49	90.98	88.75	87.31	88.28	90.40	93.86	96.05
Malaysia	N/A	N/A	65.15	64.83	64.86	65.43	70.92	72.02	68.73	N/A
Philippines	N/A	N/A	50.73	N/A	52.40	56.31	59.04	60.81	60.22	60.38
Singapore	93.00	91.00	91.00	92.00	93.00	92.00	94.00	93.00	94.00	95.00
Taiwan	90.80	91.68	92.56	92.19	92.92	93.74	93.83	93.63	93.66	94.93
Thailand	N/A	66.80	68.70	69.70	70.60	71.20	72.00	N/A	N/A	71.01

Source: IMD World Competitiveness Online.

Table 7.4 Percentage of population that has attained at least tertiary education for persons 25-34 in East Asia, 1997-2006

Countries	1997	1998	1999	2000	2001	2002	2003	2004	2005	2006
China	N/A	5.00	N/A	N/A	N/A	N/A	N/A	N/A	21.00	22.00
Hong Kong	28.50	29.30	30.30	32.00	34.40	36.80	37.90	37.90	39.80	40.50
Indonesia	N/A	3.00	6.00	6.00	4.60	5.00	5.00	N/A	N/A	N/A
Japan	45.24	45.42	45.14	47.25	47.68	50.00	52.00	52.00	53.00	54.00
Korea	N/A	34.02	35.10	37.19	39.51	41.00	47.00	49.00	51.00	53.00
Malaysia	N/A	11.00	11.40	11.00	13.00	16.00	18.00	18.50	19.86	19.92
Philippines	N/A	26.00	N/A	N/A	N/A	24.00	27.70	27.70	27.70	N/A
Singapore	29.90	33.50	36.40	35.30	42.50	45.40	49.00	51.90	51.40	56.70
Taiwan	29.70	31.70	33.50	36.20	37.80	40.60	43.20	45.00	47.80	51.20
Thailand	N/A	12.00	13.00	13.80	14.50	14.00	18.00	N/A	N/A	N/A

Source: IMD World Competitiveness Online.

Chapter Seven: Developing Education and Human Resources in East Asian KBEs 97

secondary and tertiary enrollment rates, there has been a particular emphasis on science education both in the secondary and tertiary levels. This effort has been very successful, as there has been growing emphasis on science in schools (See Figure 7.1) and, consequently, youth interest in science (See Figure 7.2) has been increasing in recent years in most East Asian countries.

Holders of degrees in science have increased as a consequence of new policies introduced by governments in East Asia. Table 7.5 shows a clear indication that East Asian countries have produced more skilled human resources over the years. The private and public R&D sectors also have been positively affected by

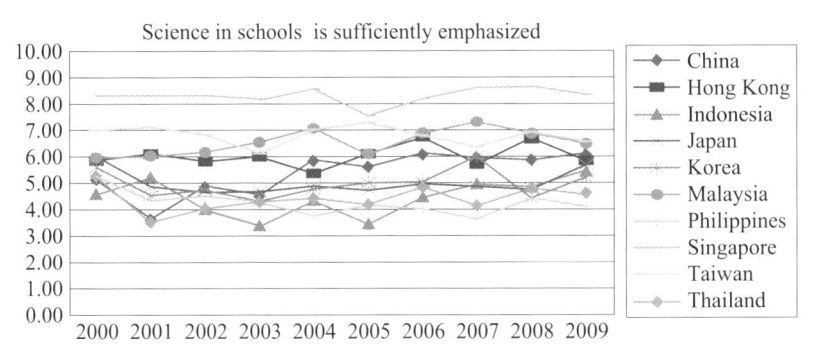

Figure 7.1   Science in Schools, East Asia*
*IMD WCY Executive Opinion Survey based on an index from 0 to 10.
Source: Computed from data collected from IMD World Competitiveness Online.

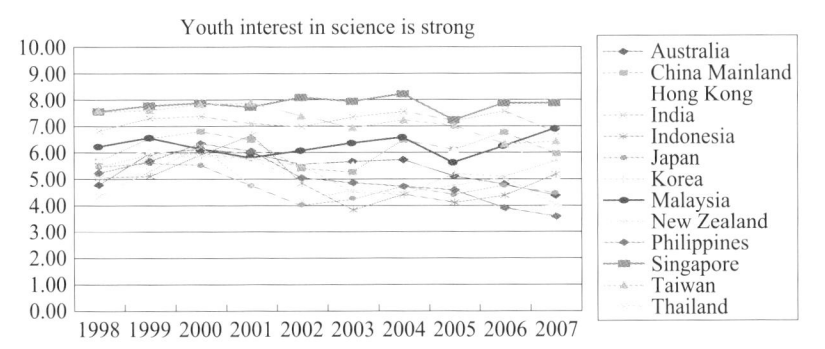

Figure 7.2   Youth Interest in Science, Asia and Pacific**
**IMD WCY Executive Opinion Survey based on an index from 0 to 10.
Source: Computed from data collected from IMD World Competitiveness Online.

Table 7.5 Science Degrees, East Asia
(Percentage of total first university degrees in science and engineering)

Countries	1997	1999	2001	2002	2004
China	72.30	73.29	59.41	57.40	56.21
Hong Kong	47.70	47.75	47.75	37.28	37.74
Indonesia	67.30	67.28	67.28	67.28	N/A
Japan	66.50	65.84	66.20	64.00	63.34
Korea	46.40	44.92	47.35	47.16	44.69
Malaysia	45.30	45.29	45.29	45.29	N/A
Philippines	N/A	N/A	N/A	N/A	25.46
Singapore	N/A	N/A	N/A	N/A	58.50
Taiwan	39.20	39.72	41.41	41.21	40.75
Thailand	26.10	26.13	26.13	26.13	68.90

Source: *National Science Foundation Science & Engineering Indicators 2008.*

increase of science-degree holders at the tertiary level.

Quality Education System for a Competitive Economy

As East Asian countries have been shifting towards the KBE, they have sought to realize an efficient education system more and more, so as to remain competitive in the global market. All the major KBEs have achieved great success in this regard; with the four tigers even outperforming Japan, the leading KBE in East Asia (See Figure 7.3).

The competitive education system is molding the future of the East Asian KBEs by providing the best education required to create the best human resources to compete at the global level. Today, international student mobility is heading not only towards the Western countries but also to the advanced East Asian KBEs. Singapore's education system is considered as one of the best educational systems in the world. Other economies are also greatly influenced by Singapore's development in this regard and are moving rapidly towards creating a competitive educational system in the region.

Countries like Singapore, Hong Kong, Taiwan, Korea and Japan have been

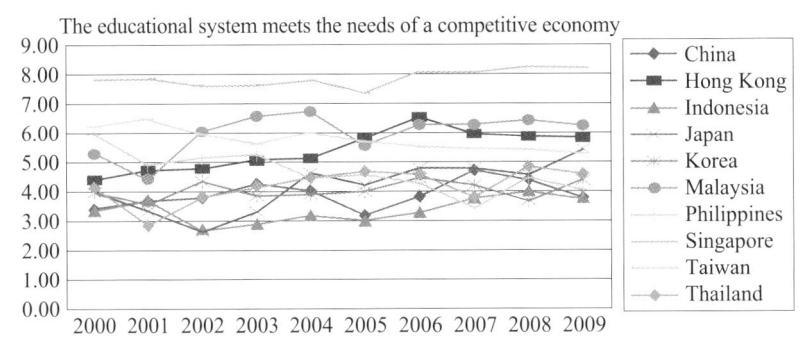

Chapter Seven: Developing Education and Human Resources in East Asian KBEs   99

Figure 7.3 Educational System in Asia-Pacific Countries, 2000-2009*
* IMD WCY Executive Opinion Survey based on an index from 0 to 10.
Source: Computed from data collected from IMD World Competitiveness Online.

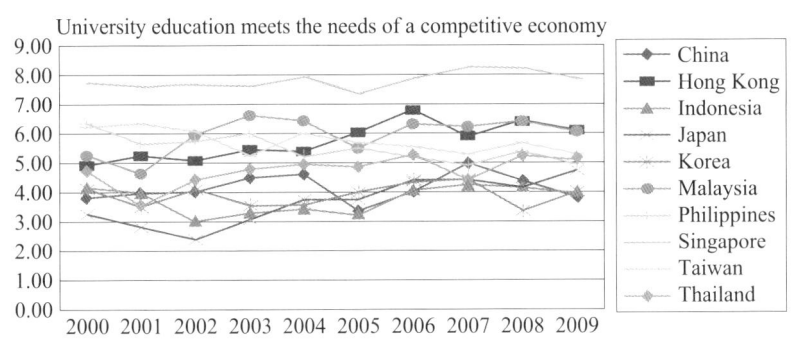

Figure 7.4 University Education in the Countries of East Asia, 2000-2009**
** IMD WCY Executive Opinion Survey based on an index from 0 to 10.
Source: Computed from data collected from IMD World Competitiveness Online.

keen in maintaining world-class quality university education for the last 10 years (See Figure 7.4). The ability to provide world-class university education in East Asia is playing a significant role in the development of the KBE by supplying the high skilled human resources required for the advanced and growing KBEs in the region.

One key concern in the development of the KBE is how to transfer knowledge between companies and universities. The education policies of advanced KBEs in East Asia clearly indicate that universities are the training places for students aiming to be placed later in companies, and thus, the universities serve the interests of these

Knowledge transfer is highly developed between companies and universities

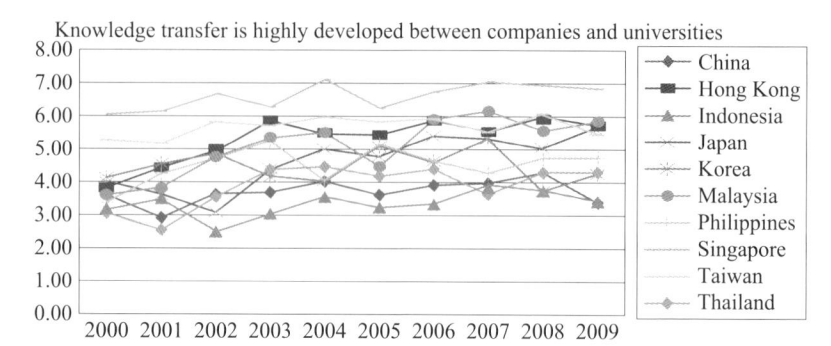

Figure 7.5 Knowledge Transfer in the Countries of East Asia, 2000-2009*
* IMD WCY Executive Opinion Survey based on an index from 0 to 10.
Source: Computed from data collected from IMD World Competitiveness Online.

companies. Keeping this in mind, the governments' involvement has been creating new and dynamic avenues for easy knowledge transfer between universities and companies. Over the last ten years, knowledge transfer between companies and universities has significantly increased in all the major KBEs (See Figure 7.5).

East Asia's Human Capital Development

In the late 20th century, four East Asian tigers, such as Korea, Taiwan, Hong Kong and Singapore, led by Japan achieved unprecedented economic growth. Indeed, today, the region is one of the most dynamic economic zones in the world, where the development of the KBE is shaping the development patterns of both the economic giant Japan as well as the other Asian tigers. One aspect of this is that, there is a close connection between demographic dynamics, human capital and economic growth in East Asia. Another aspect is that all the advanced KBEs have been committed to the development of human capital since the end of World War II. Third, there has been strong government involvement in human capital development. Finally, strong government commitment has led to rapid adoption and adaption of foreign technology through FDI, quickly improving the productivity of East Asian economies. The last two facets of this phenomenon have been so prominent that some scholars, like Wade, have argued that 'the East

Asian development model' is a 'state interventionist development model' clearly different from the so-called 'Western free market economy'. Ogawa *et al.* (1993) also stated that the four factors above have been instrumental in East Asia and the Pacific during the high growth era.

It is evident from various studies (Lucas, 1988, and Ogawa *et al.*, 1993) that public intervention has been the most influential factor in the development of human capital in the East Asian economies. Governments in East Asia have directed human capital development by subsidizing the supply of human capital, giving favor to the expansion of selected sectors, sectors that promised most to develop workers' skills through learning by doing, twisting the terms of trade in order to receive FDI and so on (Krugman, 1987; Locus, 1988 and Ogawa *et al.*, 1993).

Lucas (1988) argued that the rate of human capital accumulation is an increasing function of the level of human capital. Educational investment has created strong and permanent effects on long-run growth potential in advanced East Asian economies by passing on the available stock of knowledge from generation to generation (Ogawa *et al.*, 1993). Barro's (1991) empirical research also shows that above average schooling achievement greatly contributed to the annual growth in the advanced East Asian economies in the 1960s. Conversely, it is also true that countries with poor human capital endowment cannot keep pace with the advanced East Asian economies. Thus, it is evident that human resource development has consistently contributed to the economic growth of the major East Asian countries during the high growth era, and that it is still contributing to the development of the region's KBE.

As the governments of the advanced East Asian countries put more emphasis on secondary and tertiary education to keep pace with the development of the KBE, a stable supply of labor force, equipped with secondary and tertiary education skills has appeared in the countries concerned. Table 7.6 shows the consistency in labor supply with secondary and tertiary education in some East Asian economies.

Table 7.6 Labor with Secondary and Tertiary Education in East Asia, 2004-2007

Country	Labor force with secondary education (% of total)				Labor force with tertiary education (% of total)			
	2004	2005	2006	2007	2004	2005	2006	2007
Hong Kong	44.4	45.0	44.6	44.4	22.7	24.0	25.0	25.6
Indonesia	N/A	N/A	20.6	20.6	N/A	N/A	5.6	6.5
Japan	N/A	N/A	N/A	N/A	N/A	39.5	38.3	39.9
Korea	43.6	43.2	42.5	42.0	21.5	32.3	33.7	35.0
Malaysia	N/A	N/A	N/A	56.3	N/A	N/A	N/A	20.3
Philippines	37.9	N/A	38.6	38.7	26.5	N/A	27.5	27.7
Singapore	N/A	24.8	48.3	48.6	N/A	19.4	23.4	23.7

Source: World Bank and National Sources.

As most of the advanced East Asian economies had a consistent supply of secondary and tertiary education-equipped labor, the skill of the overall labor force has also increased. This has helped domestic industries to grow, as well as to attract more FDI from developed countries both within and outside the region. Figure 7.6 shows the overall availability of skilled labor force in East Asian economies for the 2000-2009 period; these data reveal most of the economically advanced East Asian countries have been very successful in creating the skilled labor force needed for the development of the KBE.

Early achievements in higher education have boosted the number of engineers in most East Asian economies. The IMD carried out surveys (IMD World Competitiveness Yearbook Executive Opinion Survey) for each year from 2000 to 2009 to study the availability of qualified engineers in all participating countries. The surveys for 2000-2009 period show that the advanced East Asian KBEs have clear advantages in the region, and that the availability of qualified engineers has steadily increased over the years (See Figure 7.7).

Data from Figures 7.7 and 7.8 suggest that the consistent supply of skilled and educated labor force has contributed to an increase in labor productivity in East Asia. If we consider growth in labor productivity for the 1999-2008 period, we see that the advanced KBEs in East Asia are far ahead of other East Asian economies.

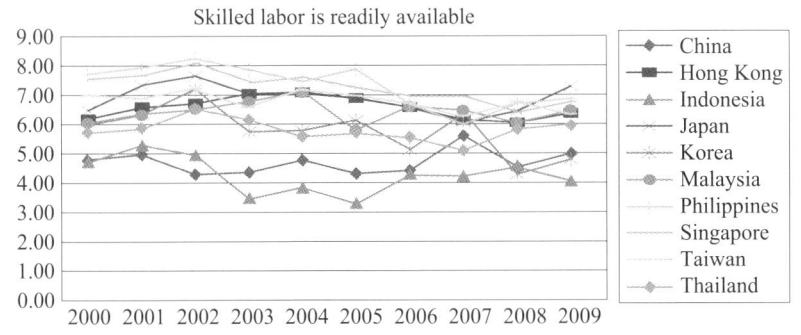

Chapter Seven: Developing Education and Human Resources in East Asian KBEs   103

Figure 7.6 Skilled Labor in the Countries of East Asia, 2000-2009*
* IMD WCY Executive Opinion Survey based on an index from 0 to 10.
Source: IMD World Competitiveness Online.

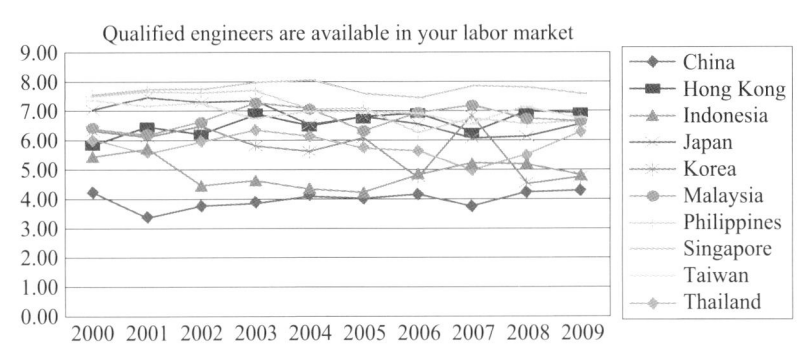

Figure 7.7 Qualified Engineers in the Countries of East Asia, 2000-2009**
** IMD WCY Executive Opinion Survey based on an index from 0 to 10.
Source: IMD World Competitiveness Online.

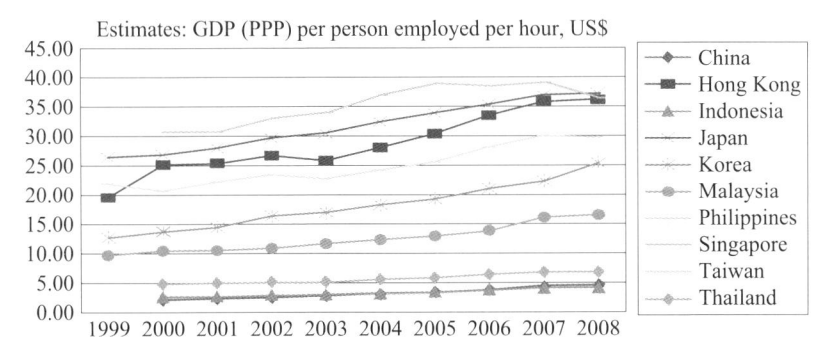

Figure 7.8 Labor Productivity in the Countries of East Asia, 1999-2008
Source: World Development Indicators, World Bank, April 2009, National Sources.

This indicates that the advanced economies of Japan, Korea, Taiwan, Hong Kong and Singapore have been quite successfully capitalizing on the availability of a skilled labor force in their markets to boost overall productivity (See Figure 7.8).

Demographic Transition

Population size and growth are both in transition in most of the East Asian KBEs. During the high growth era of East Asia, for the period of 1970s to 1990s, many scholars argued that population growth and the growth of real GNP per capita had a negative correlation, meaning that economic development in East Asia is by and large faster when population growth is low (Ogawa and Tsuya, 1993:24). However, such a conclusion is not consistent with actual conditions in East Asia now, where most of the advanced economies face the problem of a declining population. Kelly (1988a) argued that the net impact of population growth varies over time for any nation, and that it varies from nation to nation. So, it would not be wise to conclude that population growth over time has a negative correlation with economic growth.

The fertility rate in most of the advanced KBEs in East Asia has dropped sharply, while life expectancy at birth has gradually increased (See Tables 7.7 and 7.8). This, indeed, is changing the demographic structure of the concerned economies. In recent years, the governments of all the advanced KBEs have started paying special attention to sustainable population growth whereby the economies will be able to keep balance with the demand and supply of human resources, badly needed for a growing economy.

As a result of a rapid decline in fertility rate and increase in life expectancy at birth, the age composition of advanced East Asian economies has been changing very fast. There has been a decrease in the population of those between 0 and 15 years of age, while there has been a consistent increase in the population of those, age 65 and above (See Table 7.9). Although the population of those between 15 and

Table 7.7 Fertility Rate in the Countries of East Asia, 1999-2007
Total (Births per Woman)

Country	1999	2000	2001	2002	2003	2004	2005	2006	2007
China	N/A	1.73	N/A	1.70	N/A	N/A	1.72	1.72	1.73
Hong Kong	0.98	1.04	0.93	0.94	0.90	0.93	0.97	0.97	0.97
Japan	1.34	1.36	1.33	1.32	1.29	1.29	1.26	1.32	1.34
Indonesia	N/A	2.45	N/A	2.38	N/A	N/A	2.26	2.22	2.18
Korea	1.42	1.47	1.30	1.17	1.19	1.16	1.08	1.13	1.26
Malaysia	N/A	2.96	N/A	2.87	N/A	N/A	2.71	2.65	2.60
Philippines	N/A	3.49	N/A	3.34	N/A	N/A	3.20	3.16	3.11
Singapore	1.48	1.44	1.41	1.37	1.27	1.26	1.26	1.28	1.29
Taiwan	N/A	N/A	N/A	N/A	1.57	1.57	1.57	1.57	1.12
Thailand	N/A	1.83	N/A	1.81	N/A	N/A	1.81	1.81	1.81

Source: World Bank and National Sources.

Table 7.8 Life Expectancy at Birth in the Countries of East Asia, 1999-2007
Total (Years)

Country	1999	2000	2001	2002	2003	2004	2005	2006	2007
China	N/A	71.41	N/A	72.06	N/A	N/A	72.62	N/A	73.00
Hong Kong	80.38	80.88	81.42	81.48	81.33	81.78	81.58	82.38	82.28
Japan	80.57	81.08	81.42	81.56	81.76	82.03	81.93	82.32	82.51
Indonesia	N/A	67.53	N/A	68.55	N/A	N/A	69.79	N/A	70.61
Korea	75.37	75.86	76.34	76.82	77.26	77.85	78.43	78.97	78.97
Malaysia	N/A	72.65	N/A	73.09	N/A	N/A	73.81	74.05	74.29
Philippines	N/A	69.60	N/A	70.31	N/A	N/A	71.14	71.42	71.70
Singapore	77.55	78.05	78.35	78.70	79.04	79.49	79.99	80.14	80.49
Taiwan	N/A	N/A	N/A	N/A	76.87	77.26	77.26	77.43	77.56
Thailand	N/A	68.26	N/A	68.28	N/A	N/A	68.57	68.67	68.76

Source: World Bank and National Sources.

65 did not change that much, there have been downward trends for this age group in some advanced East Asian countries, such as Japan. This is a very important issue for all the advanced economies in East Asia, as they will have to work out how to increase the population of those between 0 and 15 years of age, so that labor supply remains consistent with the demands of the market.

As all the economically developed countries in East Asia have an aging population, the dependency ratio in them has also been changing very fast. Table 7.10 shows the change in the aging index for 1960, 1990 and predicted values for 2025.

Table 7.9 Demographic Composition in East Asia
(Population by Age (% of Total))

Ages Country	2000			2005			2008		
	0-14	15-64	>/=65	0-14	15-64	>/=65	0-14	15-64	>/=65
China	25.72	67.49	6.79	22.00	70.43	7.57	20.53	71.53	7.94
Hong Kong	16.85	72.12	11.02	14.39	73.38	12.23	12.57	74.89	12.54
Japan	14.60	68.16	17.24	13.79	66.29	19.92	13.44	65.15	21.41
Indonesia	30.33	64.79	4.87	28.39	66.09	5.52	27.35	66.77	5.87
Korea	20.85	71.82	7.33	19.06	71.63	9.31	17.38	72.27	10.35
Malaysia	33.47	62.66	3.87	31.34	64.30	4.36	29.95	65.43	4.62
Philippines	37.76	58.74	3.51	35.57	60.58	3.85	34.28	61.60	4.12
Singapore	21.77	71.05	7.18	19.56	71.93	8.51	17.11	73.48	9.41
Taiwan	21.11	70.27	8.62	18.70	71.56	9.74	16.95	72.62	10.43
Thailand	25.14	68.51	6.35	22.94	69.96	7.10	21.96	70.60	7.44

Source: World Bank and National Sources.

Table 7.10 Age Composition Changes in East Asia, 1960, 1990, and 2025

	1960			1990			2025		
	Dependency Ratio		Age Index	Dependency Ratio		Age Index	Dependency Ratio		Age Index
	Young	Aged		Young	Aged		Young	Aged	
China	69.1	8.6	12.4	38.6	8.6	22.3	26.5	18.9	71.4
Hong Kong	72.6	5.0	6.8	31.8	12.7	39.8	25.2	33.2	131.6
Japan	47.2	9.0	19.0	26.5	16.8	63.3	24.8	38.7	156.1
Malaysia	88.2	6.6	7.5	60.3	6.4	10.6	33.5	13.8	41.0
Korea	76.6	6.1	7.9	38.5	6.9	17.9	25.5	20.2	79.5
Singapore	79.0	3.8	4.8	31.9	7.7	24.3	25.7	29.7	115.5
Thailand	85.0	5.2	6.2	51.4	6.2	12.0	30.5	14.7	48.3

Source: Adapted from Ogawa and Tsuya (1993:42).

From this table, it is very clear that by 2025, the East Asian economies will all be fast-ageing societies; forcing governments to take special measures to increase the work force. One of them is to increase the fertility rate, while another is to bring in skilled foreign labors.

It is thus quite understandable how advanced KBEs are facing the challenge of a rapidly aging population and must address this issue by creating a highly skilled workforce along with a high rate of automation. In addition to this, there has been a gradual increase in labor movement across the region, particularly in

Table 7.11 Foreign Labor Force in the Countries of East Asia, 2000-2007 [10]
(% of Total Labor Force)

Country	2000	2001	2002	2003	2004	2005	2006	2007
Indonesia	0.48	0.34	0.48	0.29	0.24	N/A	N/A	N/A
Japan	0.23	0.25	0.27	0.28	0.29	0.27	0.33	N/A
Korea	1.29	1.47	1.58	1.69	1.80	1.46	1.77	2.62
Malaysia	12.35	16.12	16.49	22.31	19.46	16.08	16.19	15.88
Singapore	30.63	28.75	27.05	25.94	26.53	28.35	29.15	33.24
Taiwan	3.34	3.10	3.05	2.98	3.07	3.15	3.22	3.34
Thailand	0.31	0.27	0.26	0.29	0.34	0.42	0.46	0.57

Source: National Sources and OECD StatExtracts available at http://stats.oecd.org.

the advanced KBEs (See Table 7.11).

Summary

From the discussion and analysis above, it is evident that advanced KBEs, such as Japan, Korea, Taiwan, Hong Kong and Singapore have been leaders in the region in developing education and human resources. Public spending on education and other policies in these economies have helped to increase secondary and tertiary level enrollment, and, at the same time, these countries were also able to develop a high-quality education system, a high-quality university education system, qualified engineers for the labor market, and efficient management in knowledge transfer between companies and universities. These factors have contributed greatly to the development of human resources in the region. There has been a very consistent supply of skilled labor force, equipped with secondary and tertiary education skills, in most of the advanced economies in the region. Due to the demographic transition now underway, some economies have started considering foreign labor force as an additional solution to supply the human resources needed for their continued economic development.

Chapter Eight

Information and Communications Technology in East Asian KBEs

Introduction

The presence of functioning information communications technology (ICT) has grown to be more important than ever before in terms of expanding economic activities. The widespread use of ICT in economic and social sectors has drastically shaped the so-called KBE. ICT has transformed the world especially in the last couple of decades. This is more so in the case of KBEs where the generation, diffusion, absorption and application of new technology and knowledge flow at a faster speed spurring on ever greater economic development. ICT, according to many scholars, has been a major factor in this faster flow of technology and knowledge in KBEs. ICT, by providing well-needed connectivity among places and people in East Asia, is playing a very important role at all levels, be it on national, regional or global level. The movement of new inventions or innovations or their impacts reach other countries within very short time frames; this, in turn, pushes all the KBEs towards continuous innovation so as to remain competitive in the global market. Experiences over the past decades in East Asia have shown that a competitive ICT sector is extremely important. Subsequently, KBEs in East Asia have been launching new policies to create a better ICT infrastructure and thereby maximize their economic progress in a globally competitive world. This chapter examines the diverse policy approaches to ICT development adopted by East Asian economies, and the outcomes achieved. Here, ICT has been considered as a general-purpose technology similar to power delivery systems and other technological infrastructures.

Building the ICT Infrastructure in East Asia

During the high growth period of Japan in the 1960s and 1970s, the telecommunication sector, by increasing productivity and marketing, greatly contributed to economic development. Japan realized the importance of communications technology in the early stages of its economic rise after World War II, while many other East Asian economies, such as Korea, Taiwan, Hong Kong and Singapore began only later. In most of the East Asian economies, the development of the telecommunications sector received well-needed attention when Japanese FDI was flowing in huge volume. The industrial hollowing out in Japan made this process occur even faster. By the 1980s, many scholars started recognizing information as a crucial factor in production, along with capital and labor. Finally, in the 1990s, with rapid technological advancement, ICT became one of the most critical factors for competitiveness and growth in the East Asian KBEs. During the 1990s, the availability of computers further added value to the ICT infrastructure in East Asia. Later, the widespread use of the Internet and mobile phone revolutionized the ICT sector in East Asia. Today, ICT has become one of the most important sectors in furthering economic growth in most East Asian countries.

It will not be exaggerating to say that the East Asian economies have received technology and knowledge transfer needed for ICT infrastructure development from more advanced countries, and they later, improved on the transferred technologies and knowledge. In East Asia, Japan was considered to be a country of imitation, as it highly depended on the U.S. or European technologies and know-how to make highly needed technological progress. In terms of building up the ICT infrastructure, the long experience of adopting and adapting foreign technology has helped Japan to design its own ICT infrastructure, an infrastructure that best fits the Japanese market. Later, other East Asian countries followed a similar path by adopting technology and know-how from Japan to build up their own ICT infrastructure. East Asian countries, in this regard, have employed three main channels to acquire advanced foreign technologies and knowledge: international trade, FDI, and disembodied knowledge flows in the ICT sector. So, it is clear that East Asian countries, especially, the advanced KBEs in the region, such as Japan, Korea, Taiwan, Hong Kong and Singapore, have been investing in the development of ICT infrastructure in their pursuit of knowledge-based economic growth. The 2000-2007 ICT expenditure data in East Asia show a similar pattern (See Figure 6.18 in Chapter Six).

Relationship between FDI and ICT in East Asia

Until the 1980s, ICT services, such as telecommunications, had been a monopoly business owned either by the state or by heavily regulated private entities throughout the world (Guislain, P. *et al.*, 2006). Japan and other East Asian economies were no exception to this. As the ICT industry is capital-intensive, its initial growth in East Asia was very slow. Although FDI had been a great source of capital for other sectors in East Asian countries, the ICT sector received the lowest amount of FDI. Since the mid-1980s, many countries realized the importance of privatizing the ICT sector to receive FDI and thereby accelerate growth. Japan was first among the developed East Asian economies to open this sector for private investment and competition in 1985 (Guislain *et al.*, 2006). Many other East Asian economies followed a similar pattern to allow FDI to flow into the telecommunications services branch of the ICT sector. With the introduction of mobile phone technology, a huge amount of FDI flowed into East Asian countries. The cost-effectiveness of mobile networks and promotional policies for new technology quickly made the wired telephone industry a thing of the past in many East Asian countries.

There is also a growing acknowledgment that ICT acts as a strong catalyst, attracting FDI, and this has been the single most important factor in East Asia's knowledge-based economic growth. Available literature on the relationship between ICT and FDI looks at ICT as a 'location' factor for attracting FDI, also influencing other determinants of FDI (Economou, 2008). A recent study on the relationship between ICT and FDI found that ICT and the diffusion of new ICT instruments are significant 'pull' factors for attracting FDI (Gani and Sharma, 2003). Gholami, Lee, and Heshmati (2006) also mention in their study on '*The Causal Relationship between Information and Communication Technology and Foreign Direct Investment*' that there is a causal relationship between ICT investment and increase in FDI flow. There is strong evidence that ICT development causes FDI inflow, whereas there is only partial evidence that inflow of FDI helps the development of ICT.

ICT, in many ways, influences other determinants of FDI inflow in East Asian KBEs. Both East Asia's FDI-based and domestic innovations have been extensively supported by the ICT. Many studies show a positive correlation between the availability of ICT infrastructure and innovation. Persephone Economou (2008:6) points out the following: ICT exerts a positive influence on innovation and entrepreneurship, which are particularly important determinants of FDI, especially technologically intensive investments and FDI in R&D and technology intensive strategic alliances. This enhances the attractiveness of countries to export-oriented FDI as ICT provides the logistical support to facilitate exporting, and this contributes to a country's attractiveness to foreign investors (these investors seek to establish a presence in order to serve regional or global markets). Another study by Vinod (2005) states that ICT improves transparency in host countries and reduces corruption, which would otherwise hinder FDI.

Superior ICT infrastructure in the East Asian KBEs, especially in Korea, Taiwan, Hong Kong and Singapore, is allowing for the absorption of spillovers arising from FDI. This occurs because superior ICT infrastructure enhances knowledge and skills related to the R&D and other business activities of multinational corporations. The countries mentioned above, including the East Asian giant Japan, have the privilege to connect the economic activities of different regions, businesses or communities due to strong ICT infrastructure present within their borders.

ICT's Investment Facilitating Role in East Asia

As ICT becomes more widely available in the East Asian KBEs, its use evolves to better suit the changing needs of an increasingly sophisticated investment climate. Investors benefit from ICT-based investment promotion because they often rely on the easy and cheap access it offers to evaluate projects in different locations. Increased access to ICT by enterprises in East Asia is helping them to have better and more efficient access to information on the one hand, and to utilize ICT infrastructure to increase productivity on the other. The presence of strong ICT infrastructure in host countries helps companies to expand business. ICT applications are facilitating investments in East Asia by significantly increasing productivity. This is creating potential investment space by calling for reconfiguration of work organization both within firms and among firms, as well as with the rest of the economy (Information Economy Report 2007-2008).

Expanding ICT Services in East Asia

Investment in telecommunications has been declining since 2002 (See Table 8.1) in all the major KBEs in East Asia. One of the major reasons behind this is the decreasing rate of investment in the saturated, fixed telephone market (See Figure

Table 8.1 Investment in Telecommunications, East Asia

Country	1998	1999	2000	2001	2002	2003	2004	2005	2006	2007
China	N/A	N/A	N/A	N/A	1.72	1.63	1.37	1.15	1.04	0.95
Hong Kong	N/A	N/A	N/A	N/A	0.65	0.65	0.60	0.68	0.41	N/A
Indonesia	N/A	N/A	N/A	N/A	N/A	N/A	0.66	0.55	0.43	N/A
Japan	N/A	N/A	N/A	N/A	0.49	0.47	0.44	0.42	0.40	0.42
Korea	N/A	N/A	1.49	1.09	0.97	0.81	0.75	0.67	0.74	N/A
Malaysia	2.09	1.86	1.56	1.42	1.33	0.82	0.67	0.88	0.83	N/A
Philippines	N/A	N/A	N/A	N/A	0.91	N/A	1.02	N/A	N/A	N/A
Singapore	N/A	N/A	N/A	N/A	0.49	N/A	0.39	0.38	0.33	N/A
Taiwan	N/A	N/A	N/A	N/A	0.88	1.16	0.75	0.47	0.45	N/A
Thailand	N/A	N/A	N/A	N/A	1.19	0.28	0.32	0.37	0.37	0.39

Source: International Telecommunication Union, www.itu.int, World Telecommunication/ICT Indicators Development, and National Sources.

Chapter Eight: Information and Communications Technology in East Asian KBEs   113

8.1); there is very little possibility of further growth in this sector. Another reason is that the mobile telephone has taken the place of the fixed telephone in many cases, because of convenience of use and the availability of different applications.

Since the mid-1990s, the mobile telephone has emerged as a crucial ICT tool in the East Asian economies. The continued and substantial growth of mobile phone subscribers can be confirmed from 2002 to 2007 (See Figure 8.2). The major East Asian KBEs (Japan, Korea, Taiwan, Hong Kong and Singapore) have shown a very high level of mobile phone penetration for the period of 2002-2007. This increase in the use of mobile phones drastically reduced the so-called 'digital divide' among

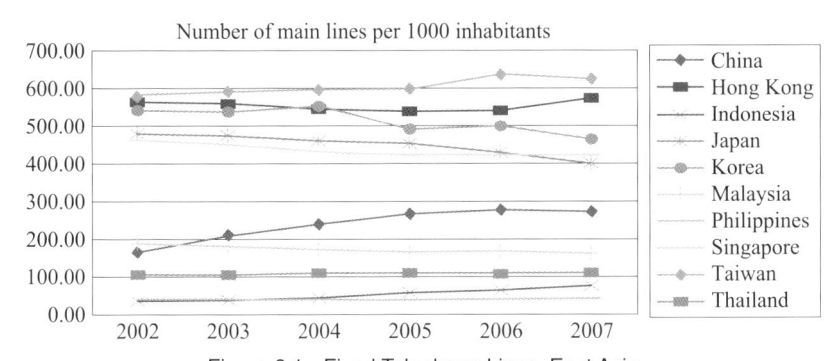

Figure 8.1   Fixed Telephone Lines, East Asia
Source: International Telecommunication Union (www.itu.int), World Telecommunication/ICT Indicators Development, and National Sources.

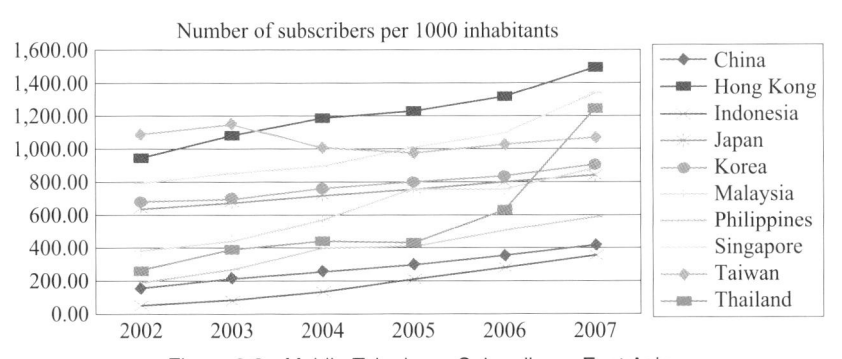

Figure 8.2   Mobile Telephone Subscribers, East Asia
Source: International Telecommunication Union, www.itu.int, World Telecommunication/ICT Indicators Development, and National Sources.

people who previously had limited access to fixed phone lines. Mobile phones are being used increasingly not only for personal purposes, but also for business purposes through mCommerce, mEnterprise (enterprise solutions enabled through mobile phones, such as logistics) and mServices (applications in mobile phones such as mobile banking) (O'Donnel *et al.*, 2007).

The availability of computers, in many ways, indicates the level of infrastructural development of a country aiming to become a KBE. Many studies have found a strong relationship between the availability of computers and the level of knowledge in a country. The East Asian KBEs are no exception to this. The availability of computers (See Figure 8.3) has also increased in the past few years throughout East Asia. The five advanced KBEs of East Asia such as, Japan, Korea, Taiwan, Hong Kong and Singapore, have achieved phenomenal success in this regard, with the number of computers reaching almost 700 per 1000 people in 2008.

The growing use of the Internet has raised production capacity in East Asian countries, which, in turn, has increased domestic investment as well as FDI inflow. A study by Changkyu Choi (2003) found a direct correlation between the growth of Internet use and FDI inflow, whereby a ten percent increase in Internet use is

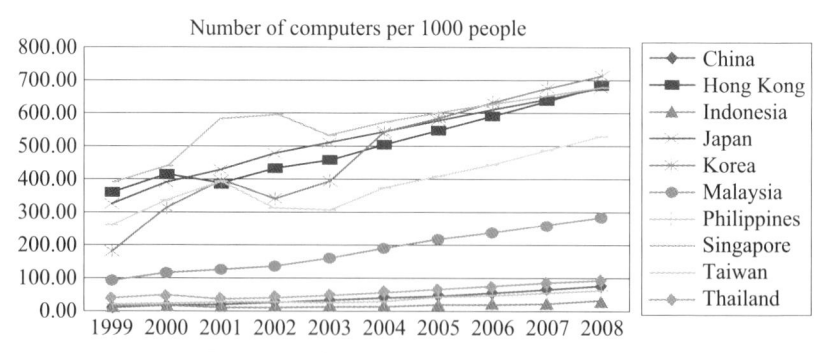

Figure 8.3 Computers per Capita, East Asia
Source: Computer Industry Almanac Inc. April 2009 (http://www.c-i-a.com) and National Sources.

correlated with a two percent increase in FDI inflow. In East Asia, the Internet is helping to lower prices by reducing search costs for business to business, as well as business to consumers, and it is contributing to the efficient functioning of both domestic and export markets (Persephone Economou, 2008:6).

The findings of Ko (2007) also supported the strong relationship between the Internet and FDI: positive network externalities associated with Internet usage encourage FDI inflow. The increase in Internet use has a positive impact on the growth of exports, as the Internet shortens transaction and other business-related costs. One study has found that in recent years, a ten percentage point increase in the growth of Web hosting in a country leads to about a 0.2 percentage point increase in export growth (Freund and Weinhold, 2004). In observing the use of Internet in East Asia, we see that Internet use in most countries in the region has drastically increased in the past few years (See Figure 8.4). Japan, Korea, Singapore, Hong Kong and Taiwan are the top countries in the region in terms of Internet use.

It is now well-known that broadband access has significant impact on the productivity of enterprises, enabling them to adopt whatever applications they require to grow. Many industries are now adopting e-business solutions by using broadband Internet in East Asia, exploring new business opportunities as well as reducing costs.

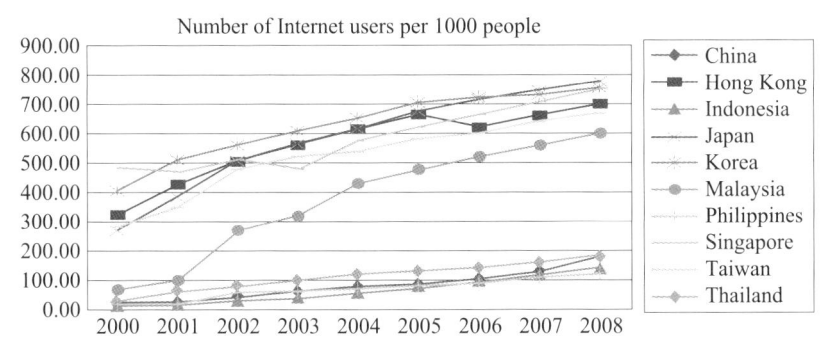

Figure 8.4   Internet Users, East Asia

Source: Computer Industry Almanac Inc. April 2009 (http://www.c-i-a.com) and National Sources.

Table 8.2 Broadband Subscribers, East Asia
(Number of Subscribers per 1000 Inhabitants)

Country	2002	2003	2004	2005	2006	2007
China	4.18	8.14	19.84	28.68	38.73	50.26
Hong Kong	146.66	182.83	224.04	243.51	261.95	274.17
Indonesia	0.18	N/A	N/A	N/A	0.88	1.14
Japan	73.74	116.89	116.83	N/A	206.84	221.39
Korea	218.50	233.56	248.16	253.25	290.76	303.57
Malaysia	0.79	4.40	9.88	19.20	33.75	37.21
Philippines	0.26	0.68	N/A	N/A	1.39	5.48
Singapore	64.66	102.48	122.98	156.03	180.97	195.07
Taiwan	93.25	134.63	165.33	190.64	196.96	208.65
Thailand	0.24	0.70	0.69	N/A	1.61	13.89

Source: International Telecommunication Union (www.itu.int), World Telecommunication/ICT Indicators Development and National Sources.

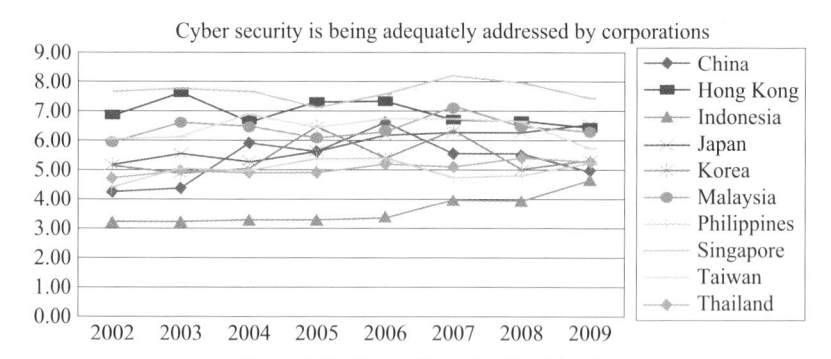

Figure 8.5 Cyber Security, East Asia*

* IMD WCY Executive Opinion Survey based on an index from 0 to 10.
Source: Computed from data collected from IMD World Competitiveness Online 1995-2009.

Consequently, in terms of the number of broadband subscribers per 1000 people since 2002, there has been a huge annual increase every year in almost all the East Asian countries under analysis. However, here, too, Japan, Korea, Singapore, Hong Kong and Taiwan are the leaders in the region (See Table 8.2).

With increasing developments in information technology (IT), companies face increasing problems related to cyber security. Without an appropriate cyber security system, IT might rise to a technological disaster in both private and public sectors. It is usually expected that corporations will develop their own cyber security systems to protect themselves. In most of the East Asian KBEs, enterprises have developed cyber security systems that can protect against technological uncertainties (See Figure 8.5).

Role of ICT in Enhancing a Competitive Business Environment

A competitive ICT infrastructure is one key factor in the development of the KBE in East Asia. The use of the computer, the Internet and other ICT tools to enhance business and production efficiency has been quite extensive. ICT, while helping other industries flourish rapidly, has by itself become one of the major

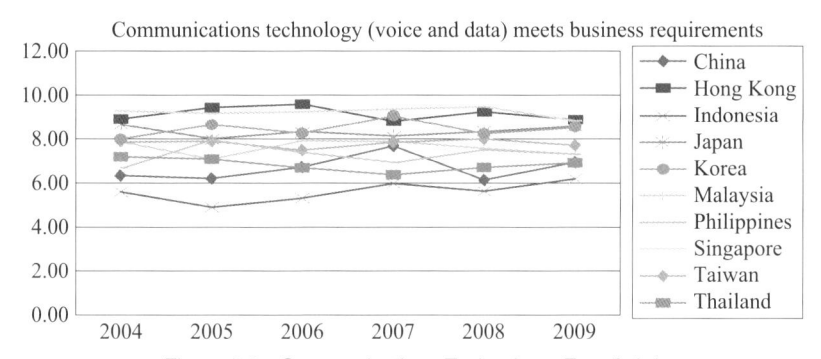

Figure 8.6   Communications Technology, East Asia*
* IMD WCY Executive Opinion Survey based on an index from 0 to 10.
Source: Computed from data collected from IMD World Competitiveness Online 1995-2009.

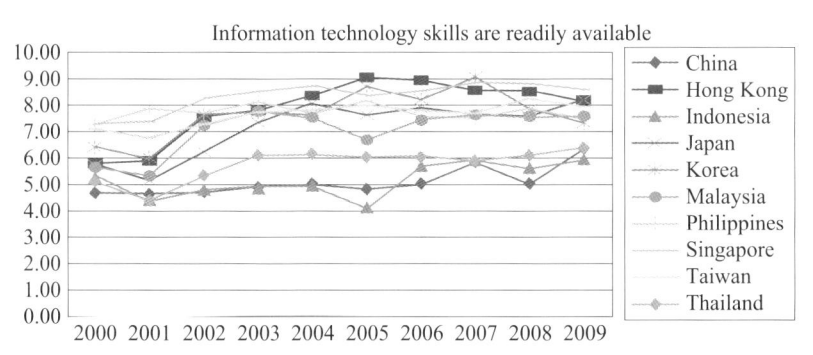

Figure 8.7   Information Technology Skills, East Asia**
** IMD WCY Executive Opinion Survey based on an index from 0 to 10.
Source: Computed from data collected from IMD World Competitiveness Online 1995-2009.

industries of the East Asian KBEs. In today's competitive and ever-globalizing world, ICT is providing a competitive business environment in East Asia, ideal for many enterprises based here. Communications technology for data and voice have met and exceeded business requirements in Japan, Korea, Taiwan, Hong Kong and Singapore for the last six years (See Figure 8.6).

Along with the increase in the number of available computers, computer users, Internet users and broadband subscribers, information technology skills have also improved significantly in the major KBEs in East Asia (See Figure 8.7). The availability of computers and the Internet now require people to develop IT

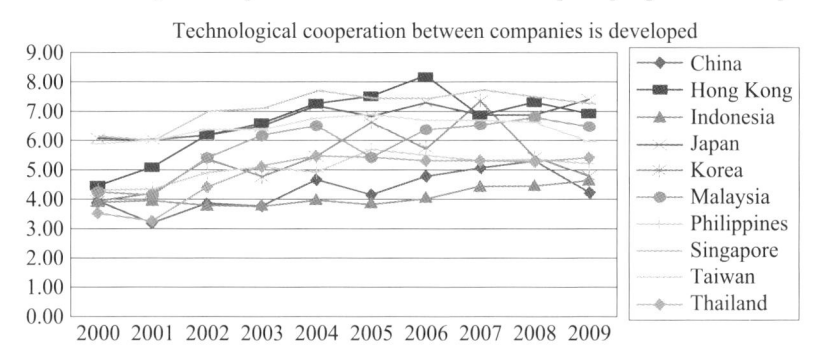

Figure 8.8   Technological Cooperation, East Asia*
* IMD WCY Executive Opinion Survey based on an index from 0 to 10.
Source: Computed from data collected from IMD World Competitiveness Online 1995-2009.

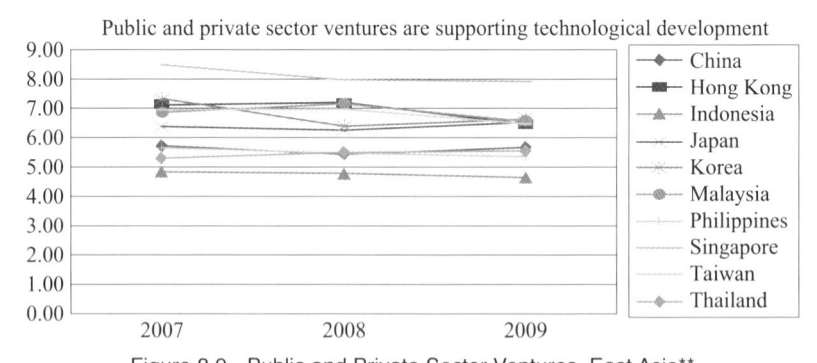

Figure 8.9   Public and Private Sector Ventures, East Asia**
** IMD WCY Executive Opinion Survey based on an index from 0 to 10.
Source: Computed from data collected from IMD World Competitiveness Online 1995-2009.

skills needed in a KBE. Educational institutions and other professional training institutions are playing an important role in this regard, training young people with well-needed information technology skills.

Technological cooperation among companies in East Asia has also increased in the last few years (See Figure 8.8), showing that the companies are preparing to meet increased competitions from the other KBEs. Not only are private companies cooperating with each other in technology development, but also public and private sector ventures are actively supporting technological development. In recent years, the trend for private-public partnerships in technological development has increased (See Figure 8.9).

The development and application of technology largely depend on the legal environment of a country. The advanced KBEs realized this at the early stage of their journey towards the KBE. The legal environment (including legal protections like patent rights) for technological development and application has improved during the last ten years (See Figure 8.10). In addition to the legal environment for developing and applying technology, technological regulations to support business development and innovation have also been fine-tuned, in most East Asian countries, but particularly in Japan, Korea, Taiwan, Hong Kong and Singapore

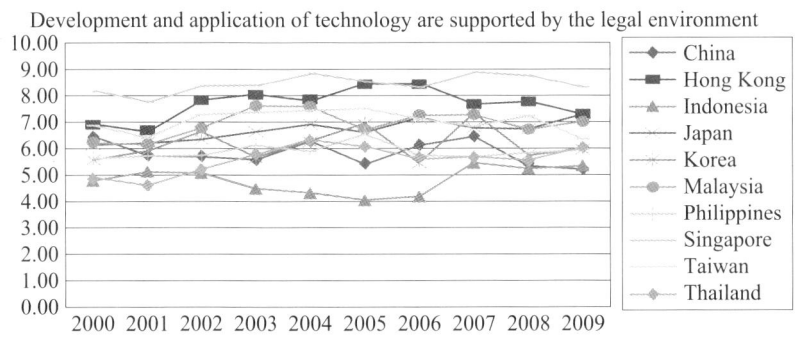

Figure 8.10 Development and Application of Technology, East Asia*
* IMD WCY Executive Opinion Survey based on an index from 0 to 10.
Source: Computed from data collected from IMD World Competitiveness Online 1995-2009.

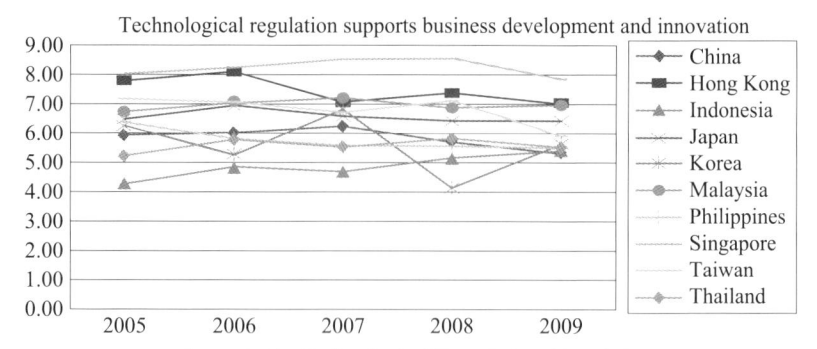

Figure 8.11 Technological Regulation, East Asia*

* IMD WCY Executive Opinion Survey based on an index from 0 to 10.
Source: Computed from data collected from IMD World Competitiveness Online 1995-2009.

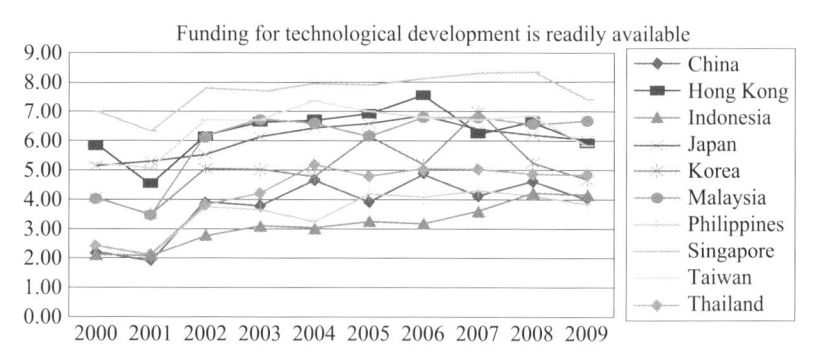

Figure 8.12 Funding for Technological Development, East Asia**

** IMD WCY Executive Opinion Survey based on an index from 0 to 10.
Source: Computed from data collected from IMD World Competitiveness Online 1995-2009.

(See Figure 8.11).

On the top of improving the legal environment for technological development, the funding for technological development, both by governments and private initiatives, has also significantly increased since 2000 in most of the advanced KBEs in East Asia (See Figure 8.12). This is playing a crucial role in the rapid development of ICT in the region.

ICT as Industry

In the past few years, the advanced East Asian KBEs have experienced strong growth in the ICT sector in many ways, such as through ICT production, trade and investment. The ICT-producing sector itself is very globalized because ICT components and parts, telecommunication equipment and computer equipment are manufactured in different locations because there has been a significant shift in production from high labor cost countries to low labor cost countries in East Asia (Information Economy Report 2007-2008, 101). During the past decade, there has been clear growth in the production of electronics in East Asia. In fact, East Asia, when combined with the Pacific nations (Australia and New Zealand), continues to be the fastest growing region in terms of electronic production (See Table 8.3). Among the five major KBEs of East Asia, Japan alone experienced 7.6 percent growth during the 2002-2005 period. On the other hand, Asia's total share in the electronics industry grew from 48 percent of world production in 2002 to 52 percent in 2005.

ICT plays an important role in the division of regional and global value-added chains, as well as in the shifting of production segments to different geographical locations. By using ICT, enterprises are able to exchange knowledge and information online from anywhere in the world, communicate just-in-time with clients and suppliers and deliver goods and services efficiently and promptly (Information Economy Report 2007-2008, 101). ICT, in many cases, has created opportunities

Table 8.3 Global Production of Electronics, 2002-2005 (USD in billions)

Region	2002	2003	2004	2005	Compound Annual Growth Rate 2002-2005
Europe	220.4	247.5	279.1	285.8	9.0%
Americas	317.6	314.1	334.3	341.9	2.5%
Asia-Pacific	343.1	386.9	448.8	492.7	12.8%
Japan	162.4	180.2	197.8	202.3	7.6%
Rest of the world	13.2	14.3	15.7	16.2	7.2%
World	1056.8	1143.0	1275.6	1338.9	8.2%

Source: Adapted from Reed Research, presented by Ernie Santiago, SEIPI, WTO ITA Symposium, 28 March 2007, Geneva.

for businesses to be more cost effective through outsourcing and offshoring. In the East Asian KBEs, the share of ICT sector value in total business-sector value continues to grow (UNCTAD Information Economy Database, 2007). Among the five advanced KBEs, Japan's performance has been the most extraordinary.

The growth of ICT as an industry has contributed greatly towards better employment in the region, as employment in the ICT sector has experienced stable growth over recent years. Japan has the highest employment in the electrical and electronic products manufacturing industry, a major part of the ICT sector, followed by Korea (Information Economy Report, 2007-2008, 110). Taiwan, Hong Kong and Singapore have also experienced huge employment growth in this sector in recent years.

Trade of ICT Goods and Services in East Asia

The past few decades have witnessed stable growth in ICT-related trade in the East Asian economies, as most of these economies have been the recipients of a huge volume of FDI. Since 1996, the value of world exports of ICT goods has more than doubled, reaching 1.5 trillion USD in 2005 (Information Economy Report 2007-2008, 115). Among the various regions of world, East Asia and the Pacific are leading in exports of ICT goods (See Figure 8.13). East Asia dominates world trade in ICT goods. The advanced KBEs of East Asia, along with still developing China, Malaysia, Thailand and the Philippines, are among the top 10 exporters of ICT goods or have significant export shares compared to other developed economies (Information Economy Report 2007-2008, 117). In the years since 1996, most East Asian KBEs have experienced growth in ICT goods exported, except for Japan, which experienced a decline in 2005 (See Table 8.4). Other developing economies in East Asia also experienced growth in ICT goods exported since 1996. This reveals the fact that the developed and developing countries of East Asia together lead exports of ICT goods.

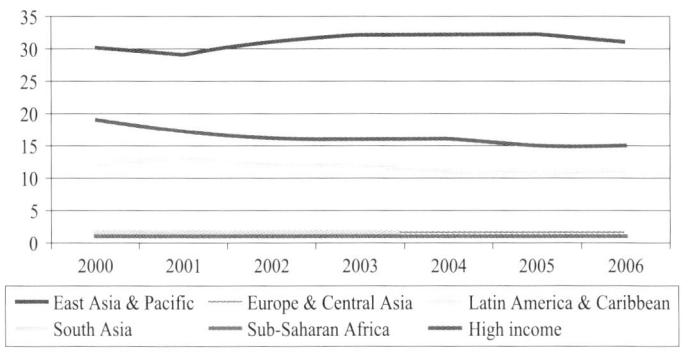

[Chart showing lines over 2000-2006 with legend: East Asia & Pacific, Europe & Central Asia, Latin America & Caribbean, South Asia, Sub-Saharan Africa, High income]

Figure 8.13   Exports of ICT Goods as a Share of Total
Goods Exports (Percentage), 2000-2006
Source: World Development Indicators 2009.

Table 8.4   Exports of ICT Goods, 1996, 2000 and 2005 (USD in millions)

Country	1996	2000	2005	Compound Annual Growth Rate 1996-2005	Compound Annual Growth Rate 2000-2005
China	18584	46996	235167	32.6%	38.0%
Hong Kong	37643	55313	118237	13.6%	16.4%
Indonesia	3287	7844	7911	10.2%	0.2%
Japan	103213	123548	121474	1.8%	-0.3%
Korea	34316	61525	87163	10.9%	7.2%
Malaysia	36987	55582	64472	6.4%	3.0%
Philippines	10294	26422	24418	10.1%	-1.6%
Singapore	67742	77345	106576	5.2%	6.6%
Taiwan	N/A	64409	66506	N/A	0.6%
Thailand	14208	20318	26169	7.0%	5.2%

Source: Adapted from the Information Economy Report 2007-2008.

On the importing side, the advanced KBEs contribute significant shares to world imports of ICT goods and services. The developing economies in East Asia, such as China, Malaysia, Thailand and the Philippines, also experienced significant growth in ICT goods imported, similar to the advanced economies of East Asia (See Table 8.5). On the other hand, high-tech exports have been increasing for the last eight years (See Figure 8.14).

In this case, it is notable that China has surpassed all the East Asian economies and is the number one exporter of ICT goods today. China's phenomenal success in

Table 8.5 Imports of ICT Goods, 1996, 2000 and 2005 (USD in millions)

Country	1996	2000	2005	Compound Annual Growth Rate 1996-2005	Compound Annual Growth Rate 2000-2005
China	16850	50597	183025	6.7%	3.8%
Hong Kong	44831	64403	119967	12.9%	11.2%
Indonesia	2851	1001	2426	5.9%	8.1%
Japan	47858	66871	76454	5.3%	2.3%
Korea	23482	39086	47037	8.6%	9.2%
Malaysia	27024	37249	46105	10.0%	4.8%
Philippines	9911	12621	23333	8.2%	8.7%
Singapore	50429	59769	80417	5.8%	1.1%
Taiwan	N/A	44851	45068	19.2%	10.5%
Thailand	13160	15660	23213	5.3%	6.1%

Source: Adapted from Information Economy Report 2007-2008.

this regard is largely due to fact that the country is the highest recipient of FDI in East Asia. Many advanced East Asian economies have even shifted their production sites to China for its cheap labor costs. Again, if we look at the percentage of high-tech exports versus total manufactured exports, we see that most advanced East Asian KBEs have maintained steady figures, though in some countries, this percentage has dropped since 2000 (See Figure 8.15). This indicates that exports of manufactured products are still increasing, parallel to the high-tech exports in the East Asian economies.

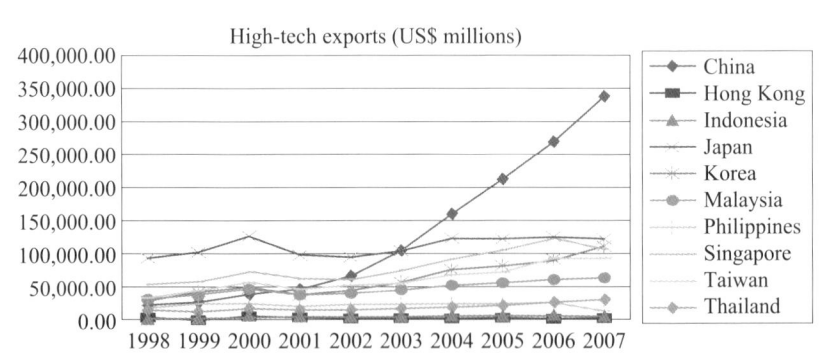

Figure 8.14 Total Volume of High-tech Exports Per Year, East Asia
Source: World Development Indicators Database March 2009, World Bank and National Sources.

High-tech exports (Percentage of manufactured exports)

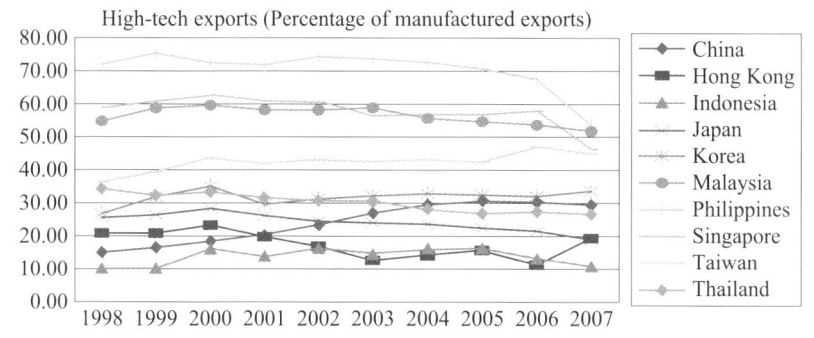

Figure 8.15   Percentage of High-tech Exports Per Year, East Asia
Source: World Development Indicators Database March 2009, World Bank and National Sources.

Macroeconomic Impact of ICT in East Asia

The impact of ICT on the economic development of the East Asian countries has been enormous. During the last two decades, ICT has evolved, improved and become more prevalent not only in advanced KBEs in East Asia but also in the developing economies of the region. Exports of ICT goods and services have grown continuously in most of the economies in the region. Simultaneously, ICT-related jobs have grown over the years, as both FDI and domestic investments have flowed into the ICT sector. In the advanced KBEs of East Asia, economic gain derives both from the ICT-producing sector and from other sectors, which are using ICT for production efficiency and cost reduction. However, the developing East Asian countries, while enjoying some growth in ICT use in different sectors, still depend on the ICT-producing sector for profit.

The UNCTAD Information Economy Report of 2007-2008 summarizes how ICT use leads to growth in productivity: first, it increases the efficiency of factor inputs (capital and labor); and, second, it fosters technological innovation as a source of total factor productivity growth. Since the mid-1990s, the advanced East Asian countries of Japan, Korea, Taiwan, Hong Kong and Singapore, along with other countries in the region started to invest in ICT at faster rates and have acquired a stock of ICT capital considerable enough to match the ICT capital intensity of the early

1990s' United States (Information Economy Report 2007-2008, 155). Countries like Japan, Korea, Taiwan, Hong Kong and Singapore have specialized in the production of ICT goods to mainly meet domestic demand, and the ICT-producing sector has had a sizeable, positive effect on total factor productivity growth in the countries mentioned above (Information Economy Report 2007-2008, 159).

Summary

From the analysis in this chapter, it is clear that the relationship between the ICT and the creation of KBE in East Asia is positively correlated. From the discussion above and from the data analysis of the East Asian countries, it is evident that advanced KBEs, such as Japan, Korea, Taiwan, Hong Kong and Singapore, have been highly successful in the development of ICT. Over the years, there has been greater public and private ICT expenditure in the countries mentioned above, a boom in ICT development in the region. The number of main telephone lines and mobile telephones per 1000 people, computers per capita, number of Internet users, and appropriate cyber security measures are major contributing factors to ICT development in East Asian countries. They have made local businesses much more competitive by providing more sophisticated communications technology. The availability of superior IT skills, better technological cooperation between and among the companies, supporting public and private sector ventures for technological development, an appropriate legal environment for the development and application of technology, suitable technological regulations to support business development and innovation, as well as availability of sound funding for technological development are also key factors contributing to ICT development in East Asian countries. These factors have enhanced the rapid growth of the region's ICT industry. There has been an enormous positive impact from these factors on the growth of global production of electronics in the region, making East Asia, along with the Pacific, the number one regional producer of electronics. In the years from 2002 to 2005, East Asia experienced more than 12% annual growth in this sector. East Asia and the Pacific also recorded the highest volume of exports in ICT goods for the 2000-2006 period. Again, the volume of high-tech exports also has substantially increased over the years in the East Asian countries under the analysis. It is therefore evident that the key factors of ICT development identified in this chapter have significantly improved the ICT sector of the East Asian economies.

Chapter Nine

Innovations in East Asian KBEs

Introduction

The generation, diffusion, absorption and application of new technology, knowledge or ideas are crucial drivers of economic development for any KBE. Knowledge flows from advanced countries remain the primary source of new ideas for the East Asian KBEs. This chapter examines the diverse policy approaches towards innovation adopted by the East Asian economies and the outcomes achieved. Three main channels for knowledge flows in East Asia, such as international trade, acquisition of disembodied knowledge and foreign direct investment are discernible. The exceptionally fast growth of domestic innovation efforts in Japan, Korea, Taiwan, Hong Kong and Singapore, drawing on R&D data, are used to illustrate outcomes.

Historical Background of Innovation in East Asia

Many East Asian countries achieved the status of middle or high income countries in the last two decades of the 20th century. The four tigers (Korea, Taiwan, Hong Kong and Singapore), led by Japan, enjoyed unprecedented economic growth during that period. Although the long-term goal of R&D is to take the lead in innovation, most R&D activities in East Asia have been more to innovate on the existing technologies of developed countries rather than inventing new things through systematic research. East Asia's efforts to make existing technology more sophisticated and cheaper, and then reselling it to the world, were the main force behind high economic growth. The earlier absorption of knowledge and technology from abroad has contributed to today's system of innovation in many East Asian countries. Countries like Japan, Korea, Taiwan, Hong Kong and Singapore, have created modern innovation infrastructure through the experience of absorbing foreign technology and knowledge, and they now create better and cheaper products through innovation of this absorbed knowledge and technology. While absorbing external technology and knowledge, these countries have also developed the ability to innovate new knowledge and technology on their own. These combined efforts have helped them to move to the frontier of innovation, where they carry out R&D activities to invent new technology and knowledge, and then patent it just as any advanced economy of the world might.

East Asia's heavy engagement in international trade has been a key source of technology transfer from developed countries to East Asian ones. This engagement in international trade has intensified as FDI has flooded into East Asian countries. The rapid growth of the Japanese economy, changing business environment due to globalization and the growing availability of cheap but capable human resources in many East Asian countries have caused FDI to flow to unprecedented levels within East Asia; this is a true blessing for economic growth.

Initial Absorption of Foreign Technology and Knowledge

Innovations into new technology and knowledge are still centered in certain geographical locations which lead the global frontier of innovation. Spillover effects and technology transfer result in further improvement of initial innovations in many advanced countries. The advanced countries of the world do not always perform equally well at the global frontier of innovation. For example, at least 80% of the domestic productivity growth in most OECD countries is from foreign sources of technology (Eaton and Kortum, 1996). Only a few advanced countries, such as the U.S. and Japan, are exceptions and are able to lead the global frontier of innovation. Almost 80% of the world's R&D is still carried out in developed nations (Brahmbhatt and Hu, 2007:6). However, due to globalization, the speed of technology and knowledge transfer to other countries has become faster than before. This creates opportunities to increase or improve on newly invented technology and knowledge by the participation of other countries. This process, indeed, is now contributing to the total increase of knowledge worldwide. One study shows that a one percent increase in R&D in the U.S. contributes to an increase of 0.35% in knowledge creation in other OECD countries within 10 years (Bottazi and Peri, 2005).

Thus, developing countries receive much needed technology and knowledge from advanced countries and most of the time; they, then, innovate on existing technologies and knowledge. Instead of spending R&D money to create frontier innovation, developing nations pay more attention to how to catch up with frontier knowledge through the adoption and adaption of existing technologies. The same is true for most East Asian countries. Many studies have showed that East Asian countries, in this regard, have employed three main channels to acquire advanced foreign technologies and knowledge: international trade, foreign direct investment and disembodied knowledge flows. Keller (2002) found that all of these three channels have been significant for technological development in East Asia, and, that among the three, imports of advanced capital equipment through international trade are the most important, accounting for two-thirds of the estimated impacts. In comparison, FDI and disembodied knowledge flows account for about one-sixth each on average. Both FDI and disembodied knowledge flows are relatively new in East Asia when compared to International Trade. It is therefore not surprising to see that the contribution of FDI and disembodied knowledge flows is relatively low compared to the imports of advanced capital equipment through international trade. However, FDI has changed the speed, depth and mode of technological innovation in East Asia to a great extent, further contributing to the development of disembodied knowledge flows in East Asia.

Getting Hold of Foreign Technology through Imports
　　　Table 9.1 shows the share that machinery imports occupy out of total imports in East Asian countries. Though indigenous technology innovation was the norm in China and India during the 1950s and 1980s, the table below shows the growing importance of applied technological knowledge transfer in the early periods of technology adaption in the selected East Asian countries.

Table 9.1 Machinery Import Share out of Total Imports

	1980	1990	1997
Developed Countries	0.256	0.355	0.378
Developing Countries	0.310	0.348	0.348
1. East Asia and the Pacific	0.297	0.344	0.406
(1) ASEAN 4	0.325	0.421	0.501
Indonesia	0.376	0.411	0.425
Malaysia	0.370	0.525	0.616
Philippines	0.296	0.320	0.487
Thailand	0.260	0.428	0.473
(2) NIEs	0.254	0.383	0.438
Hong Kong	0.237	0.308	0.371
Korea	0.227	0.351	0.355
Singapore	0.281	0.441	0.553
Taiwan	0.273	0.434	0.474
(3) China	0.251	0.351	0.365
2. South Asia	0.257	0.244	0.254
3. Latin America and the Caribbean	0.295	0.339	0.373
4. Europe and Central Asia	0.274	0.320	0.364
5. Middle East and North Africa	0.323	0.341	0.335
6. Sub-Saharan Africa	0.330	0.373	0.325

Sources: Urata, 2003: 85.

Figure 9.1, for instance, highlights the imports of machinery in the industrial sector. This has strengthened growing firms in many East Asian economies by providing them with access to advanced technologies and knowledge, without which, they could not have developed domestically. This has, indeed, helped the East Asian economies to develop their technological expertise and build up technological capabilities through 'reverse engineering' of capital equipment imported from Japan and Korea; they are the two largest exporters in the industrial sector when compared to other East Asian countries.

Brahmbhatt and Hu (2007) show that East Asian ratios to GDP for imports of machinery and transport equipment (including much of what is classified as 'high technology' goods) are mostly well above the levels associated with other countries at similar per capita income levels (See Figure 9.2). This reveals that the advanced East Asian economies heavily depended on the import of machinery and

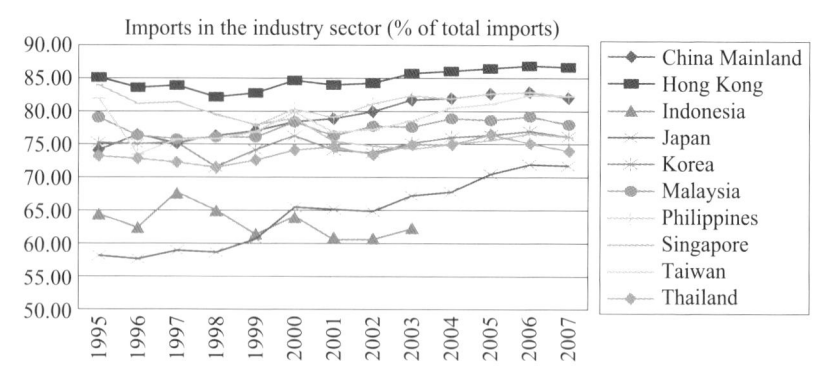

Figure 9.1 Imports in the Industry Sector in East Asia, 1995-2007
Source: Computed from data collected from IMD World Competitiveness Online.

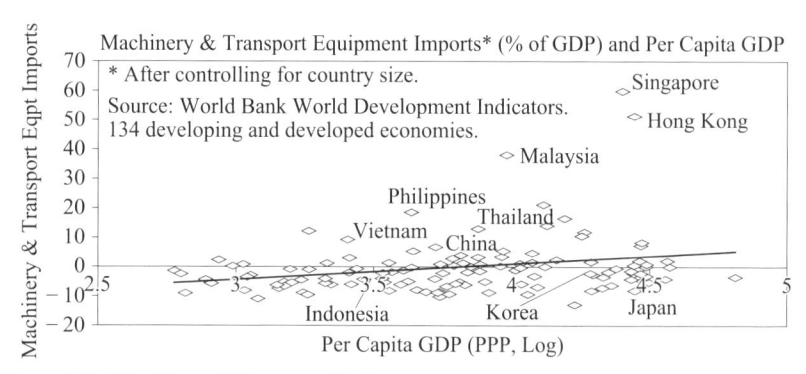

Figure 9.2 Machinery & Transport Equipment Imports (% of GDP) and Per Capita GDP
Source: Brahmbhatt and Hu, 2007: 9.

transport equipment during the high growth era; they thereby were able to achieve high GDP growth.

Creating Initial Innovation System through Exporting

The export of industrial goods has been the most important contributor to the East Asian Miracle. In recent decades, the countries that have shown superior strength in exports have achieved unprecedented economic growth. Industrial exports dominate exports in many East Asian countries (See Figure 9.3). This has, in fact, validated earlier attempts of importing advanced capital equipment and technologies from developed countries. Initially, Korea, Taiwan, Hong Kong and

Singapore followed this path, importing advanced capital equipment and technologies from developed countries, and then, exporting manufactured industrial products to achieve rapid economic growth.

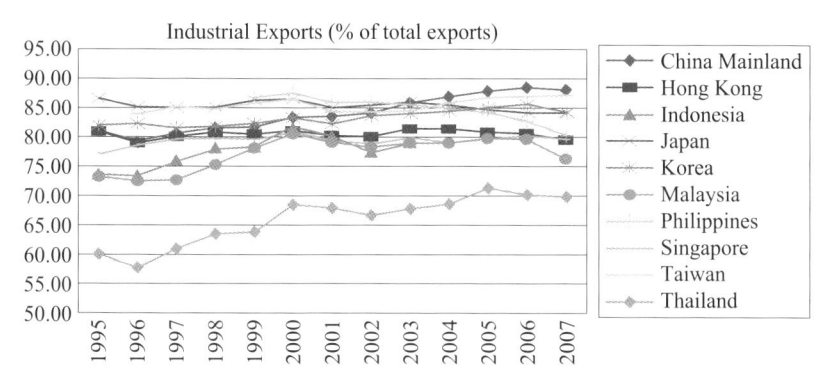

Figure 9.3 Industrial Exports in East Asia, 1995-2007
Source: Computed from data collected from IMD World Competitiveness Online.

Revenues earned from exports have been used to import more advanced capital equipments and technologies. Figure 9.4 corroborates evidence that East Asian exports of machinery and transport equipment (containing much of what are classified as high technology products) are generally much higher than other economies at similar income levels (Brahmbhatt and Hu: 2007). The analysis in Figure 9.4 has been controlled for country size, and thus, the positions of the East

Figure 9.4 Machinery & Transport Equipment Imports (% of GDP) and Per Capita GDP-2003
Source: Brahmbhatt and Hu, 2007: 10.

Asian countries do not represent their actual performance.

Most East Asian countries have maintained a relatively higher rate of high-tech exports compared to many other countries (See Table 9.2). This signifies how the East Asian economies have used imported machineries and technologies to produce better high-tech products and then, to export them at higher margins. This has led to the growth of many Original Equipment Manufacturing (OEM) industries in the advanced East Asian countries. Hobday (1995, 2000) emphasized the role of OEM subcontracting in fostering industrial exports and technology transfer in East Asia, especially in Korea and Taiwan. During the last three decades of the 20th century, OEM production and exports in the four tigers drastically increased. For instance, by 1990, almost 70-80% of Korea's electronics exports were under OEM type contracts, while over 40% of Taiwan's computer hardware exports were of this form. Over the past 15 years, OEM type contracting has been central to the enormous expansion of manufactured exports from China (Brahmbhatt and Hu, 2007: 10).

As firms in many East Asian countries have enhanced technological capability through OEM production and exports, they have moved towards making more sophisticated technologies by making Original Design Manufacturing (ODM) products. In this process, the firms themselves took over the responsibility for

Table 9.2 High-tech Exports in East Asia, 1998-2007
(Percentage of manufactured exports)

Country	1998	1999	2000	2001	2002	2003	2004	2005	2006	2007
China	15.08	16.76	18.57	20.56	23.30	27.09	29.79	30.59	30.28	29.69
Hong Kong	20.90	20.92	23.28	19.65	16.93	12.65	14.33	15.59	11.35	19.33
Indonesia	10.05	10.16	16.17	13.97	16.40	14.49	16.22	16.36	13.27	10.83
Japan	25.75	26.28	28.31	26.21	24.44	24.03	23.66	22.45	21.58	18.94
Korea	26.82	31.92	34.82	29.55	31.30	32.15	32.77	32.34	32.02	33.47
Malaysia	54.88	58.90	59.54	58.09	58.19	58.91	55.65	54.61	53.78	51.66
Philippines	71.90	74.96	72.58	71.86	74.14	73.60	72.62	70.73	67.64	53.59
Singapore	58.84	60.68	62.58	60.69	60.39	56.31	56.72	56.74	57.98	46.47
Taiwan	36.26	39.20	43.36	41.97	42.93	42.52	43.02	42.51	46.84	44.74
Thailand	34.30	32.29	33.37	31.54	30.78	30.29	28.21	26.66	27.41	26.56

Source: IMD World Competitiveness Online.

post-conceptual design and development of the products. This led the firms to step into Original Brand Manufacturing (OBM), whereby they captured the entire product cycle of R&D, innovation, design, development, production and marketing using their own brand name (Brahmbhatt and Hu, 2007). Sturgeon and Lester (2004) have described this OEM-ODM-OBM mode of technological development as 'supplier-oriented industrial upgrading'. With respect to this, Brahmbhatt and Hu (2007) mention the case of Samsung in Korea by saying:

> Samsung Electronics of Korea is a rare example of a developing country firm that has successfully traveled the whole of this road, building on OEM and technology licensing deals with advanced country MNCs like Sony, Toshiba, Philips and GTE in the 1980s, making huge efforts to build up its design capabilities, R&D and independent brand in the 1990s, till the present, when it has annual R&D expenditures of $4-5 billion (representing 8-9 percent of sales and employing close to a quarter of the workforce), and has the largest global market share for sales of DRAM and SRAM semiconductors, flash memories, TVs, monitors and LCD panels, as well as the second or third largest market shares for mobile phones and DVD players.
>
> Brahmbhatt and Hu (2007: 11).

It is thus quite evident that exporting has helped the East Asian economies to adopt, adapt and finally, produce new technologies. However, this process of learning through exports did not bring comparable results to all the economies of East Asia. Nabeshima (2004) pointed out that to be selected as an OEM supplier, firms needed to possess production and technological capabilities to produce quality products at lower costs through a competent distribution channel. In the case of ODM and OBM, the requirements were even higher. Not all the firms in the East Asian economies were capable of meeting the high requirements to be selected as OEM, then as ODM and finally as OBM. This explains why there are few firms like Samsung in East Asia that have successfully walked through the transition from being an unknown OEM supplier to a global brand today. This clearly indicates that importing advanced capital equipment and technologies in the earlier stages of development helped the firms in East Asia to develop the technological capability they needed to be selected as an OEM producer. Later, further capability building as OEM producers helped those firms to be selected as ODM suppliers, pushing them on towards the final stage of OBM production.

Developing Competitive Technological Capabilities

As the financial capability of many East Asian firms grew rapidly, they started purchasing disembodied external knowledge through acquisition of patents, non-patented inventions, licenses, disclosures of know-how and trademarks. These activities helped the firms to have access to a broader and more competitive level of foreign technology, enabling them to grow much faster than during their earlier stages of development in OEM production. Consequently, East Asian economies, especially the newly industrializing economies of Korea, Taiwan, Hong Kong and Singapore, have been spending a good percentage of their GDP in royalty payments (See Table 9.3).

Table 9.3 Royalty Payments (Percentage of GDP)

	1970	1980	1990	1997
Developed Countries	0.124	0.124	0.178	0.231
Developing Countries	0.112	0.086	0.137	0.172
1. East Asia and the Pacific	0.075	0.128	0.259	0.292
(4) ASEAN 4	NA	0.098	0.162	0.357
Indonesia	NA	NA	NA	NA
Malaysia	NA	0.152	NA	NA
Philippines	NA	0.058	0.086	0.192
Thailand	NA	0.092	0.200	0.539
(5) NIEs	NA	0.195	0.472	0.467
Hong Kong	NA	NA	NA	NA
Korea	NA	0.195	0.540	0.507
Singapore	NA	NA	NA	0.460
Taiwan	NA	NA	0.363	0.405
(6) China	NA	NA	NA	0.060
2. South Asia	0.016	0.008	0.021	0.034
3. Latin America and the Caribbean	0.158	0.055	0.090	0.115
4. Europe and Central Asia	0.050	0.050	0.050	0.227
5. Middle East and North Africa	0.186	0.177	0.183	0.215
6. Sub-Saharan Africa	0.181	0.155	0.074	0.131

Sources: National Sources and Kawai and Urata, 2003: 72.

Royalty payments made abroad for East Asia are much higher relative to other economies at similar income levels (Figure 9.5). This indicates that some measure of the technology transfer is going on in East Asia. However, in addition to this, the East Asian economies have also developed disembodied knowledge flows through technological spillovers, benefiting from open source information such as scientific, technical and industrial journals, informal contacts and communications through networks of researchers and specialists, trade and industry associations, and trade fairs (Brahmbhatt and Hu, 2007:13). As the East Asian countries have adopted and adapted new technologies and knowledge from abroad, they have basically been imitating rather than innovating new technologies.

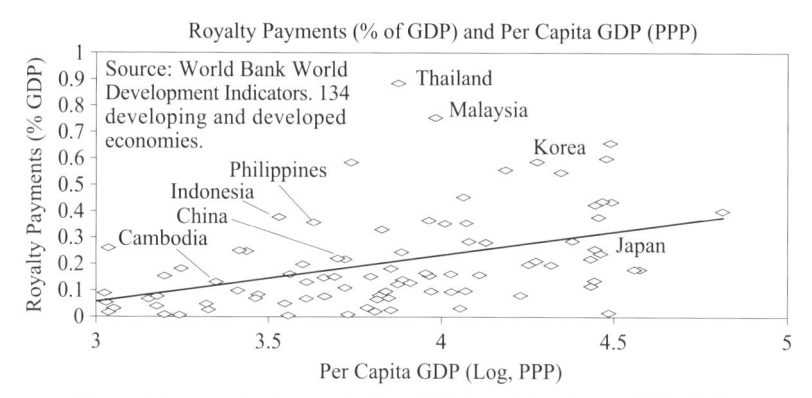

Figure 9.5   Royalty Payments (% of GDP) and Per Capita GDP (PPP)
Source: Brahmbhatt and Hu, 2007: 13.

Foreign Direct Investment – A Major Contributor to East Asia's Innovation

FDI has been the most important external source used to enhance technology and upgrade technological capabilities in East Asian countries. In some East Asian countries, however, a growing learning capacity, correlated to competitive education and training of the labor force, extensive and high-quality domestic R&D, as well as domestic innovation efforts in domestic economies, attracted more FDI than in others. With respect to this, Brahmbhatt and Hu (2007) mention how domestic R&D not only generates new knowledge, but also enhances firms' ability to assimilate and exploit existing knowledge, and how as a result, they are more likely to benefit from FDI spillovers. This, in turn, helps them to be selected as suppliers to sophisticated global production networks, provided they possess significant in-house design, engineering and other capabilities. It is thus quite apparent that domestic innovation and FDI are mutually supportive. It is also to be noted that stocks of inward FDI in manufacturing in East Asia are generally higher than in other developing or developed regions (See Figure 9.6). This clearly indicates the contribution of FDI to the development of innovation in East Asia.

In recent decades, FDI has become, for many East Asian countries, one of the most important means for receiving advanced technologies and knowledge from developed countries. Multinational corporations (MNCs) play a very important role in this regard, as through FDI, they can use advanced technology in many East Asian countries at low-production cost and with high-quality results. In many cases, the MNCs are the pioneers in introducing new product and process innovations, maintaining quality standards, and accessing a capacity for the global export markets for the countries they bring FDI into. The logic of MNCs suggests that the MNCs' choice of FDI is related to fully protecting its intangible assets (knowledge) in liberal transactions, which leads them to deploy those assets within the shielding boundaries of their own affiliates through FDI (Caves, 1996 and Markusen, 2002). This protects the firms from licensing their technologies through liberal market

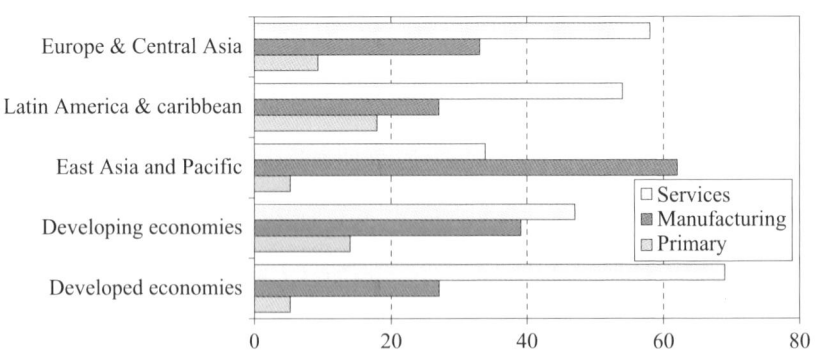

Figure 9.6 Sectoral Composition of FDI Stock in 2002
Source: Brahmbhatt and Hu, 2007: 15.

transactions because, technologies, many a times, involve considerable amount of knowledge, which may have the characteristics of public goods making it very difficult to license them in the liberal markets. Another reason for the MNCs to opt for FDI is that as the technology gets more sophisticated, selling it to other firms at appropriate prices becomes difficult, because external buyers may not be able to evaluate the value of the technology properly (Urata, 2003:80). In the case of East Asia, another major reason for large volume of FDI inflow is the increasing importance and appearance of East Asia in the global market.

As the MNCs bring in new technologies and managerial know-how, host countries in East Asia have two benefits: first, intra-firm technology transfer, in which the technology transfer is between the parent company and its affiliates; and, second, technology spillover to other domestic firms. The affiliate of the MNCs achieves higher productivity by accessing the parent company's superior technological know-how at relatively lower costs. As they produce high quality products, a standard set by the parent companies, the affiliates have an advantage in competing more efficiently in the market, and, this, in turn, increases consumer choice in the market. As one would expect, this also enhances productivity in the rest of economy in the host country by increasing competition and as technological spillovers take place alongside the spread of expertise to different corners of the economy.

Domestic firms in FDI recipient countries get spillover effects by imitating superior products, technologies, and processes from MNC affiliates (Das, 1987, and Wang and Blomström, 1992); they also acquire skills by hiring human resources well-trained in MNC affiliates (Djankov and Hoekman, 2000 and Fosfuri *et al.*, 2001). In East Asia, both vertical and horizontal spillover effects have been observed in innovation through FDI inflows. In the initial stage, vertical spillovers have been observed more, since the R&D level in host country firms was very weak compared to foreign firms. However, as the R&D level rose, there has been increasing horizontal spillover in many East Asian economies, such as Korea, Taiwan, Hong Kong and Singapore.

From Imitation to Innovation

Rapid industrialization during the 'East Asia Miracle' in the 1960s and 1970s occurred largely due to imitation of foreign technologies, a kind of reverse engineering. In the beginning, East Asian economies reverse-engineered relatively simple products that did not require advanced or specialized R&D capability. However, this process enabled them to realize the potential of technological know-how for competing in the global market. This helped firms in East Asia to take risks and to learn from experience and considerable trial and error that was involved in achieving an advanced technology. Creative imitations, along with innovation, helped Japan to become a global economic giant within a relatively short period of time after World War II. By adopting and adapting advanced technologies from abroad, Japanese firms excelled in later stages by gaining access to newer technology and using it with an understanding of the growing market that was more accurate than the original innovators possessed – this process is often referred to as 'technological leapfrogging'. A similar sequence came later for many East Asian economies, most notably Korea, Taiwan, Hong Kong and Singapore. Many scholars have called this pattern of development the 'flying geese' model.

Status of Research and Development in East Asia

In a KBE, research and development (R&D) counts most as it directly involves creating and diffusing new knowledge through innovation. R&D involves a variety of factors such as innovation, private and public initiatives in R&D, the availability of R&D personnel, and scientific education. The long-term aim of developing a proper innovation infrastructure is to support continuous innovation and thereby create new knowledge; this enables a country to remain competitive in a KBE. Many countries are spending a huge amount of money on R&D in order to support continuous innovation. The OECD countries are leaders in this race. Together with the development of the education and ICT sectors, development in innovation infrastructure is also extremely important for becoming a KBE. The two other sectors of education and human resources, and ICT, help innovation infrastructure to grow. Thus, any country trying to become a KBE must also strive to build up its innovation system.

Creating the Human Resources for R&D

The availability of scientists and engineers is a very important pre-requisite for creating a functional innovation system. The East Asian KBEs, being benefitted from KBE-oriented government policy, are capable to guarantee themselves a steady supply of science graduates (See Table 7.5 in Chapter Seven). In this regard, even latecomers in East Asia, such as China, Malaysia and Thailand, have also been performing consistently well. There has been an increasing emphasize on science education in schools throughout East Asia (See Figure 7.1 in Chapter Seven).

R&D Expenditures

In the process of becoming a KBE, expenditures on R&D in East Asian countries have risen, although the total amount is still far below than that of Japan (See Table 9.4). Investment in R&D largely increases when the country has already become a KBE. In this region, Japan was the first country to reach this goal, after 1945, and, as a consequence, R&D expenditures are highest in Japan. Japan's high growth was followed by the four tigers of East Asia; and they, too, have successfully allocated greater funds for R&D so as to become a part of the KBE. All other countries in the region are still at the beginning of their economic transformation

Table 9.4   Total Expenditure on R&D (USD in millions)

Country	1998	1999	2000	2001	2002	2003	2004	2005	2006	2007
China	6,656.5	8,201.0	10,819.7	12,595.1	15,556.4	18,600.9	23,756.8	29,898.5	37,662.7	48,770.3
Hong Kong	723.1	760.5	795.8	910.4	961.7	1,098.0	1,221.1	1,404.1	1,531.9	N/A
Indonesia	53.1	90.2	111.7	76.3	N/A	N/A	N/A	N/A	N/A	N/A
Japan	115,884.7	131,973.5	142,013.3	127,924.5	124,114.2	135,318.4	146,001.3	151,431.7	148,397.4	N/A
Korea	8,104.1	10,022.7	12,248.7	12,480.8	13,846.3	15,998.7	19,381.4	23,582.1	28,619.0	N/A
Malaysia	287.5	N/A	439.9	N/A	658.1	N/A	N/A	N/A	993.7	1,060.1
Philippines	N/A	N/A	N/A	N/A	111.8	109.0	105.4	115.7	123.3	N/A
Singapore	1,489.2	1,567.1	1,745.5	1,804.3	1,901.4	1,965.6	2,403.1	2,752.7	3,152.9	N/A
Taiwan	5,276.0	5,904.7	6,329.3	6,064.3	6,491.1	7,058.6	7,877.2	8,735.0	9,438.3	10,090.3
Thailand	N/A	314.4	308.9	303.2	309.3	373.2	411.5	413.9	503.6	497.6

Source: OECD Main Science and Technology Indicators 2/2008, UNESCO http://stats.uis. unesco.org and National Sources.

towards the KBE, and, as a result, R&D expenditures there have yet to reach the level of the OECD KBEs.

Total expenditure on R&D per capita provides a comprehensive picture of the availability of R&D funding rather than the amount of total R&D spending. In Table 9.4, we see that China spends the second largest amount on R&D, while in terms of R&D expenditure per capita, China ranks seventh in East Asia (See Table 9.5). From Table 9.5, it is quite evident that the newly industrialized economies (NIEs), such as Korea, Taiwan, Hong Kong and Singapore, led by Japan are having the highest expenditures on R&D per capita in East Asia.

Table 9.5 Total Expenditure on R&D Per Capita (USD in millions)

Country	1998	1999	2000	2001	2002	2003	2004	2005	2006	2007
China	5.3	6.5	8.5	9.9	12.1	14.4	18.3	22.9	28.7	36.9
Hong Kong	110.5	115.1	119.4	135.6	142.6	163.1	180.0	206.1	223.4	N/A
Indonesia	0.3	0.4	0.5	0.4	N/A	N/A	N/A	N/A	N/A	N/A
Japan	916.7	1,042.0	1,119.4	1,005.0	973.9	1,060.3	1,143.4	1,185.3	1,161.0	N/A
Korea	175.1	215.0	260.6	263.6	290.8	334.3	403.5	489.9	592.6	N/A
Malaysia	12.9	N/A	18.7	N/A	26.8	N/A	29.3	N/A	37.3	39.0
Philippines	N/A	N/A	N/A	N/A	1.4	1.4	1.3	1.4	1.4	N/A
Singapore	379.2	395.8	433.4	436.0	455.3	477.7	576.7	645.3	716.4	N/A
Taiwan	240.6	267.2	284.1	270.7	288.2	312.3	347.2	383.6	412.6	439.5
Thailand	N/A	5.1	5.0	4.8	4.9	5.8	6.3	6.4	7.7	7.6

Source: OECD Main Science and Technology Indicators 2/2008, UNESCO http:///stats.uis. unesco.org and National Sources.

The role of R&D expenditure in East Asian KBEs is quite large. Parallel to the government's continuous efforts to increase the investment in R&D in the country, the business sector has also been playing a very important role in overall advancement of R&D in the private sector. R&D performance in the business sector is higher than R&D performance in the government and higher education sectors (See Table 9.6 and Table 9.7) in most East Asian countries. Guellec and Potterie (2004) mentioned that higher flow of business R&D increases an economy's ability to absorb benefits from accumulated stocks of all types of R&D, business, public and foreign. In East Asia, higher R&D expenditure in business sectors is especially beneficial to firms that wish to be innovative domestically as well as have easier access to knowledge from abroad.

Table 9.6   Business Expenditure on R&D (USD millions)

Country	1998	1999	2000	2001	2002	2003	2004	2005	2006	2007
China	2,983.9	4,066.7	6,487.3	7,611.8	9,517.9	11,601.3	15,875.3	20,426.6	26,770.8	34,321.4
Hong Kong	206.6	181.8	143.8	266.7	321.8	455.9	589.4	722.6	809.7	781.95
Indonesia	N/A	N/A	29.4	10.9	N/A	N/A	N/A	N/A	N/A	N/A
Japan	82,506.7	93,323.4	100,774.5	94,247.0	92,393.0	101,457.6	109,780.5	115,766.0	114,496.5	N/A
Korea	5,698.9	7,155.4	9,070.0	9,508.3	10,370.0	12,173.7	14,868.8	18,123.7	22,110.5	N/A
Malaysia	190.3	N/A	254.7	N/A	442.9	N/A	535.2	N/A	843.7	900.0
Philippines	41.0	46.9	61.8	71.3	80.4	79.8	77.2	67.3	72.2	N/A
Singapore	917.8	985.8	1,082.4	1,141.4	1,168.0	1,194.6	1,532.3	1,821.1	2,072.5	N/A
Taiwan	3,388.4	3,786.0	4,025.6	3,854.9	4,036.7	4,434.1	5,095.2	5,856.6	6,370.5	6,976.6
Thailand	N/A	146.8	115.9	125.1	138.4	142.7	149.6	165.8	198.4	237.5

Source: OECD Main Science and Technology Indicators 2/2008, UNESCO http://stats.uis.unesco.org and National Sources.

Table 9.7   R&D Performance in Different Sectors in East Asia

Country	Business	Government	Higher Education
China	62.4	27.1	10.5
Hong Kong	33.2	3.1	63.6
Indonesia	14.3	81.1	4.6
Japan	75.0	9.3	13.7
Korea	76.1	12.6	10.1
Malaysia	65.3	20.3	14.4
Philippines	58.6	21.7	17.0
Singapore	63.8	10.9	25.4
Taiwan	62.2	24.8	12.3
Thailand	43.9	22.5	31.0

Source: UNESCO Science and Technology Statistics 2006.

Human Resources in R&D

During the period from 1998 to 2007, most East Asian KBEs experienced growth in total R&D personnel nationwide per capita (See Table 9.8). Increasing investments in R&D by the business sector have helped to increase the total number of R&D personnel working in business enterprises over the last ten years (See Table 9.9) in most of the countries. Japan, Korea, Taiwan, Hong Kong and Singapore have showed very noteworthy growth in this regard among all the economies of East Asia.

Table 9.8 Total R&D Personnel Nationwide Per Capita
(full-time work equivalent per 1000 people)

Country	1998	1999	2000	2001	2002	2003	2004	2005	2006	2007
China	0.61	0.65	0.73	0.75	0.81	0.85	0.89	1.04	1.14	1.31
Hong Kong	1.38	1.53	1.47	1.64	1.91	2.50	2.77	3.24	3.35	N/A
Indonesia	N/A	N/A	0.27	0.25	N/A	N/A	N/A	N/A	N/A	N/A
Japan	7.32	7.26	7.07	7.01	6.73	6.91	7.02	7.21	7.32	N/A
Korea	2.78	2.96	2.94	3.50	3.62	3.89	4.04	4.47	4.92	N/A
Malaysia	0.30	N/A	0.43	N/A	0.44	N/A	0.70	N/A	0.56	0.55
Philippines	N/A	N/A	N/A	N/A	0.12	0.17	0.16	0.16	0.16	N/A
Singapore	3.51	3.81	4.81	4.70	5.24	5.71	6.12	6.70	6.85	N/A
Taiwan	N/A	4.73	4.69	4.81	5.33	5.65	6.11	6.55	7.05	7.65
Thailand	N/A	0.32	N/A	0.51	N/A	0.66	N/A	0.57	N/A	0.65

Source: OECD Main Science and Technology Indicators 2/2008, UNESCO http://stats.uis. unesco.org and National Sources.

Table 9.9 Total R&D Personnel in Business Per Capita
(full-time work equivalent per 1000 people)

Country	1998	1999	2000	2001	2002	2003	2004	2005	2006	2007
China	0.25	0.28	0.36	0.42	0.47	0.51	0.54	0.68	0.75	0.90
Hong Kong	0.42	0.49	0.39	0.49	0.68	1.11	1.40	1.79	1.85	1.83
Indonesia	N/A	N/A	0.03	0.01	N/A	N/A	N/A	N/A	N/A	N/A
Japan	4.85	4.77	4.59	4.41	4.36	4.55	4.60	4.77	4.84	N/A
Korea	1.68	1.80	1.85	2.47	2.53	2.68	2.76	3.19	3.55	N/A
Malaysia	0.09	N/A	0.14	N/A	0.26	N/A	0.24	N/A	0.21	0.21
Philippines	N/A	N/A	N/A	N/A	N/A	0.07	0.06	0.06	0.06	N/A
Singapore	2.22	2.44	2.54	2.40	2.74	3.04	3.56	4.00	4.00	N/A
Taiwan	3.21	3.17	3.14	3.23	3.31	3.56	3.96	4.25	4.64	5.14
Thailand	N/A	0.09	N/A	0.11	0.11	0.11	0.10	0.12	0.12	0.13

Source: OECD Main Science and Technology Indicators 2/2008, UNESCO http://stats.uis. unesco.org and National Sources.

Quality of R&D

Many scholars argue that the quality of R&D in the major KBEs in East Asia has rapidly increased due to developments in microeconomic stability, financial systems, high-quality public research institutions and the protection of intellectual rights. Economies like Japan, Korea, Taiwan, Singapore and Hong Kong have achieved more success than other East Asian countries in terms of high-quality R&D (See Figure 9.7). A reflection of this development can be seen in the number of scientific articles published by authors in different countries in East Asia. From

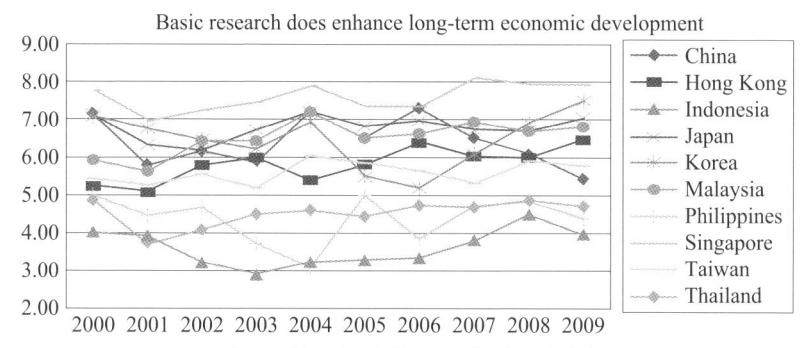

Basic research does enhance long-term economic development

Figure 9.7   Basic Research, East Asia*
* IMD WCY Executive Opinion Survey based on an index from 0 to 10.
Source: Computed from data collected from IMD World Competitiveness Online 1995-2009.

Table 9.10   Scientific Articles Published According to Author's Origin

Country	1997	1998	1999	2000	2001	2002	2003	2004	2005
China	12,172	13,781	15,715	18,479	21,134	23,269	28,768	34,846	41,596
Hong Kong	2,548	N/A	1,817	N/A	N/A	N/A	N/A	N/A	N/A
Indonesia	146	136	163	182	189	178	157	182	205
Japan	51,462	53,838	55,274	57,101	56,082	56,346	57,228	56,534	55,471
Korea	5,802	7,057	8,478	9,572	11,007	11,735	13,401	15,255.00	16,396
Malaysia	349	387	471	460	472	494	479	586	615
Philippines	170	171	176	185	141	182	184	163	178
Singapore	1,339	1,584	1,897	2,361	2,434	2,632	2,939	3,384	3,609
Taiwan	6,016	6,355	6,643	7,190	7,912	8,123	8,929	10,133	10,841
Thailand	405	541	549	663	727	834	1,019	1,131	1,249

Source: NSF Science & Engineering Indicators 2008 and National Sources.

Table 9.10, we see that the number of publications has increased steadily in most East Asian KBEs.

Capacity for Innovation in East Asia

East Asian KBEs have made great leaps in capacity building by increasing R&D expenditures and creating greater number of R&D personnel. Figure 9.8 indicates whether companies in East Asia obtain technology exclusively from licensing or imitating foreign companies (1 on the scale), or by conducting formal research and pioneering their own new products and processes (7 on the scale) for the year

Capacity for Innovation

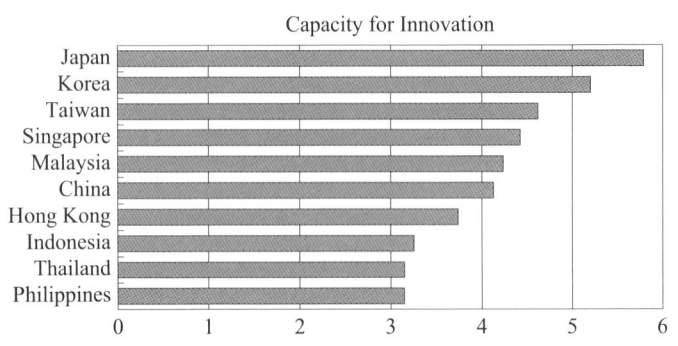

Japan	~5.8
Korea	~5.2
Taiwan	~4.7
Singapore	~4.5
Malaysia	~4.2
China	~4.1
Hong Kong	~3.7
Indonesia	~3.2
Thailand	~3.1
Philippines	~3.1

Figure 9.8 Capacity for Innovation in East Asia, 2007-2008
Source: World Economic Forum, Executive Opinion Survey 2007, 2008.

Quality of scientific research institutions

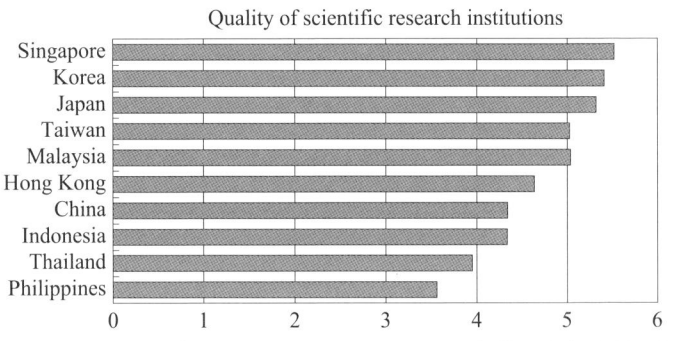

Singapore	~5.6
Korea	~5.3
Japan	~5.3
Taiwan	~5.0
Malaysia	~5.0
Hong Kong	~4.6
China	~4.3
Indonesia	~4.3
Thailand	~4.0
Philippines	~3.6

Figure 9.9 Quality of Scientific Research Institutions in East Asia, 2007-2008
Source: World Economic Forum, Executive Opinion Survey 2007, 2008.

2007-2008. From Figure 9.8, it is apparent that capacity for innovation has been much higher in the major KBEs of East Asia, where countries obtain technology by conducting formal research and pioneering their own new products and processes rather than from licensing or imitating foreign companies. Japan, Korea, Taiwan and Singapore lead this trend, while Hong Kong lags behind Malaysia and China.

Efforts for capacity building have been further strengthened by institutional improvements, reducing microeconomic instability and improving overall human capital status in East Asia. Research institutions have been playing a key role in advancing innovation capacity in East Asia. Figure 9.9 shows scientific research institutions in East Asian countries are nonexistent (1 on the scale) or are the best in

University-industry research collaboration

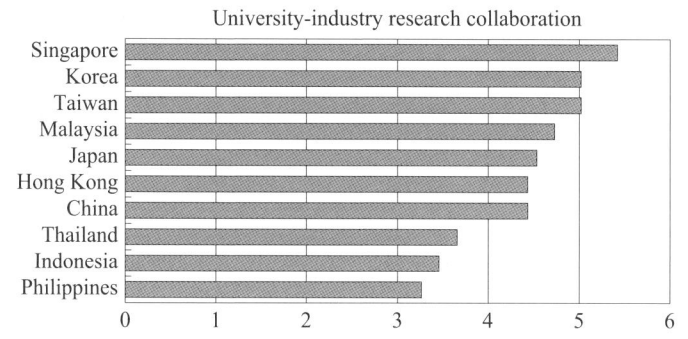

Singapore	~5.5
Korea	~5
Taiwan	~5
Malaysia	~4.7
Japan	~4.5
Hong Kong	~4.3
China	~4.3
Thailand	~3.7
Indonesia	~3.5
Philippines	~3.2

Figure 9.10   University-Industry Research Collaboration in East Asia, 2007-2008
Source: World Economic Forum, Executive Opinion Survey 2007, 2008.

their fields internationally (7 on the scale). From the figure, it is evident that scientific research institutions in East Asian KBEs have been very active in internationally competitive research. This trend is also visible in latecomers to the KBE.

Again, in the area of R&D, collaboration between the business community and local universities (1 = minimal or nonexistent, 7 = intensive and ongoing) has been very strong in most of the East Asian countries (See Figure 9.10). The major East Asian KBEs have shown superior performance in this regard, except for Hong Kong, which lags behind Malaysia.

East Asian KBEs realized the importance of innovation as they approached the frontiers of knowledge, where they have lesser opportunities to integrate and adapt exogenous technologies. They now strive to create cutting-edge products and processes to maintain a competitive edge among other developed countries around the globe. Public and private sectors are jointly building an environment conducive to competitive innovation in East Asia. Government procurement decisions have been facilitating technological innovation in major East Asian KBEs. Figure 9.11 shows an executive opinion survey carried out by the World Economic Forum (1 = strongly disagree, 7 = strongly agree). From the figure, we see that Malaysia also performed well in this regard, along with the advanced East Asian KBEs.

Government procurement facilitates technological innovation

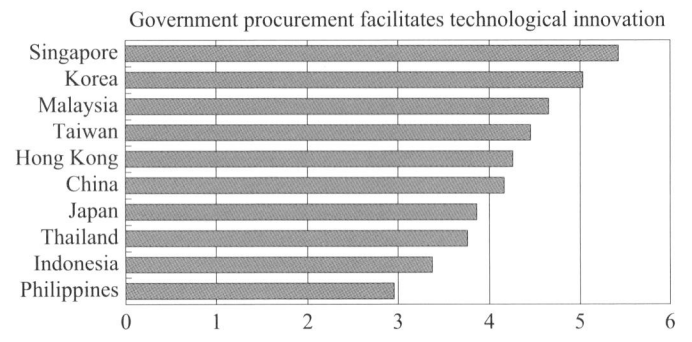

Singapore
Korea
Malaysia
Taiwan
Hong Kong
China
Japan
Thailand
Indonesia
Philippines

Figure 9.11   Government Procurement for Technological Innovation, East Asia
Source: World Economic Forum, Executive Opinion Survey 2007, 2008.

Moving Towards the Global Frontier of Innovation

Creating the human resources for R&D, R&D expenditures, availability of R&D personnel, and high-quality of R&D provide the input for a system of innovation in East Asia. This system has led, over time, to the growing innovation capacity of the region. Thus, it is important to look at the outcome of these inputs in East Asian economies. Patents and patent citations provide a very strong indication of the innovation output of an economy. Although historically, most innovations in East Asia (except in Japan) involve adoption and adaptation of existing knowledge, and mostly have derived from abroad, nevertheless, patentable innovations are of growing importance in East Asia, where several advanced economies now patent at around the same rate as advanced economies (Brahmbhatt and Hu, 2007: 22). In this section, we investigate patenting and the determining factors of patenting in East Asia. This provides us with an understanding of patent quality and patent concentration in the region.

Patenting in East Asian KBEs

Many scholars have argued that there is a significant relationship between innovation inputs, such as R&D expenditures and innovation outputs, such as patents. In addition to R&D expenditures, openness to foreign knowledge has been a contributing factor in East Asian innovation. As the innovation infrastructure of East Asian KBEs has developed, there has been a great increase in patent applications in most of the countries. If we look at Table 9.11, we find that since 2000, there has been a steady increase in the number of patent applications filed for residents and non-residents in all of the East Asian economies. This trend is most prevalent in Japan, China, Korea, Taiwan, Hong Kong and Singapore.

In terms of patents granted to residents, Japan, Korea, Taiwan and China are the leading economies in East Asia (See Table 9.12). If we compare the change in patents per 1000 people between 1990-1994 and 2000-2004, we see that the

Table 9.11   Number of Patent Applications Filed for Residents and Non-residents, East Asia

Country	2000	2001	2002	2003	2004	2005	2006	2007
China	51,906	63,450	80,232	105,317	130,384	173,327	210,501	245,161
Hong Kong	8,295	8,914	9,130	9,102	10,005	11,763	13,790	13,766
Indonesia	3,889	3,922	3,837	3,300	3,667	4,303	4,606	N/A
Japan	419,543	440,248	421,805	413,093	423,081	427,078	408,674	396,291
Korea	102,010	104,612	106,136	118,651	140,115	160,921	166,189	172,469
Malaysia	6,227	5,934	4,937	5,062	5,442	6,286	4,800	N/A
Philippines	3,636	2,605	854	1,873	2,696	2,351	3,265	N/A
Singapore	8,236	8,656	8,199	7,906	8,585	8,605	9,163	9,951
Taiwan	61,231	67,860	61,402	65,742	72,082	79,442	80,988	81,834
Thailand	5,049	5,332.	4,489	5,131	5,373	6,340	6,248	1,388

Source: World Intellectual Property Organization and the WIPO Patent Report, 2008 Edition (http://www.wipo.int/ipstats/fr/statistics/patents).

Table 9.12   Total Number of Patents Granted to Residents, East Asia

Country	1998	1999	2000	2001	2002	2003	2004	2005	2006	2007
China	1,592.0	2,091.7	3,640.3	4,887.7	5,813.3	7,555.7	11,837.7	16,783.3	21,341.0	25,909.0
Hong Kong	25.5	25.0	34.7	27.3	27.0	22.7	29.7	51.0	59.0	65.3
Indonesia	N/A	N/A	N/A	N/A	N/A	N/A	N/A	N/A	N/A	N/A
Japan	127,820.5	129,867.0	123,977.7	118,534.7	110,053.0	109,575.0	110,625.7	111,483.3	116,806.3	127,644.0
Korea	25,188.0	31,219.7	34,035.3	29,353.0	24,983.7	27,511.0	31,994.7	39,742.7	59,335.3	78,122.3
Malaysia	36.5	37.3	28.0	27.0	24.7	27.0	29.0	30.7	82.7	187.3
Philippines	15.5	12.0	6.3	7.7	10.0	9.7	11.7	12.7	23.0	N/A
Singapore	25.0	32.7	62.7	109.3	174.3	196.0	272.7	376.7	464.3	487.3
Taiwan	17,984.0	18,006.7	19,402.0	24,699.7	26,964.3	29,370.3	29,772.7	35,598.7	36,538.0	36,721.7
Thailand	35.5	33.3	39.0	44.0	47.3	51.0	50.7	58.3	79.0	98.7

Source: World Intellectual Property Organization, the WIPO Patent Report, 2008 Edition (http://www.wipo.int/ipstats/fr/statistics/patents)and National Sources.

Table 9.13   USPTO Patents Granted, East Asia *

Country	Patents per 1000 People 1990-1994	2000-2004	% Change
China	0.00	0.03	22.9
Hong Kong	3.15	9.32	11.4
Indonesia	0.00	0.01	8.8
Japan	18.23	28.54	4.6
Korea	1.44	8.67	19.7
Malaysia	0.07	0.28	15.3
Philippines	0.01	0.02	10.4
Singapore	1.09	9.87	24.6
Taiwan	6.30	30.17	17.0
Thailand	0.01	0.07	20.9

* Annual averages.
Source: *US Patent and Trade Office*.

newly industrialized economies (See Table 9.13) have had tremendous success.

Areas of Innovations in East Asian KBEs

Using the six broad categories of patents - chemicals, computers and communications, drugs and medical items, electrical items and electronics, mechanical items and all others - Brahmbhatt and Hu (2007) found that a major area of innovation concentration in East Asia has been in electrical items and electronics. The median share of patenting in this technological field for seven East Asian economies in 2002 is 38%, ranging from a low of 25% in Hong Kong to 45%-50% in Taiwan and Singapore. The second most important area of concentration is computers and communications, with a median East Asian share of 15%, ranging from a low of 12% for China and Malaysia to 25%-30% percent for Korea and Singapore. The share of East Asian patenting in these two areas has generally risen since the early 1990s. According to Figure 9.12, compared to other areas of concentration, East Asian patenting in electrical items and electronics is higher relative to the world average share of patenting in this sector - in other words, East Asian Revealed Comparative Advantage (RCA) indices in this sector are substantially greater than one, reflecting world class levels of sophistication in specific areas of specialization (for example, Korea in DRAM technology and LCD manufacturing, or Taiwan in the wafer foundry

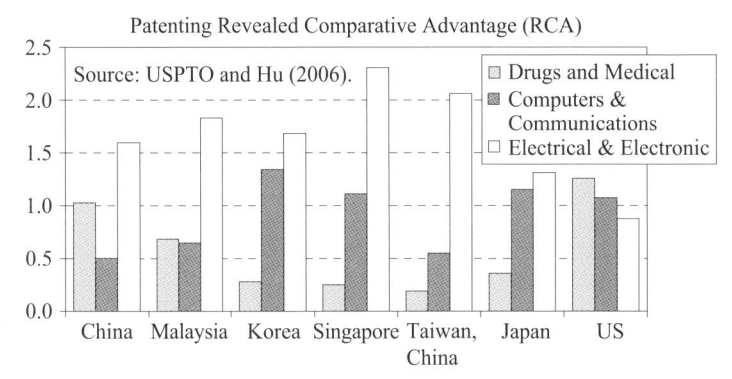

Figure 9.12 Patenting Revealed Comparative Advantage in East Asia
Source: Brahmbhatt and Hu, 2007: 26.

industry, testing and packaging services) (Brahmbhatt and Hu, 2007: 25).

Patent Quality in East Asian KBEs

Patent quality provides us with a more comprehensive view of a country's real innovation output, as the technological and economic values of patents differ significantly. Scherer and Harhoff (2000) have surveyed this and found that in the case of the U.S. and Germany, the top 10% of patents account for over 80% of economic value, indicating that the number of patents alone is not sufficient to judge true patent quality. While patent productivity in most East Asian KBEs has increased over the years (See Table 9.14), patent quality differs significantly across the region. Although the volume of patenting in economies such as Korea and Taiwan equals or exceeds that of most developed economies, quality varies greatly among East Asian countries. Patent quality in the U.S. is much higher than in many East Asian countries. In East Asia, Japan comes closest to U.S. quality, with a quality rating of 80%-90% of the U.S. while Korea comes close to Japan in most technological field, even matching or exceeding it in some. Korea is followed by Taiwan, with a score of 70%-80% compared to the U.S. (Brahmbhatt and Hu, 2007: 27).

Table 9.14   Patent Productivity, East Asia*

Country	1998	1999	2000	2001	2002	2003	2004	2005	2006	2007
China	5.33	8.82	13.40	10.14	9.76	17.38	26.18	23.45	25.39	26.92
Hong Kong	14.18	7.45	15.59	5.17	5.04	3.76	4.01	7.14	4.10	4.49
Indonesia	N/A	N/A	N/A	N/A	N/A	N/A	N/A	N/A	N/A	N/A
Japan	205.01	221.59	192.99	194.71	195.25	190.89	191.56	182.17	204.79	N/A
Korea	460.82	514.84	263.37	186.58	249.96	237.66	266.25	348.23	520.28	N/A
Malaysia	10.52	N/A	7.15	N/A	5.03	N/A	3.92	N/A	33.23	60.06
Philippines	N/A	N/A	N/A	N/A	N/A	1.31	2.99	3.04	7.44	N/A
Singapore	3.44	4.97	10.74	17.12	21.21	13.98	26.95	32.50	24.86	N/A
Taiwan	233.36	257.93	339.57	445.85	333.44	384.41	372.90	437.62	317.83	288.70
Thailand	N/A	5.48	N/A	8.34	5.41	7.99	8.40	8.00	15.27	13.42

* Patents granted to residents / R&D personnel in business ('000s).
Source: World Intellectual Property Organization, the WIPO Patent Report, 2008 Edition (http://www.wipo.int/ipstats/fr/statistics/patents), OECD Main Science and Technology Indicators 2/2007, UNESCO Web and National Sources.

Patent Citation and Knowledge Flows

Brahmbhatt and Hu (2007) reveal that the U.S. remains by far the largest source of citations for East Asian innovators, providing close to 60%. This proportion has risen slightly between 1992-1994 and 2002-2004, with Japan being the second largest source, contributing close to 20% (See Figure 9.13).

The share of citations made by East Asian economies with respect to other East Asian economies has picked up from 1.7% of citations in 1992-1994 to 5.9% in 2002-2004. This has occurred although most of these intra-East Asian patent citations have been made with respect to patents held by Korea and Taiwan, the two largest innovators in the region besides Japan. The share of citations with respect to other East Asian economies is highest - around 7%-8% - in China, Hong Kong, Malaysia and Singapore, while the share of 'own' or 'compatriot' patents is highest in Korea and Taiwan (See Figure 9.14).

We found earlier that East Asia has been particularly good in innovation in terms of electrical items and electronics technology. Surprisingly, in terms of patent citation among the U.S., Japan, Korea and Taiwan, each of these four economies, as a result of geographical localization, cites compatriot patents from

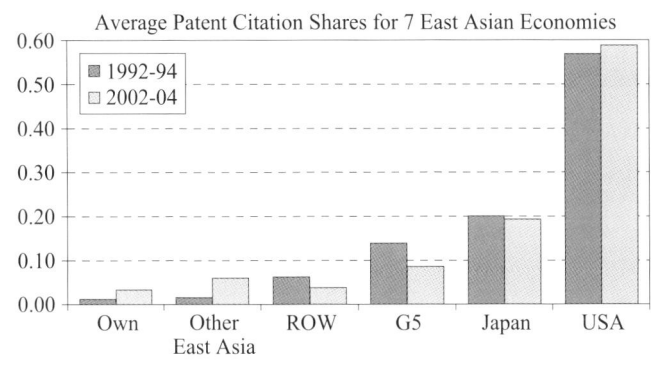

Figure 9.13 Patent Citation in East Asia
Source: Brahmbhatt and Hu, 2007: 28.

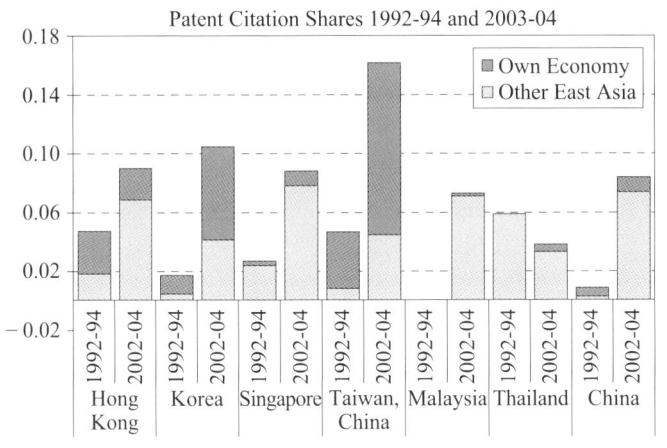

Figure 9.14 Patents Citation Share in East Asia
Source: Brahmbhatt and Hu, 2007: 28.

the same economy much more than patents from the rest of the world (See Figure 9.15). For instance, Korean patents cite other Korean patents almost 5 times as often as they do U.S. patents. Brahmbhatt and Hu (2007) use the term 'tacitness of knowledge' to describe the factors behind this localization. They further point out that tacitness and geographical localization help explain the economic usefulness of cities and industrial clusters, which facilitate face-to-face interactions and knowledge spillovers. In most East Asian KBEs, industrial clusters can be seen where governments also provide incentives for companies. Audretsch and

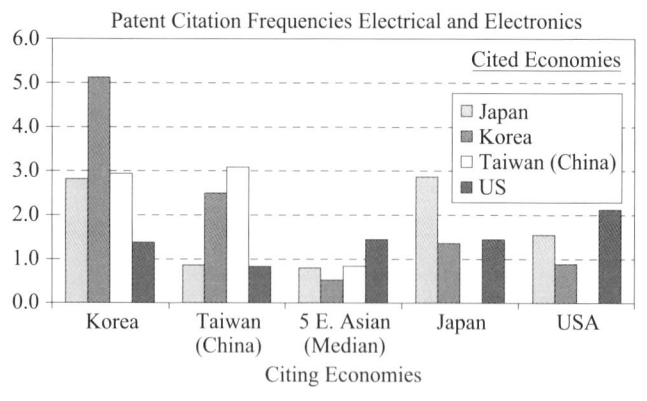

Figure 9.15 Patent Citation Frequencies
Source: Brahmbhatt and Hu (2007: 29).

Feldman (1996) also mention how geographical clustering is greatest in industries with high intensity of R&D and high employment of skilled labor, as well as in industries at an early stage in their life cycle, where most of the knowledge about the industry is still in the heads of skilled workers and less has been codified in manuals and protocols. From Figure 9.15, we also see that there is a high intensity of intra-East Asian cross-border knowledge flows. The citation frequency from Korea with respect to both Taiwanese and Japanese patents is more than twice as high as citation frequency for U.S. patents, while Taiwanese citation frequency with respect to Korean patents is also nearly three times the frequency of citation for Japanese and the U.S. Even Japan's frequency with respect to Korean patents is almost as high as its citation frequency for U.S. This trend indicates that there is a growing regional dimension in East Asian knowledge flows, especially in the field of electrical items and electronics technology.

Preserving Intellectual Property Rights in East Asian KBEs

As the East Asian economies move towards the global frontier of innovation, there is an even greater need for intellectual property rights and other legislative supports for innovation. Over the past ten years, efforts made to enforce intellectual property rights (See Figure 9.16) as well as the development of legislation to facilitate scientific research have been extremely good (See Figure 9.17) in most

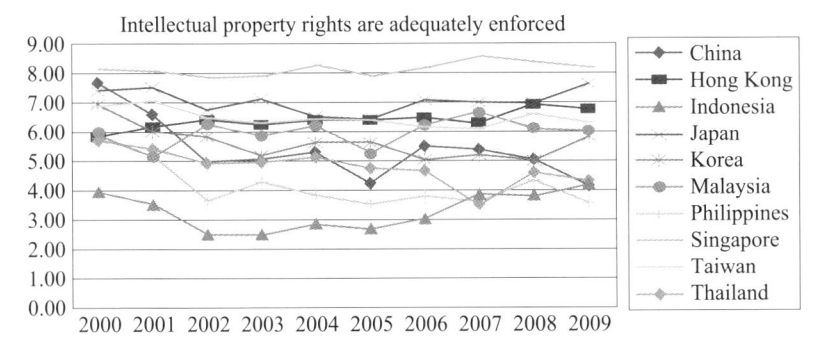

Figure 9.16 Intellectual Property Rights, East Asia*
* IMD WCY Executive Opinion Survey based on an index from 0 to 10.
Source: Computed from data collected from IMD World Competitiveness Online 1995-2009.

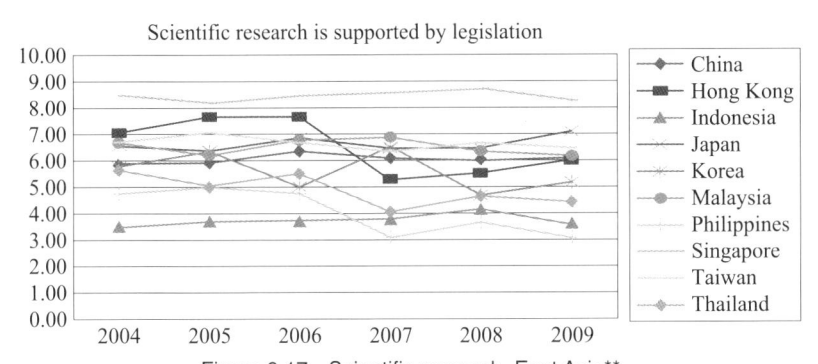

Figure 9.17 Scientific research, East Asia**
** IMD WCY Executive Opinion Survey based on an index from 0 to 10.
Source: Computed from data collected from IMD World Competitiveness Online 1995-2009.

East Asian KBEs.

In the 2009 IMD rankings, Singapore, Japan, Hong Kong, Taiwan and Korea are the leading East Asian economies in terms of both appropriate enforcement of intellectual property rights and development of legislation to facilitate scientific research. Proper enforcement of intellectual property rights and legislative support for scientific research play crucial roles in developing a well-educated workforce, a workforce that East Asia needs to further excel in scientific research and development.

Summary

From the analysis in this chapter, it is clear that East Asian economies have made enormous efforts to achieve greater innovation, create a KBE and become competitive on the global stage. From the discussion and analysis of East Asian countries in this chapter, it is quite evident that advanced KBEs such as Japan, Korea, Taiwan, Hong Kong and Singapore, have been highly successful in innovation. Imports of machinery and transport equipment in the earlier stages of East Asian development helped the East Asian economies gain access to external technologies. As the economies' growth has accelerated, there has been greater public and private expenditure in R&D, leading to crucial innovations and spurring on the creation of the KBE. Consequently, there has been a continuous increase in exports of both manufactured and high-tech goods. Huge investments both in public and private sectors have increased total R&D personnel in most of the advanced economies of the region. In the meantime, the quality of basic research has also improved to a great extent in order to meet the demands of long-term economic growth. There has been rapid growth in the number of scientific articles published by East Asian countries, indicating their growing research capability. As the quality of scientific research institutions has risen, there have been stronger and stronger industry-university collaborations on research in most of the countries in the region, further contributing to R&D. The governments of the concerned economies have allocated appropriate funds to further enhance technological innovations. All these factors have contributed to concentrated or diversified R&D in the East Asian economies. Consequently, the number of patents application and the number of patents granted have increased drastically over the years in the advanced economies of East Asia. Intellectual property rights enforcement, along with appropriate legislation for scientific research, has contributed to the overall increase in patent productivity in the region. It is therefore clear that the key factors for innovation identified in this chapter have significantly improved innovation infrastructure in East Asian economies as they move towards a KBE.

Chapter Ten

Economic Ramifications of the KBE in East Asia

Introduction

From discussions in earlier chapters, it is clear that discourse on the KBE in East Asia is prevalent. Economic growth in the last two or three decades of the twentieth century laid the infrastructural foundation for most East Asian KBEs. The economic bubble bursting in Japan in the 1990s, as well as the Asian financial crisis occurring in 1997, forced the East Asian KBEs to re-affirm their commitment to transforming their economies into KBEs. The first decade of the twenty-first century has seen drastic growth of East Asian KBEs. The world financial crisis, beginning in 2008, tested the economic strength of successful East Asian KBEs. Although many Western countries, including the U. S., the world's number one economy, suffered greatly during this historic financial crisis, East Asian countries showed resilience. Although most East Asian economies were also affected by the crisis, their recovery was much better compared to what happened after the Asian financial crisis of 1997. This final chapter attempts to put together basic facts about KBE development in East Asian countries in order to investigate the economic ramifications of the KBE in the region. Based on discussions of KBE development and its economic ramification in East Asia, this chapter also forecasts future trends for KBEs in East Asia. This forecast is then complemented with policy recommendations.

Key Factors for KBE Development in East Asia

Through discussions in Chapters Six, Seven, Eight and Nine, the key factors for each pillar of the KBE in East Asia are very evident. From the analysis in the above chapters, we also found that there has been a trend for high growth in most of the factors. This indicates that, in fact, all the selected countries in East Asia have made tremendous efforts in developing all pillars of the KBE. In their pursuit to become KBEs, some East Asian countries have performed extraordinarily well, while others are still in the process of development.

From the discussions in Chapter Six, we found that there are some key factors of economic incentives and institutional regimes that are very important to build up the initial infrastructures of KBE and to maintain and update those infrastructure to remain competitive in the global competition. Openness, a supportive business environment, a suitable business environment, a functional monetary system, a sound financial system, and the protection of property rights have been the key factors for economic incentives in East Asian countries while in terms of institutional regimes, the key factors identified are voice and accountability, political stability, government effectiveness, regulatory quality, rule of law and control of corruption.

In Chapter Seven, we discussed and analyzed the contributing factors of education and human resources development in the East Asian economies. In this regard, the main contributing factors identified are gross secondary and tertiary level enrollments, a high-quality education system, high-quality university education, sufficient supply of qualified engineers for the labor market, and efficient management in knowledge transfer between companies and universities.

Then, in Chapter Eight, we discussed and analyzed the various factors contributing to ICT development in the East Asian economies. Here, we identified the main contributing factors for this pillar in East Asia. The key factors for ICT development are: main telephone lines and mobile telephones per 1000 people, computers per 1000 people, the number of Internet users, appropriate cyber security, high-quality communications technology that meets business requirements, the availability of high-level information technology skills, technological cooperation between and among companies, supportive public and private sector ventures for technological development, an appropriate legal environment for the development and application of technology, and suitable technological regulations to support business development and innovation.

Finally, in Chapter Nine, we analyzed the factors that have contributed to the development of innovation in East Asia. They are as follows: total R&D personnel nationwide per capita, quality of basic research, number of scientific articles published, quality of scientific research institutions, industry-university collaboration, government funding to help along technological innovation, number of patent applications, number of patents granted, intellectual property rights, appropriate legislation for scientific research, and patent productivity.

Present Status of the East Asian KBEs

From empirical data analysis and discussion in Chapters Six, Seven, Eight and Nine, we see that Japan, Korea, Taiwan, Hong Kong and Singapore have been the most successful in East Asia in their pursuit to become KBEs. These countries have made significant improvements in all four pillars of the KBE described in the KBE framework proposed in Chapter Three. Moreover, from analysis and discussion in Chapter Six, we have realized that FDI has greatly contributed to the initial development of the KBE in most countries in East Asia. Only Japan is an exception to this trend. However, Japanese FDI inflow to the other East Asian countries has been one of the very strong forces contributing to the growth of the region's KBE.

To further understand our findings, we compared our findings with the World Bank's knowledge economy indices as to whether Japan, Korea, Taiwan, Hong Kong and Singapore are indeed the most successful KBEs in the region or not. The Knowledge Economy Index (KEI) provided by the World Bank takes into account whether the environment is conducive for use of knowledge in economic development. The KEI score is an aggregate index representing the overall progress of a country on its way to becoming a KBE. The index is calculated based on the average of the normalized performance scores of a country on all four pillars described in Figure 3.5 of Chapter Three - economic incentives and institutional regimes, education and human resources, ICT and the innovation system.

Scrutinizing the overall KEI index of all the East Asian countries, as shown in Table 10.1, we observed that indeed Japan, Korea, Taiwan, Hong Kong and Singapore are the most successful KBEs in the region. Among the latecomers, Malaysia has also showed remarkable success. Thanks to the twenty-two year leadership of Mahathir Mohammad and his 'Vision 2020' policy formulation that led the transformation of Malaysia's product-economy into KBE. Later, the 'KBE Master Plan 2001' put forth by the Malaysian Government helped the country to become the leader among the latecomer KBEs in the region. The Philippines and Thailand have shown greater success compared to the other developing economies in the region, but political instability and corruption have hindered their transformation into functional KBEs. Indonesia's trailing behind is also the result of political instability and corruption, followed by natural disasters, such as earthquakes, volcanic bursts and tsunami. On the other hand, China has shown steady improvement and is slowly moving towards a KBE. The most important factors for China in this regard were a stable political situation and the government's policy towards economic growth.

Table 10.1 KBE Index for the East Asian KBEs

Country	1995	2000	Most Recent
Japan	8.35	8.36	8.02
Hong Kong	8.23	7.91	8.24
Singapore	8.18	8.33	8.1
Taiwan	7.61	8.01	8.52
Korea	7.25	7.92	7.61
Malaysia	5.76	5.66	5.51
Philippines	5.01	4.36	4.11
Thailand	4.96	5.14	4.93
China	3.74	3.63	4.37
Indonesia	3.47	2.9	3.14

Source: World Bank Online (Knowledge for Development).

Tracking the Overall Development of the East Asian KBEs

The purpose of creating a KBE is to have a globally strong and competitive economy that can maintain sustainable economic growth. The East Asian economies have been pursuing policies necessary to create KBEs in order to continue their economic development in the post-industrial era. In the process, some economies in the region have become exceptionally successful in creating a functional KBE, while some others are still lagging behind. Economies like Japan, Korea, Taiwan, Hong Kong and Singapore have had remarkable achievements in creating a successful KBE. To understand the development trends in East Asian KBEs, we did not investigate GDP growth, because the bigger the economy grows, the lower the GDP growth rate becomes, although the absolute value of GDP is always higher in advanced countries. For this reason, we considered the human development index (HDI), which is a composite measure of three components: longevity (measured by life expectancy); knowledge (adult literacy rate and mean years of schooling); and standard of living (real GDP per capita in purchasing power parity) to understand the development pattern in the East Asian KBEs. HDI provides information on the human development aspect of economic growth (World Bank, 2010).

Table 10.2 shows the HDI for the East Asian economies for the years 1980, 1985, 1990, 1995, 2000, 2005, 2006, and 2007. From the table, we observe that

Table 10.2 Human Development Index Trends in East Asia

Country	1980	1985	1990	1995	2000	2005	2006	2007
China	0.533	0.556	0.608	0.657	0.719	0.756	0.763	0.772
Hong Kong	N/A	N/A	N/A	N/A	N/A	0.939	0.943	0.944
Indonesia	0.522	0.562	0.624	0.658	0.673	0.723	0.729	0.734
Japan	0.887	0.902	0.918	0.931	0.943	0.956	0.958	0.960
Korea	0.722	0.760	0.802	0.837	0.869	0.927	0.933	0.937
Malaysia	0.666	0.689	0.737	0.767	0.797	0.821	0.825	0.829
Philippines	0.652	0.651	0.697	0.713	0.726	0.744	0.747	0.751
Singapore	0.785	0.805	0.851	0.884	N/A	N/A	0.942	0.944
Taiwan	N/A	N/A	N/A	N/A	N/A	N/A	N/A	0.943
Thailand	0.658	0.684	0.706	0.727	0.753	0.777	0.780	0.783

Source: *Human Development Report 2009*[11].

there has been a positive growth trend in human development in all the economies of East Asia. The advanced KBEs have achieved incredible success in this regard, even when compared to the most advanced nations of the world. From these findings, it is obvious that most of the East Asian KBEs have achieved excellent growth in life expectancy, adult literacy rate and mean years of schooling, and real GDP per capita in purchasing power parity.

Proposed Framework for the KBE in East Asia

The purpose of the proposed KBE framework was to establish the collective nature of the foundations of a KBE such as education and human resources, ICT and innovation that are in the initial stage facilitated by government through economic incentives and institutional regimes. However, once there is substantial development in education and human resources, ICT and innovation, along with positive influence from economic incentives and institutional regimes, all these four pillars quite independently contribute to the development of a KBE. From our discussion in Chapter Six, we realize how the role of government, through economic incentives and institutional regimes, facilitated the development of the other three pillars of the KBE in East Asia. However, once the economies started transforming into KBEs, we observed that various factors of all four pillars quite discretely and independently contribute to the growth of the KBE in the region. Overall economic growth in a KBE is affected by different factors of the four pillars, while there is a spillover effect of economic growth on each pillar reversely, too. Thus, the findings from this book also provide a test of the proposed framework. From the findings, we realize that the proposed framework for the KBE in East Asia is very relevant and explains the development mechanism of the KBE in East Asia to a great extent.

Future Trends for the KBE in East Asia

The future trends for East Asian countries for becoming KBEs will be to further reshape present factors contributing to KBE, while working on other factors that have not yet developed so significantly in the region. From the discussions and analysis in Chapter Six, Seven, Eight, and Nine, it is quite obvious that all the countries given are already making considerable efforts to promote the KBE. In the last ten years, the advanced economies in East Asia, such as Japan, Korea, Taiwan, Hong Kong and Singapore, have performed extraordinarily well in creating a KBE, while the other East Asian economies, such as China, Indonesia, Malaysia, the Philippines, and Thailand, though performing positively in many of the key factors for the KBE, still remain far behind the advanced East Asian economies. Among the late-comers, Malaysia and China have been growing rapidly in the recent years in terms of creating a KBE. Through the discussions and analysis in Chapter Six, Seven, Eight, Nine and in this Chapter, it is predictable that the advanced economies will continue to lead the race of knowledge-based economic development in East Asia while the latecomers will try to reduce the gap with their more advanced counterparts.

Through the study, it is apparent that Japan, Korea, Taiwan, Hong Kong and Singapore are already ahead of other East Asian countries in terms of building the necessary KBE infrastructure. As a result, these countries' future policy formulations will be to create new avenues for knowledge workers so that the country can make the best use of KBE infrastructure already available domestically. In the future, the ability to supply world-class knowledge workers and attract the world-class companies for research and development in advanced East Asian economies will bring more benefits to their KBEs. The availability of functional economic incentives and institutional regimes, an excellent world-class educational system and human resources, sophisticated and highly capable information and communications technology and top class innovation facilities supported by both governments of the concerned countries and the world's leading corporations, will provide Japan, Korea, Taiwan, Hong Kong and Singapore with the triangular knowledge flow among government, university and companies, which will, in the future, help these nations to build a highly globally competitive KBE in East Asia. Based on the discussions, analysis and findings from this book, it can be predicted that in the coming years, these countries will maintain their regional lead in the race towards the KBE.

In the case of China, Indonesia, Malaysia, the Philippines and Thailand, economic development differs greatly, and political stability has become one of the major issues calling out for solution so that KBE infrastructure can be built at a faster speed. Although China's political system has guided China's miraculous GDP growth over the last two decades, it has to readjust to absorb the rapid changes a KBE is bringing to its borders. Until now, the country has been more a production economy than a KBE. The country has to address the issue of allowing different key actors in the KBE to work independently, but responsibly, to create a functioning KBE in China. On the other hand, Malaysia experienced huge economic growth by pursuing the 'Vision 2020' policy, which also led to Malaysia's attempt to become a KBE. Malaysia's continuous efforts to build up the KBE infrastructure have put Malaysia ahead of many other East Asian nations in their race to become a KBE. Despite remarkable efforts by the Malaysian government and private sector, the country is far behind the advanced East Asian KBEs in creating a KBE. As a consequence, the future trend in policy formulations for Malaysia to become a KBE involve reducing gaps with its neighbor, Singapore, in terms of attracting talented foreigners and large foreign companies for R&D advancement. In this regard, the country also has to reconsider the quality of education to create enough domestic qualified knowledge workers for its future KBE. Any additional efforts, on the top of current efforts to become a KBE, will push Malaysia to become a KBE rather than a petroleum-based, rent-seeking economy. This will, in turn, help Malaysia to reduce the gap with leading KBEs in the region while creating a functional KBE in the Malaysian context.

Other East Asian countries, such as Indonesia, Thailand and the Philippines, are still struggling to establish the greater political stability required for creating a functional KBE. Military interventions and weak government effectiveness in these countries have been given by many scholars as major hurdles for steady

KBE growth. Moreover, the availability of a large, semi-skilled labor force in these countries attracts low-technology-oriented mass production, rather than high-technology-oriented R&D via FDI. In addition to this, weak ICT puts up barrier to the steady growth of a KBE in these countries. However, these countries, along with China to some extent are in the initial developmental stage of building KBE infrastructure. This development pattern resembles the growth experience of the four tigers of East Asia. It can thus be said that these countries have to work on creating functioning economic incentives and institutional regimes in the first place to help the other three pillars, such as education and human resources, ICT and innovation, to flourish so that they can contribute to the creation of a KBE in these countries.

Policy Recommendations for the East Asian KBEs

To pursue pro-KBE policies in the future, Japan, Korea, Taiwan, Hong Kong and Singapore, have to address how to increase the birth rate and how to attract more foreign talented nationals to work in these countries. Singapore, which attracts the most foreign nationals in East Asia, has to motivate both foreigners and Singaporeans to work and live in Singapore for longer periods of time. The efforts by these advanced KBEs to create an excellent education system to domestically supply well-needed qualified human resources have to continue in the future. This will, in turn, further improve the quality of university education in the concerned countries. This will play a very important role in providing continuous support to the growth of the KBE. Moreover, efforts towards creating excellent ICT and innovation infrastructures will continue to be an integral part of future policy formulations for these countries.

In the case of China, Indonesia, Malaysia, the Philippines and Thailand, work on all four pillars of the KBE is needed to rapidly transform their economies. The future policy of these countries in terms of creating a KBE should thus be to build up effective economic incentives and institutional regimes, a high-quality education system and human resources, functional ICT and an output-oriented innovation system. Among these countries, Malaysia, which is ahead of these five economies in terms of creating a KBE, may have to create a level playing field for all talented people regardless their ethnic identity. This will encourage the talented people of all ethnic groups in Malaysia to work domestically rather than looking for job opportunities abroad. In many cases, the country may also like to follow some of the steps taken by neighboring Singapore in its pursuit to become a KBE.

Summary

From the discussions in this chapter, it is clear that discourse of the KBE in East Asia is prevalent and that the economic growth of most East Asian countries heavily depends on it. Although the East Asian countries are at different stages in terms of creating a KBE, efforts towards transforming product economies into KBEs can be observed even in the region's latecomers. The KBE and HDI indices show a direct correlation between the growth of KBE and the overall development of East Asian countries. The advanced East Asian economies of Japan, Korea, Taiwan, Hong Kong and Singapore have shown exemplary performance in terms of achieving knowledge-based economic growth.

In this book, we studied the knowledge-based economies in East Asia from a general perspective to understand their general development patterns. However, all these East Asian countries have unique and diverse cultures, which may also provide powerful input to the KBE. Certain cultural traits may have contributed to the high growth of some East Asian countries, while others may have blocked development in some other East Asian countries. This may explain why some countries in East Asia are more successful than others in terms of creating a KBE. As this book does not study the cultural ramifications of the East Asian KBEs individually, there remains enormous scope for future research.

References

APEC Economic Committee (2000). *Towards Knowledge-based Economies in APEC*. APEC Secretariat, Singapore.

Abramovitz, M. (1979). Rapid growth potential and its realization: The experience of capitalist economies in the postwar period. In Mainvaud, E. (ed.), *Economic Growth and Resources* (pp. 1-30). Volume 1, London: Macmillan.

Aoki, M., Murdock, K. and Okuno-Fujiwara, M. (1997). Beyond The East Asian Miracle: Introducing the Market-Enhancing View. In Aoki *et al*. (eds.), *The role of government in East Asian economic development: comparative institutional analysis*. Oxford: Clarendon Press.

Audretsch, D. and Feldman, M. (1996). R&D Spillovers and the Geography of Innovation and Production. *American Economic Review*. 86(3). 630-640.

Address by Prime Minister Dr. Mahathir Mohamad in the Second Global Knowledge Conference 2000, 8 March, Kuala Lumpur, Malaysia.

Bateira, J. (2006). Beyond the codification debate: a 'Naturalist' view of knowledge. In Dolfsma, W. and Soete, L. (eds.), *Understanding the Dynamics of a Knowledge Economy*. Edward Elgar, Massachusetts.

Bercuson, K., Carling, R. G., Hussain, A. M., Rumbaugh, T. and Elkan, R. V. (1995). Singapore: A Case Study in Rapid Development. *IMF Occasional Paper No. 119*, Washington, DC: IMF, February.

Booth, A. (1999). Education and Economic Development in Southeast Asia: Myth and Realities. *ASEAN Economic Bulletin 16*, No. 3.

Bottazi, L. and Peri, G. (2005). The International Dynamics of R&D and Innovation in the Short Run and the Long Run. *NBER Working Paper 11524*, Cambridge: National Bureau of Economic Research.

Betcherman, G. (c1997). Human-resource aspects of the changing nature of the firm: issues, evidence and public policy implications. In OECD Proceedings, *Industrial competitiveness in the knowledge-based economy: the new role of governments*. OECD.

Bray, M. and Lee, W. O. (2001). Education and Political Transition in East Asia: Diversity and Commonality. In Bray, M. and Lee, W. O. (Eds), *Education and Political Transition: Themes and Experiences in East Asia*. Hong Kong.

Barro, R. J. (1991). Economic Growth in a Cross-section of Countries. *NBER Working Paper No. 3120*, Cambridge: National Bureau of Economic Research.

Brahmbhatt, M. and Hu, A. (2007). Ideas and Innovation in East Asia. *Policy Research Working Paper 4403*, World Bank, November 2007.

Braverman, H. (1974). *Labor and Monopoly Capital: The Degradation of Work in the Twentieth Century*. New York and London: Monthly Review Press.

Brusoni, S., Prencipe, A. and Pavitt, K. (2000). Knowledge Specialization and the Boundaries of the Firm: Why Do Firms Know More Than They Make? *Administrative Science Quarterly*, 46, pp. 597-621.

Chartrand, H. H. (2006). The Competitiveness of Nations in a Global Knowledge-Based Economy. *Ph.D. Dissertation*, University of Saskatchewan.

Cowan, R., David P.A. and Foray, D. (2000). The Explicit Economics of Knowledge: Codifcation and Tacitness. *Industrial and Corporate Change*, 9 (2): 211-253.

Colecchia, A. and Schreyer, P. (2001). ICT Investment and Economic Growth in the 1990s: Is the United States a Unique Case? A Comparative Study of Nine OECD Countries. *STI Working Papers*, 2001/7.

Chen, D. H. C. and Dahlman, C. J. (2005). The Knowledge Economy, the KAM Methodology and World Bank Operations. The World Bank, Washington DC, 19 October, 2005.

Chen, D. H. C. and Gawande, K. (2007). Underlying Dimensions of Knowledge Assessment: Factor Analysis of the Knowledge Assessment Methodology Data, *World Bank Policy Research Working Paper 4216*, April 2007.

Castells, M. and Himanen, P. (2002). *The Information society and the Welfare State: The Finish Model*. Oxford University Press, New York.

Castells, M. and Hall, P. (1994). *Technopoles of the World: The Making of 21st Century Industrial Complex*. Routledge, New York.

Choi, C. (2003). Does the Internet stimulate inward foreign direct investment? *Journal of Policy Modeling*, Vol. 25, Issue 4 (June), pp. 319-326.

Caves, R. (1996). *Multinational Enterprises and Economic Analysis (2nd Ed.)*. Cambridge, UK: Cambridge University Press.

David, P. A. and Foray, D. (2002). An Introduction to the Economy of the Knowledge Society.

International Social Science Journal, 54(171): 9-23.

Drucker, P. (1969). *The Age of Discontinuity: Guidelines to Our Changing Society*. New York: Harper and Row.

--------------. (1985). *Innovation and Entrepreneurship*. New York: Harper & Row.

Dunning, J.H. (c1997). Technology and the Changing Boundaries of Firms and Governments. In OECD Proceedings, *Industrial competitiveness in the knowledge-based economy: the new role of governments*. OECD.

Drake, K. (c1997). *Industrial competitiveness in the knowledge-based economy: the new role of governments*. OECD.

Dunnewijk, T. and Wintjes, R. (2006). Governance forces shaping economic development in a regional information society: a framework and application to Flanders. In Dolfsma, W. and Soete, L. (eds.), *Understanding the Dynamics of a Knowledge Economy*. Edward Elgar, Massachusetts.

Dolfsma, W. and Soete, L. (2006). Dynamics of a knowledge economy: introduction. In Dolfsma, W. and Soete, L. (eds.), *Understanding the Dynamics of a Knowledge Economy*. Edward Elgar, Massachusetts.

Dolfsma, W. (2006). Knowledge, the knowledge economy and welfare theory. In Dolfsma, W. and Soete, L. (eds.), *Understanding the Dynamics of a Knowledge Economy*. Edward Elgar, Massachusetts.

Davenport, T. H. and Prusak, L. (c1998). *The Working Knowledge: how companies manage what they know*. Boston, Mass: Harvard Business School Press.

Dosi, G. (1982). Technological Paradigms and Technological Trajectories: A Suggested Interpretation of the Determinants and Directions of Technical Change. *Research Policy*, 11: 147-162.

Denzin, N. (1984). *The Research Act*. Englewood. NJ: Prentice Hall.

Debnath, S. C. (2007). Emerging Knowledge-based Economies in the Southeast Asia and Their Impact on the Trade. *Environment and Trade Under the WTO System*, Volume 1, No. 1, pp 5-42.

----------------. (2008). Policy Formulations for a Knowledge-based Economy- A Comparative Study of Malaysia and Singapore. *International Journal of Knowledge, Culture and Change Management*, Volume 8, No. 1, pp 146-157.

Dufrane, A. L. S. (2001). A Higher Education Perspective on Identification of Characteristics that Determine Effectiveness in Collaborations between American Higher Education and Business.

PhD Book. The George Washington University,Washinton DC, U.S.

Das, S. (1987). Externalities and Technology Transfer through Multinational Corporations: A Theoretical Analysis. *Journal of International Economics*, Vol. 22, pp.171-182.

Djankov, S. and Hoekman, B. (2000). Foreign Investment and Productivity Growth in Czech Enterprises. *World Bank Economic Review* 14 (1): 49–64.

Eliasson, G. (c1989). The Economics of Coordination, Innovation, Selection, and Learning- a theoretical framework for research in industrial economics. *IUI Working Paper*, No. 235, Stockholm.

--------------. (1990). The knowledge based information economy. In Gunnar Eliasson *et al.* (eds.), *The knowledge based information economy*. Industrial Institute for Economic and Social Research.

Evans, P. (1995). *Embedded Autonomy: States and Industrial Transformation*. New Jersey: Princeton University Press.

Edigheji, O. (2005). A Democratic Developmental State in Africa? A concept paper, *Research Report 105*, Center for Policy Studies, Johannesburg, South Africa.

Economic Planning Unit. (2001). *Knowledge-Based Economy Master Plan*, Prime Minister's Department, Malaysia.

Economic Social and Commission for Asia and the Pacific (1999). Promotion of foreign direct investment: lessons for economies in transition. New York: United Nations.

European Commission. (2000). *Preparing the Transition to a Competitive, Dynamic, and Knowledge-based Economy: An information society for all*. Retrieved from http://ue.eu.int/ueDocs/cms_Data/docs/pressdata/en/ec/00100-r1.en0.htm on June 20, 2007.

Easterly, W. and Levine, R. (2000). It's not factor accumulation: Stylized facts and growth models. *World Bank Working Paper*, Development Research Group.

Economou, P. (2008). Harnessing ICT for FDI and Development. *OECD Global Forum on International Investment III*, March 27-28, 2008, Paris, France.

Eaton, J. and Kortum, S. (1996). Trade in ideas: patenting and productivity in the OECD. *Journal of International Economics*, vol. 40, no. 3/4, May 1996, pp. 251-278.

Etzkowitz, H. and Leydesdorff, L. (1998). The Endless Transition: A "Triple Helix" of University-Industry-Government Relations. *Minerva*, 36, 203-208.

---------------. (1988). Introduction. In Giovanni Dosi *et al.* (eds.), *Technological Change and Economic Theory*. Pinter, London.

Freeman, C. (1982). *The Economics of Industrial Innovation*. Penguin: Harmondworth.

Freeman, C. and Perez, C. (1998). Structural Crisis of Adjustment. In Giovanni Dosi *et al.* (eds.), *Technological Change and Economic Theory*, Pinter, London.

Ferne, G. (c1997). Collective Research and IPRs in the Global Environment. In OECD Proceedings, *Industrial competitiveness in the knowledge-based economy: the new role of governments*. OECD.

Fort, B. and Webber, D. (2006). *Regional integration in East Asia and Europe: convergence or divergence?* London: Routledge.

Foray, D. (2004). *The Economics of Knowledge. Cambridge*, MA/London: MIT Press.

Friedman, T. L. (2006). *The World is Flat: A Brief History of the Twenty-first Century*. New York: Farrar, Straus and Giroux.

Fukuyama, F. (1999). *The Great Disruption: Human Nature and the Reconstitution of Social Order*. New York: Simon & Schuster.

Freund, C. L. and Weinhold, D. (2004). The effect of the Internet on international trade. *Journal of International Economics*, Vol. 62, Issue 1 (January), pp. 171-189.

Fosfuri, A., Motta, M. and Rønde, T. (2001). Foreign Direct Investment and Spillovers through Workers' Mobility. *Journal of International Economics*, 53 (1): 205–22.

Guinet, J. (c1997). Knowledge Flows in National Innovation Systems. In OECD Proceedings, *Industrial competitiveness in the knowledge-based economy: the new role of governments*. OECD.

Georgescu-Roegen, N. (1971). *The Entropy Law and the Economic Process*. Cambridge, MA: Harvard University Press.

Guislain, P. and Qiang, C. Z. W. (2006). Foreign Direct Investment in Telecommunications in Developing Countries. *Information and Communications for Development- Global Trends and Policies*, World Bank, Washington.

Gani, A. and Sharma, B. (2003). The Effects of Information Technology Achievement and Diffusion on Foreign Direct Investment. *Perspectives on Global Development and Technology*, Vol. 2, No. 2 (June), pp. 161-178.

Gholami, R., Lee, S. Y. T. and Heshmati, A.(2006). The Causal Relationship Between Information and Communication Technology and Foreign Direct Investment. *The World Economy*, 29 (1), pp. 43–62.

Guellec, D. and Potterie, B. V. P. (2004). From R&D to Productivity Growth: Do the Institutional Settings and the Source of Funds for R&D Matter? *Oxford Bulletin of Economics and Statistics*, 66, 3.

Granstrand, O. (1999). *The Economics and Management of Intellectual Property: Towards Intellectual Capitalism*. Cheltenham, UK: Edward Elgar.

Galbraith, J. K. (1967). *The New Industrial State*. Penguin: Harmondsworth.

Hobday, M. 1995. *Innovation in East Asia: The Challenge to Japan*, London, Edward Elgar.

_____. 2000. East versus Southeast Asian Innovations: Comparing OEM and TNC-led Growth in Electronics. In Lim and Nelson (eds), *Technology, Learning, and Innovations: Experinces of Newly Industrializing Economies*. Cambridge University Press, pp 69-129.

Heritage Foundation. (2009). 2009 Index of Economic Freedom. Available at http://www.heritage.org/index/PDF/2009/Index2009_Chapter1.pdf.

Heritage Foundation 2009 Online available at http://www.heritage.org/index/Ranking.aspx.

Irvine, J. and Martin, B. R. (1984). *Foresight in Science: Picking the Winners*. London: Frances Printer.

IMD (2003). *The IMD World Competitiveness Yearbook*. Switzerland.

IMD World Competitiveness Online, Updated: May 2009.

International Telecommunication Union Online Database.

Jewkes, J., Sawers, D. and Stillerman, J. (1956). *The Source of Invention*. London, Macmillan.

Johnson, C. (1982). *MITI and the Japanese Miracle: The Growth of Industrial Policy*, 1925-1975. Stanford: Stanford University Press.

Johnson, R. B. (2010). Mixed Method and Mixed Model Research. *Lecture 14*, University of Southern Alabama, USA available at http://www.southalabama.edu/coe/bset/johnson/lectures/lec14.pdf.

Jaffe, A. B. and Trajtenberg, M. (2002). *Patents, Citations, and Innovations: A Window on the Knowledge Economy*. Cambridge, MA and London: MIT Press.

Kim, W. M. (1998). *The four asian tigers : economic development and the global political economy*. - San Diego, Calif.; Tokyo: Academic Press.

Khan, M. (2001). Investment in Knowledge. *STI Review*, No. 27: 19-47, OECD, Paris.

Keynes, J. M. (2003). *The economic consequences of the peace*. With a new introduction by David Felix. New Brunswick, N.J.: Transaction Publishers.

Kash, D. E. and Ryecroft, R. W. (1999). *The Complexity Challenge: Technological Innovation for the 21st Century*. Printer: London.

Kohn, M. and Marion, N. (1992). The Implications of Knowledge-Based Growth for the Optimality of Open Capital Market. *The Canadian Journal of Economics*, 25(4): 865-883.

Kaufmann, D., Kraay, A. and Zoido-Lobatón, P. (1999a). Aggregating Governance Indicators. *World Bank Working Paper*, No. 2195, available at: http://www.worldbank.org/wbi/governance.

Kong, L. (2004). Science and Education in an Asian *Tiger*. *Paper presented in Teaching and Research Conference*, 18th and 19th November 2004, Queensland, Australia.

Koh, W. T. H. and Wang, P. K. (2003). Competing at the Frontier: The Changing Role of Technology Policy in Singapore's Economic Strategy. *Social Science Research Network*. Retrieved from http://papers.ssrn.com/sol3/papers.cfm?abstract_id=626342 on 22 July 2007.

Krugman, P. (1987). The Narrow Moving Band, the Dutch Disease and the Competitive Consequences of Mrs Thatcher. *Journal of Development Economics*, Vol. 27: 41-55.

Keller, W. (2002). Knowledge Spillovers at the World's Technology Frontier. *Centre for Economic Policy Research*, Discussion Paper No. 2815.

Kelly, A. C. (1988a). Economic Consequences of Population Change in the Third World. *Journal of Economic Literature*, Vol. 26: 1685-1728.

Ko, K. W. (2007). Internet externalities and location of foreign direct investment: A comparison between developed and developing countries. *Information Economics and Policy*, Vol. 19, Issue 1 (March), pp. 1-23.

Kawai, H. and Urata, S. (2003). Competitiveness and technology: an international comparison. In Lal, S. and Urata, S. (eds.), *Competitiveness, FDI and Technological Activities in East Asia*. In Association with the World Bank. Edward Elgar.

Kojima, K. (2000). The 'flying geese' model of Asian economic development: origin, theoretical extensions, and regional policy implications. *Journal of Asian Economics*, Vol. 11, Issue 4, pp.375-401.

Knowledge Economy Forum (2002). *Building Knowledge Economies: Opportunities and Challenges for EU Accession Countries*. Paris, February 19-22.

Leydesdorff, L. (2005). *The Knowledge-based Economy: modeled, measured, simulated*. Boca Raton, Fla.: Universal Publishers.

Leydesdorff, L. (2001b). *A Sociological Theory of Communication: The Self-Organization of the Knowledge-Based Society*. Parkland, FL: Universal Publishers.

Leydesdorff, L. (2006). The knowledge-based economy and the triple helix model. In Dolfsma, W. and Soete, L. (eds.), *Understanding the Dynamics of a Knowledge Economy*. Edward Elgar, Massachusetts.

Lazaric, N. and Thomas, C. (2006). The coordination and codification of knowledge inside a network, or the building of an epistemic community: the Telecom Valley case study. In Dolfsma, W. and Soete, L. (eds.), *Understanding the Dynamics of a Knowledge Economy*, Edward Elgar, Massachusetts.

Low, L. (2001). The Singapore developmental state in the new economy and polity. *The Pacific Review*. 14(3): 411-441.

Los, B. (2006). A non-parametric method to identify nonlinearities in global productivity catch-up performance. In Pyka, A. and Hanusch, H. (eds.), *Applied Evolutionary Economics and the Knowledge-based Economy*. Edward Elgar, Massachusetts.

Lucas, R. E. (1988). On the Mechanics of Economic Development. *Journal of Monetary Economics*, Vol. 22:3-42.

Lundvall, B.-Å. and Borràs, S. (1999). *The Globalising Learning Economy: Implications for Innovation Policy*. Brussels, DG XII.

Lundvall, B.-Å. (Ed.) (1992). *National System of Innovation*. London: Pinter.

List, F. (1841). *The National Systems of Political Economy*. London: Longman, 1904.

Micossi, S. (c1997). Europe's Industrial Policy: Promoting Openness, Flexibility and Innovation. In OECD Proceedings, *Industrial competitiveness in the knowledge-based economy: the new role of governments*. OECD.

Mokyr, J. (2006). The great synergy: the European Enlightenment as a factor in modern economic growth. In Dolfsma, W. and Soete, L. (eds.), *Understanding the Dynamics of a Knowledge Economy*. Edward Elgar, Massachusetts.

Markusen, R.J. (c1997). Foregin Direct Investment, Country Characteristics and Lessons for Policy. In OECD Proceedings, *Industrial competitiveness in the knowledge-based economy: the new role of governments*. OECD.

Muller, P. (2006). Reputation, leadership and communities of practice: the case of open source software development. In Dolfsma, W. and Soete, L. (eds.), *Understanding the Dynamics of a Knowledge Economy*. Edward Elgar, Massachusetts, Page 77.

Mani, A. (2005). Creating Knowledge Based Economies in Southeast Asia. *The Ritsumeikan Economic Review*. 54(3): 114-132.

Mustapha, R. and Abdullah, A. (2004). Malaysia Transitions Toward a Knowledge-Based Economy. *The Journal of Technology Studies*. xxx(3): 51-61.

Morone, P. and Taylor, R. (2006). Knowledge diffusion with complex cognition. In Pyka, A. and Hanusch, H. (eds.), *Applied Evolutionary Economics and the Knowledge-based Economy*. Edward Elgar, Massachusetts.

McLean, B. and Shrestha, S. (2002). International financial liberalization and economic growth. *Research Discussion paper*, available at http://www.rba.gov.au/PublicationsAndResearch/RDP/RDP2002-03.html, accessed 14 November, 2008.

MITA (1998). Address by Dr. Lee Boon Yang, Minister of Manpower at the National Day Lecture 1998 of the National University of Singapore Economics and Statistics Society, Singapore Government Press Release, Ministry of Information, Communications and the Arts. Retrieved from http://stars.nhb.gov.sg/stars/public/ on 22 January 2007, paragraph 9.

Morris, P. (1996). Asia's Four Little Tigers: A comparison of the role of Education in their Development. *Comparative Education*, Vol. 32, No. 1, pp 95-109.

Markusen, J. (2002). *Multinational Firms and the Theory of International Trade*. Cambridge, MA: MIT Press.

Nonaka, I. and Takeuchi, H. (1995). *The knowledge-creating company: how Japanese companies create the dynamics of innovation*. New York: Oxford University Press.

Nonaka, I. and Takeuchi, H. (1995). *The Knowledge Creating Company*. Oxford: Oxford University Press.

Nabeshima, K. (2004). Technology Transfer in East Asia: A Survey. In Yusuf, S., Altaf, M. A. and Nabeshima, K. (eds.), *Global Production Networking and Technological Change in East Asia*. Washington, DC: World Bank; New York: Oxford University Press, pp. 395–434.

Nelson, R. R. (Ed.) (1993). *National Innovation Systems: A Comparative Analysis*. New York: Oxford University Press.

Orna, E. (1990). *Practical information policies: how to manage information flow in organizations*.

Brookfield, Vt.: Gower.

OECD (1980). *Technical Change and Economic Policy*. Paris.

OECD (c1997). *Industrial competitiveness in the knowledge-based economy: the new role of governments*. OECD Proceedings.

OECD (2005). *The Measurement of Scientific and Technological Activities: Guidelines for Collecting and Interpreting Innovation Data: Oslo Manual*. Third Edition, prepared by the Working Party of National Experts on Scientific and Technology Indicators, OECD, Paris, paragraph 71.

OECD (1996). *The Knowledge-based Economy*. Paris.

OECD (2001a). *The New Economy: Beyond the Hype*. Paris.

OECD (2001b). *OECD Science, Technology and Industry Scoreboard*. Paris.

OECD (2001c). *OECD Education at a Glance*. Paris.

OECD (2002a). *OECD Economic Outlook*. No. 71, Paris.

OECD (2002b). *OECD Information Technology Outlook*. Paris.

OECD (2002c). *Dynamising National Innovation Systems*. Paris.

OECD (2002d). *Public/private Partnerships for Innovation*. Internal working document, OECD, Paris.

OECD (2002). *OECD Science, Technology and Industry Outlook*. OECD, Paris.

Ogawa, N., Jones, G. W. and Williamson, J. G. (1993). *Human Resource Development along the Asia-Pacific Rim*. Oxford University Press, Oxford, New York.

Ogawa, N. and Tsuya, N. O. (1993). Demographic Change and Human Resources Development in the Asia-Pacific Region: Trends of the 1960s to 1980s and Future Prospects. In Ogawa, N., Jones, G. W. and Williamson, J. G. (eds), *Human Resource Development along the Asia-Pacific Rim*. Oxford University Press, Oxford, New York.

O'Donnell, J., Jackson, M., Shelly, M. and Ligertwood, J. (2007). Australian Case Studies in Mobile Commerce, *Journal of Theoretical and Applied Electronic Commerce Research*, Vol. 2, No 2, pp. 1 - 18

Porter, M. E. (1998). Clusters and the New Economics of Competition. *Harvard Business Review (November-December)*: 77-90.

------------. (1998). *On Competition*. Boston: Harvard Business Review Books.

Porter, E. M., Takeuchi, H. and Sakakibara, M. (2000). *Can Japan Compete?* New York: HarperCollins Publishers.

Poppo, L. and Zenger, T. (1998). Taking alternative theories of the firm: transaction costs knowledge based and measurement explanations in make or buy decisions in information services. *Strategic Management Journal*, 19(9): 853-877.

Pyka, A. and Hanusch, H. (2006). Introduction. In Pyka, A. and Hanusch, H. (eds.), *Applied Evolutionary Economics and the Knowledge-based Economy*. Edward Elgar, Massachusetts.

Romer P. (1986). Increasing returns and long-run growth. *Journal of Political Economy*, 94(5): 1002-1037.

Rollo, C. (2002). The Knowledge Strategy within a Business Context. *Paper presented at The Third European Conference on Organizational Knowledge, Learning and Capabilities*, OKLC 2002, Athens, Greece.

Reyment, R. and Joreskog, K.G. (1993). *Applied Factor Analysis in the Natural Sciences*. Cambridge, UK: Cambridge University Press.

Rosenberg, N. (1982). *Inside the Black Box: Technology and Economics*. Cambridge, etc.: Cambridge University Press.

Smith, A. ([1776], 1937). *An Inquiry into the Nature and Causes of Wealth of Nations*. Modern Library, New York.

------------. (1991). *The wealth of nations*. With an introduction by D.D Raphael. London: David Campbell.

Sen, A. (1999). *Development as freedom*. Oxford: Oxford University Press.

Soete, L. (c1997). Macroeconomic and Structural Policy in the Knowledge-based Economy: National Policy Challenges. In OECD Proceedings, *Industrial competitiveness in the knowledge-based economy: the new role of governments*. OECD.

Smith, K. (2002). What is the Knowledge Economy? In Institute for New Technologies Discussion Paper 2002-6, *Knowledge Intensity and Distributed Knowledge Bases*. The United Nations University.

Skolnikoff, E. B. (1993). *The Elusive Transformation: Science, Technology and the evolution of international politics*. Princeton, NJ: Princeton University Press.

Stam, E. and Garnsey, E. (2006). New firms evolving in the knowledge economy: problems and solutions around turning points. Iin Dolfsma, W. and Soete, L. (eds.), *Understanding the Dynamics of a Knowledge Economy*. Edward Elgar, Massachusetts.

Storper, M. (1997). *The Regional World – Territorial Development in a Global Economy*. New York: Guilford Press.

Stiglitz, J. E. and Yusuf, S. (Eds.) (c2001). *Rethinking the East Asian miracle*. Washington, D.C.: World Bank. New York: Oxford University Press.

Stiglitz, J. E. (1996). Some Lessons from the East Asian Miracle. *The World Bank Research Observer*, vol. 11, no. 2 (August 1996), pp. 151-77.

Sheehan, P. J. (c1997). Learning to Govern in the Knowledge Economy: Policy Co-ordination or Institutional Competition. In OECD Proceedings, *Industrial competitiveness in the knowledge-based economy: the new role of governments*. OECD.

Seddon *et al*. (1995). The political determinants of Economic Flexibility, with special reference to the East Asian NICs. In Killick Tony (ed), *The Flexible Economy: Causes and Consequences of the adaptability of national economies*. London and New York: Routledge.

Solow, R. M. (1997). *Learning from "learning by doing": lessons for economic growth*. Stanford, Calif.: Stanford University Press.

Schumpeter, J. A. ([1939], 1964). *Business Cycles: A Theoretical, Historical and Statistical Analysis of Capitalist Process*. New York: McGraw-Hill.

----------------. (1989). *Essays on entrepreneurs, innovations, business cycles, and the evolution of capitalism*. Edited by Richard V. Clemence with a new introduction by Richard Swedberg. New Brunswick, N.J.: Transaction Publishers.

Sahal, D. (1981). *Patterns of Technological Innovation*. Reading, MA: Addeson Wesley.

Salavisa, I. (2006). The state at the crossroads: from welfare to the knowledge-based society. In Dolfsma, W. and Soete, L. (eds.), *Understanding the Dynamics of a Knowledge Economy*. Edward Elgar, Massachusetts.

Saxenian, A. (1994). *Regional Advantage: Culture and Competition in Silicon Valley and Route 128*. Cambridge: Harvard University Press.

Scarpetta, S., Bassanini, A., Pilat, D. and Schreyer, P. (2000). Economic Growth in the OECD Area: Recent Trends at the Average and Social Levels. *OECD Economics Department Working Paper*, No. 248.

Scherer, F.M. and Harhoff, D. (2000). Technology Policy for a World of Skew-distributed Outcomes. *Research Policy*, 29.

The Work Foundation. Retrieved from http://www.theworkfoundation.com/futureofwork/research/knowledgeeconomy.aspx on 22 January 2007, paragraph 4.

The Conference Board and Groningen Growth and Development Centre, Total Economy Database, September 2008. Retrieved from http://www.conference-board.org/economics/ on 8th November, 2008.

Thurow, L. C. (1999). *Building Wealth: The New Rules for Individuals, Companies, and Nations in a Knowledge-Based Economy*. New York: HarperCollins Publishers.

Toner, P. and Butler, G. (2004). *Some Reflections on Governing the Market*. Issues & Studies 40, no. 1 (March 2004): 81-102.

UNCTAD. (2007). Science and technology for development: the new paradigm of ICT. *Information Economy Report 2007-2008*, New York and Geneva.

UNCTAD. (2007). Information Economy database, 2007.

Verspagen, B. (1991). A new empirical approach to catching up or falling behind. *Structural Change and Economic Dynamics*, 2, 80-359.

Vinod, H. D.(2005). Opening to the World: The Effect of Internet Access on Corruption. School of Information, University of Michigan.

Weder, B. (c1999). *Model, myth, or miracle?: reassessing the role of governments in the East Asian experience*. Tokyo: United Nations University Press.

Wade, R. (1990). *Governing the Market: Economic Theory and the Role of Government in East Asian Industrialization*. Princeton, N.J.: Princeton University Press.

Wong, P.K. (2003). *From using to creating Technology: The evolution of Singapore's National Innovation System and the changing role of public policy*. In S. Lall and S. Urata (eds.), *Foreign Direct Investment, Technology Development and Competitiveness in East Asia*. Edward Elgar.

Wolfe, D. (2002). Social Capital and Cluster Development in Learning Regions. In Holbrook, J. and Wolfe, D. (Eds.), *Knowledge, Clusters, and Regional Innovation*. Montreal: McGill-Queen's UP.

Whitley, R. D. (1984). *The Intellectual and Social Organization of the Sciences*. Oxford: Oxford University Press.

World Economic Forum. (2002-2003). *Global Information Technology Report*.

World Economic Forum. (2002-2003). *Global Competitiveness Report*.

World Bank (2008). *Knowledge Assessment Methodology*. Retrieved from http://web.worldbank.org/WBSITE/EXTERNAL/WBI/WBIPROGRAMS/KFDLP/EXTUNIKAM/0,,contentMDK:20584268~menuPK:1433162~pagePK:64168445~piPK:64168309~theSitePK:1414721,00.html on 20 June, 2008, paragraph 2.

World Bank (2009). Knowledge Assessment Methodology. Available at http://web.worldbank.org/WBSITE/EXTERNAL/WBI/WBIPROGRAMS/KFDLP/EXTUNIKAM/0,,contentMDK:20584288~menuPK:1433258~pagePK:64168445~piPK:64168309~theSitePK:1414721,00.html

Weiss, L. (1998). *The Myth of the Powerless State*. Cambridge: Polity Press.

Wentzel, A. (2006). Conjectures, constructs and conflicts: a framework for understanding Imagineering. In Pyka, A. and Hanusch, H. (eds.), *Applied Evolutionary Economics and the Knowledge-based Economy*. Edward Elgar, Massachusetts.

Wang, J. Y. and Blomström, M. (1992). Foreign Investment and Technology Transfer: A Simple Model. *European Economic Review* 36 (1): 137–55.

World Bank Working Paper (2004). *Improving Competitiveness through a knowledge-based economy*. Knowledge Economy Forum III, Budapest, March 23-26, 2004.

World Bank (1993). *The East Asian miracle: economic growth and public policy*. New York, N.Y.: Oxford University Press.

Yin, R. K. (1994). *Case Study Research: Design and Methods*. 2nd ed. Thousand Oaks, Calif.: Sage Publications.

Yashiro, N. (c1997). Human Capital Formation and Industrial Competitiveness. In OECD Proceedings, *Industrial competitiveness in the knowledge-based economy: the new role of governments*. OECD.

1 Address by Dr. Lee Boon Yang, Minister of Manpower at the National Day Lecture 1998 of the National University of Singapore Economics and Statistics Society, Singapore Government Press Release, Ministry of Information, Communications and the Arts. Retrieved from http://stars.nhb.gov.sg/stars/public/ on 22 January 2007, paragraph 9.
2 Heritage Foundation Online, 2009 available at http://www.heritage.org/index/Ranking.aspx
3 Heritage Foundation Online, 2009 available at http://www.heritage.org/index/Ranking.aspx
4 World Bank KBE online, 2009 available at http://web.worldbank.org/WBSITE/EXTERNAL/

WBI/WBIPROGRAMS/KFDLP/EXTUNIKAM/0,,contentMDK:20584288~menuPK:1433258~pagePK:64168445~piPK:64168309~theSitePK:1414721,00.html

5 World Bank KBE online, 2009 available at http://web.worldbank.org/WBSITE/EXTERNAL/WBI/WBIPROGRAMS/KFDLP/EXTUNIKAM/0,,contentMDK:20584288~menuPK:1433258~pagePK:64168445~piPK:64168309~theSitePK:1414721,00.html

6 World Bank KBE online, 2009 available at http://web.worldbank.org/WBSITE/EXTERNAL/WBI/WBIPROGRAMS/KFDLP/EXTUNIKAM/0,,contentMDK:20584288~menuPK:1433258~pagePK:64168445~piPK:64168309~theSitePK:1414721,00.html

7 World Bank KBE online, 2009 available at http://web.worldbank.org/WBSITE/EXTERNAL/WBI/WBIPROGRAMS/KFDLP/EXTUNIKAM/0,,contentMDK:20584288~menuPK:1433258~pagePK:64168445~piPK:64168309~theSitePK:1414721,00.html

8 World Bank KBE online, 2009 available at http://web.worldbank.org/WBSITE/EXTERNAL/WBI/WBIPROGRAMS/KFDLP/EXTUNIKAM/0,,contentMDK:20584288~menuPK:1433258~pagePK:64168445~piPK:64168309~theSitePK:1414721,00.html

9 Retrieved from http://www.conference-board.org/economics/ on 8th November, 2008

10 Note: Data for China, Hong Kong and Philippines are not available.

11 Human Development Report 2009 [11] available at http://hdrstats.undp.org/en/indicators/81.html and http://www.dgbas.gov.tw/public/Data/910616273671.pdf for Taiwan's data

■ About the author

Sajit Chandra Debnath

Sajit Chandra DEBNATH, Assistant Professor, College of Business Administration, Ritsumeikan University. He completed DBE (Doctor with Business Expertise) from Kyushu University in 2010 while he completed his Ph.D. in Economies from Ritsumeikan Asia Pacific University in 2011. Among his most recent publications, "Knowledge Economy Approach", "Information and Communications Technology is East Asian Knowledge-based Economies" and "Value-based Management in Japanese Keiretsu and Korean Chaebols" are notable.

The East Asian Knowledge-based Economies

2013年3月30日　初版第1刷発行

- ■著　　者──Sajit Chandra Debnath
- ■発 行 者──佐藤　守
- ■発 行 所──株式会社大学教育出版
  〒700-0953　岡山市南区西市 855-4
  電話 (086) 244-1268 (代)　FAX (086) 246-0294
- ■印刷製本──サンコー印刷㈱

© Sajit Chandra Debnath 2013, Printed in Japan
検印省略　　落丁・乱丁本はお取り替えいたします。
本書のコピー・スキャン・デジタル化等の無断複製は著作権法上での例外を除き禁じられています。本書を代行業者等の第三者に依頼してスキャンやデジタル化することは、たとえ個人や家庭内での利用でも著作権法違反です。

ISBN978-4-86429-205-4